Mealea Ro...

Dictionary entries

CW00855224

brave

You are **brave** if you are able to do something that frightens you: *The brave girl saved her brother from drowning in the wild surf.*

Word building: If you are brave, then you do things **bravely** with a lot of **bravery**.

Word use: Another word that means nearly the same is **courageous**.

break *(brake)*

1. to split into bits in a rough or sudden way.
2. to not keep something like a rule or a promise: *They often break their word and don't do what they say they will.*
3. a short rest.

Word building: I **broke**, I have **broken**, I am **breaking** | If something can break, then it's **breakable**.

Word use: Don't confuse **break** with **brake**.

bubble *(bubb-l)*

a small ball of air or gas: *A bubble from the lemonade went up my nose. | The bubble I blew with the soapy water floated away.*

budgerigar *(budge-e-ree-gar)*

a kind of small yellow and green parrot. It is found in parts of Australia away from the coast but can be kept in a cage. Some people breed them in other colours such as blue.

Word building: This word is often shortened to **budgie**.

Word use: This word comes from the Kamilaroi language of New South Wales. See the map of Australian Aboriginal languages at the end of this book.

MACQUARIE
EARLY PRIMARY
DICTIONARY
AUSTRALIA'S NATIONAL DICTIONARY

General Editor
Alison Moore

jacaranda
www.jaconline.com.au

First published 2010 by
John Wiley & Sons Australia, Ltd
42 McDougall Street, Milton, Qld 4064

Typeset in Helvetica LT Regular 11/13pt

© Macquarie Dictionary Publishers Pty Ltd

National Library of Australia
Cataloguing-in-publication data

Title:	Macquarie early primary dictionary / Alison Moore, general editor; Susan Butler, executive editor.
ISBN:	978 1 74246 070 3 (pbk.)
Target Audience:	For primary school age.
Subjects:	English language — Dictionaries, Juvenile. English language — Australia — Dictionaries, Juvenile.
Other Authors/Contributors:	Butler, Susan. Moore, Alison
Dewey Number:	423

Reproduction and communication for educational purposes
The Australian *Copyright Act 1968* (the Act) allows a maximum of one chapter or 10% of the pages of this work, whichever is the greater, to be reproduced and/or communicated by any educational institution for its educational purposes provided that the educational institution (or the body that administers it) has given a remuneration notice to Copyright Agency Limited (CAL).

Reproduction and communication for other purposes
Except as permitted under the Act (for example, a fair dealing for the purposes of study, research, criticism or review), no part of this book may be reproduced, stored in a retrieval system, communicated or transmitted in any form or by any means without prior written permission. All inquiries should be made to the publisher.

A number of words entered in this dictionary are derived from trademarks. However, the presence or absence of this indication of derivation should not be regarded as affecting the legal status of any trademark.

Editorial staff

General editor	Alison Moore
Editors	Laura Davies, Victoria Morgan
Computer systems	Andrew Doyle
Editor, Macquarie Dictionary	Susan Butler

Special acknowledgement is due to Dr Helen Fraser whose non-phonemic respelling method is used for pronunciation guides in this dictionary.

Cover adapted from a design by Natalie Bowra

Cover images: © Mark Higgins (koala), © Robyn Mackenzie (gum leaves). Both used under licence from Shutterstock

Illustrated by Glenn Lumsden, Stephen Francis and the Wiley Art Studio

MACQUARIE
DICTIONARY
AT

THE UNIVERSITY OF
SYDNEY

Typeset in India by Aptara

Printed in China by
Shenzhen Donnelley Printing Co., Ltd.

10 9 8 7 6 5 4 3 2

John Wiley & Sons Australia, Ltd, places great value on the environment and is actively involved in efforts to preserve it. The paper used in the production of this dictionary was supplied by mills that source their raw materials from sustainably managed forests.

Contents

How to use the dictionary

Welcome to the *Macquarie Early Primary Dictionary*! The next few pages show you how to get the most out of your dictionary by telling you about the different parts of an entry.

Each dictionary entry can have several parts. There is the **headword** (the word you are looking up), the **pronunciation guide** (how to say the word), the **definition** (the meaning of the word), and an **example sentence** to show how the word is used. As well as these, an entry can have a **Word building** section, giving words related to the headword, and a **Word use** section which tells you something extra about the word.

How to find the word

The word you are looking up is called the **headword**. Headwords are listed in the dictionary in alphabetical order, from A to Z. If you look down the edge of each page you'll find the whole alphabet, with the letter you are in specially marked with a green box. This makes the first step of looking up a word very easy.

If you know the correct spelling of a word, then you will find it quickly. If you are not completely certain, you may have to look for the word by using the letters that you are sure about, and then checking a few words until you find it.

If you still can't find the word, then maybe it has a tricky spelling. The word might begin with a letter you don't sound when you say the word, or a letter that is said in a different way to normal. The table below gives some helpful hints for finding those tricky words. You can also find this table inside the covers at the front and the back of the dictionary.

The sound the word begins with	The possible first letters of the word	Example
f	ph	**ph**otograph
g	gh	**gh**ost
g	gu	**gu**ide
h	wh	**wh**ole
j	g	**g**em
k	ch	**ch**aracter
k	qu	**qu**ay
kw	qu	**qu**ite
n	gn	**gn**ome
n	kn	**kn**ee
r	rh	**rh**yme
r	wr	**wr**ite
s	c	**c**ereal
s	sc	**sc**ience
sh	s	**s**ugar
sk	sch	**sch**ool
w	wh	**wh**ite
z	x	**x**ylophone

How to say the word

After many headwords you will find a **pronunciation guide** in brackets. Usually this is the headword written differently, to make it easier for you to say the word. It is also broken up into parts, so you can sound the parts out separately to start with.

If a word has more than one part, the part that you say more loudly or with more force than the others is in thicker (**bold**) letters. This is the part of the word that has the **stress** on it. Here is an example showing how a change in stress can change the meaning of a word:

> ## object[1] *(**ob**-ject)*
> something that you can touch or see: *What is that red **object** on the shelf?*
>
> ## object[2] *(ob-**ject**)*
> to say that you don't agree or that you don't like something.
> Word building: If you object to something, then you have an **objection** to it.

There are only two extra symbols used in the pronunciation guides that you have to remember. These are **dh** and **zh** — **dh** sounds like the first sound in *then*, and **zh** sounds like the middle sound in *measure*.

Sometimes a rhyming word is used to help you say the word. For example:

> ## clover *(rhymes with **over**)*
> a small plant which has leaves with three round parts. Some people say that if you find a clover leaf with four round parts, you will have good luck.

When a headword is not followed by a pronunciation guide, it means that the word is said just like it is spelt.

The meaning of the word

After each headword there is an explanation of what the word means. This is the word's **definition**.

Some words have more than one meaning. These meanings can be similar to each other or very different. When they are similar, each meaning is numbered and listed under the same headword. For example:

> ## fine[1]
> **1.** very good: *She is a **fine** writer.*
> **2.** very thin: *This cloth is so **fine** that you can almost see through it.*
> **3.** sunny and dry: *I hope it is **fine** tomorrow for our picnic.*
> **4.** healthy: *I felt sick this morning, but I'm **fine** now.*

When a word has other meanings which are very different, they are listed under separate headwords, with the headwords numbered. For example, there is another meaning of **fine** which is quite different from the meanings shown above. Because this meaning is so different, it is listed separately in the dictionary, like this:

fine²

money that you have to pay because you have done something wrong.

Example sentences

Many definitions are followed by a sentence showing how the word can be used. When there are two example sentences, they are separated by a green upright line (|).

frame

the part which fits around something or holds it up and which gives it its shape: *This picture needs a **frame** so I can hang it up. | Our house has a wooden **frame**.*

Words related to the headword

At the end of some entries there is a **Word building** section which gives words that are related to the headword. These can be forms of the headword — different verb forms, plurals, and different forms of adjectives and adverbs, when they are not formed in the usual way. Here are some examples:

forget...

Word building: I **forgot**, I have **forgotten**, I am **forgetting**

foot...

Word building: For more than one we use **feet**.

funny...

Word building: more funny = **funnier**, most funny = **funniest**

Word building also contains words which are different to the headword, but which are closely related. For example:

farm...

Word building: Someone whose job is to work on a farm is a **farmer**.

formal...

Word building: If you say or do something in a formal way, then you say or do it **formally**.

Extra information about the word

Some entries include a **Word use** section which gives extra information about the word. It could be telling you which language the word has come from, or it could be telling you a word which means nearly the same as the headword, or one which means the opposite. Sometimes Word use tells you if there is another spelling for the headword, and sometimes it gives you helpful hints about the word. Here are some examples:

brolga...

Word use: This word comes from the Kamilaroi language of New South Wales.

fragile...

Word use: Another word which means nearly the same is **delicate**.

decrease...

Word use: The opposite of this is **increase**.

didjeridu...

Word use: Some people spell this **didgeridoo**.

fowl...

Word use: Don't confuse this with **foul**.

Aa

Acrobats amuse an audience of aliens.

abbreviate *(a-**bree**-vee-ate)*
to make a word shorter by leaving out some of the letters: *You can **abbreviate** 'William' to 'Will'.*
Word building: I **abbreviated**, I am **abbreviating** | When you abbreviate a word, you get an **abbreviation**.

abdomen *(**ab**-dom-en)*
the part of your body that has your stomach in it.

ability *(a-**bil**-i-tee)*
the power to do something: *Teresa has the **ability** to swim across the pool.*
Word building: For more than one we use **abilities**. | When you have the ability to do something, you are **able** to do it.

Aboriginal *(ab-o-**rij**-i-nal)*
An **Aboriginal** person is one who is related to the first people to live in Australia.
Word building: An Aboriginal person is sometimes called an **Aborigine**.
Word use: Aboriginal people are often called **Indigenous** people.

about *(a-**bowt**)*
1. having to do with: *This story is **about** pirates.*
2. close to: *I have **about** ten dollars.*
3. around: *Let's go and walk **about** the town.*

above *(a-**buv**)*
If something is **above** something, it is higher than it: *Our plane flew **above** the clouds.*

abrasion *(a-**bray**-zhon)*
a wound or sore on your skin that is caused by severely scraping the skin against something rough: *I fell over playing netball and now I have an **abrasion** on my elbow.*

abroad
out of your own country: *My grandparents went **abroad** last summer.*

absent *(**ab**-sent)*
not where you should be or where you normally are: *Dimitri is **absent** from school today because he's sick.*
Word use: The opposite of this is **present**.

accent *(**ak**-sent)*
the way you say words: *I speak with an Australian **accent**, but Jock's **accent** is Scottish.*

accept *(ak-**sept**)*
to take what somebody gives you.
Word use: Don't confuse this with **except**. | The opposite of this is **reject**.

access *(ak-sess)*
1. a way of getting to some place: *This door gives easy **access** to the back of the stage.*
2. the chance to visit or approach: *My parents are divorced but my dad still has **access** to me every second weekend.*
3. to get in to a place: *You can **access** the basement through this door.*
4. to get to information stored in a computer: *You'll need to enter the password to **access** that file.*

accident *(ak-si-dent)*
something bad that happens when things go wrong: *She hurt her leg when she had an **accident** on her bike.*
Word building: Something that happens by accident is **accidental**, and it happens **accidentally**.

account *(a-count)*
1. the money that you have in a bank: *I have more than $100 in my online bank **account**.*
2. a story telling the important things that have happened: *Your mother is giving me an **account** of her day at the office.*

accurate *(ak-yu-ret)*
exactly right or correct.
Word building: Something that is accurate has been done **accurately** and has **accuracy**.

accuse *(a-cuze)*
to say that you blame somebody for doing something wrong: *Did you **accuse** me of stealing your diary?*
Word building: I **accused**, I am **accusing** | When you accuse someone of a crime, you make an **accusation**.

ace
1. a playing card with a single shape on it: *The **ace** of hearts has a red heart on it.*
2. a serve in tennis so good that the other player can't touch the ball with their racquet.
3. an everyday word you use to describe something excellent: *Pam's surfboard is really **ace**.*

ache *(ake)*
a pain that lasts a long time like a toothache or headache.

acrobat *(ak-ro-bat)*
someone who does daring tumbling and balancing tricks like somersaults and walking along a rope high above the ground.

across
1. from one side to the other side of: *The tree fell **across** the creek in the flood.*
2. on the other side of: *My friend lives **across** the street.*

act
1. something done or performed: *He was given a medal for his **act** of bravery during the bushfire.*
2. to do something: *She **acted** quickly during the emergency.*
3. to play the part of someone else in a play, film or television show: *He is going to **act** in a film about an Antarctic explorer.*
Word building: A person who acts is called an **actor**. Some people call a woman who acts an **actress**.

action
1. an act or deed: *His quick **action** saved the injured child.*
2. the state of being active: *The children leapt into **action** when the school bell rang.*

activity *(ak-tiv-i-tee)*
something you do, often with a lot of energy: *Walking the dog is a healthy **activity**.*
Word building: For more than one we use **activities**. | If you take part in an activity then you are **active**.

actual
real or existing: *His nickname is Ricky but his **actual** name is Richard.*
Word building: If something really happened, it **actually** happened.

adapt *(a-**dapt**)*
to change: *I will **adapt** my story to make it funnier.*
Word building: I **adapted**, I am **adapting** | If something can adapt or be adapted, it is **adaptable**.

adaptation *(a-dap-**tay**-shon)*
1. any kind of change.
2. a change in a living thing that helps it survive in a changed environment.

add
1. to join one thing to another to make it bigger: *Here is a new DVD to **add** to your collection.*
2. to find the sum or whole amount of something: *Please **add** up all these numbers and tell me what the total is.*
Word building: Something added to something else is an **addition**.

addict *(**ad**-ict)*
someone who can't do without something, especially drugs.
Word building: A person who is an addict is **addicted** to things like alcohol, drugs, or cigarettes, and is suffering from an **addiction**.

address *(a-**dress**)*
1. the number of the house, the name of the street and the suburb or town where you live: *She wrote her **address** at the top of the letter.*
2. a special talk to a group of people: *Today a police officer gave an **address** on road safety to the school assembly.*
3. the special series of numbers and letters that you key in to a computer to get to a particular website or to send email to someone.

adjective
a word which describes a noun, such as *small* in *a small room.*
Word building: If a word is used as an adjective, it is **adjectival**.

admiral *(**ad**-mi-ral)*
the most important sailor in the navy.

admire *(ad-**mire**)*
to think someone or something is really good.
Word building: I **admired**, I am **admiring** | When you admire someone, you have **admiration** for them.

admit *(ad-**mit**)*
1. to agree that you have done something wrong: *He had to **admit** that he had broken the window.*
2. to let someone or something in.
Word building: I **admitted**, I am **admitting** | When you admit you've done something, you make an **admission**.

adopted *(a-**dop**-ted)*
You're **adopted** if you were chosen by your family to belong to them after your birth.

adore *(a-**dore**)*
to feel very strong love for something or someone.
Word building: I **adored**, I am **adoring** | If you adore something, then you feel **adoration** for it.

adult *(a-**dult** or **ad**-ult)*
someone who is a grown-up: *My teacher is an **adult**, and I'm a child.*

advance *(ad-**vance**)*
to move forwards.
Word building: I **advanced**, I am **advancing**

advantage *(ad-**van**-tij)*
something that puts you ahead of other people: *Her long legs gave her an **advantage** in the high jump.*

adventure *(ad-**ven**-cher)*
something exciting that happens to you: *Sleeping overnight in the bush will be an **adventure**.*
Word building: Someone who's always looking for an adventure is **adventurous**.

a
b
c
d
e
f
g
h
i
j
k
l
m
n
o
p
q
r
s
t
u
v
w
x
y
z

adverb

a word which tells you something extra about a verb, adjective or another adverb, such as *happily* in *They played happily*.

Word building: If a word is used as an adverb, it is **adverbial**.

advertisement *(ad-**ver**-tis-ment)*

a notice that tells you that something is for sale or that something is going to happen: *When we wanted to sell our car, my parents put an **advertisement** in the paper.*

Word building: This word is often shortened to **ad**. | You use an advertisement to **advertise** something.

advice *(ad-**vice**)*

something that someone tells you when you want to know the best thing to do: *My big sister gave me **advice** about how to set up my laptop.*

Word use: Don't confuse this with **advise**.

advise *(ad-**vize**)*

to tell someone what you think they should do: *I don't know which phone to buy — could you please **advise** me?*

Word building: I **advised**, I am **advising**

Word use: Don't confuse this with **advice**.

aerobics *(air-**robe**-ics)*

exercises done to music to improve your fitness.

aeroplane *(**air**-o-plane)*

a machine with wings and propellers or jet engines, which flies through the air.

Word building: This word is often shortened to **plane**.

affect *(a-**fect**)*

to make something or someone different: *I hoped the happy music would **affect** the mood of the lonely boy.*

Word use: This word is sometimes confused with **effect**, which means 'something that happens because of something else'.

affection *(a-**fec**-shon)*

great liking for someone or something: *Heidi cuddled her new puppy with **affection**.*

Word building: If you feel or show affection, you are **affectionate**.

afford *(a-**ford**)*

to have enough money to pay for something: *I'm saving all my pocket money so that I can **afford** a new computer game.*

afraid *(a-**fraid**)*

frightened or scared.

after *(**arf**-ter)*

1. at a time later than: *You can watch television **after** you do your homework.*
2. behind: *You were **after** me in the line at the cinema, and that's why you missed out on the last movie ticket.*

afternoon

the part of the day between noon and night-time.

after-school care

a place where you can go in the afternoon when school finishes, where people look after you before you go home.

again *(a-**gen**)*

another time or once more.

against *(a-**genst**)*

1. on or next to: *Don't lean **against** the wall.*
2. in the opposite direction to: *The skateboard goes more slowly when you're riding **against** the wind.*

age

how old you are: *Children under five years of **age** can get into the circus free.*

aggressive (a-**gress**-iv)

People or animals are **aggressive** if they feel like attacking you: *Lions are* **aggressive** *when they're angry.*

Word building: When lions are aggressive, they might show their **aggression** by roaring.

ago

If something happened a particular amount of time **ago**, that amount of time has passed since it happened: *I started school five years* **ago**.

agony (**ag**-o-nee)

a lot of pain, almost too much to put up with: *When I broke my leg, I was in* **agony**.

agree (a-**gree**)

1. to say yes.
2. to think the same about something as someone else does.

Word building: I **agreed**, I am **agreeing** | When you agree to do something, you make an **agreement**.

Word use: The opposite of this is **disagree**.

agriculture (**ag**-ri-kul-cher)

farming: *Farmers work in* **agriculture**.

Word building: Farming is **agricultural** work.

ahead (a-**hed**)

If something is **ahead** of something else, it is in front or before: *Lucy is* **ahead** *of me in the line for the canteen.* | *Watch out for the bump in the road* **ahead**. | *I crossed the finish line* **ahead** *of you.*

aid

1. help: *The starving people in Africa need our* **aid**.
2. something or someone that helps: *This dictionary is an* **aid** *to spelling.*

AIDS (aids)

a very serious disease which is caused by a virus that destroys the body's ability to fight infection.

aim

1. to point something at something else: *You'll see the possum if you* **aim** *the torch at the lowest branch of the tree.*
2. to make an effort to do something: *We* **aim** *to save some of our money each week.*

air

what you breathe. It is a mixture of gases.

air conditioner (air con-**dish**-i-ner)

a machine that makes a place cooler.

aircraft

any machine that can fly, such as an aeroplane or helicopter.

air pollution (**air** po-loo-shun)

pollution of the air by things like smoke from cars and factories.

airport (**air**-port)

a large, flat place where planes land and take off. There are also buildings for people who work there, for the passengers, and for the planes.

alarm (a-**larm**)

1. a sound or signal used to warn people: *The lifesavers gave the* **alarm** *as soon as they saw the shark.*
2. to make something or someone feel scared: *Don't move too quickly — you'll* **alarm** *the horses.*

album (**al**-bum)

a book with blank pages where you can keep things like photographs, pictures or stamps.

alcohol (**al**-co-holl)

Some drinks for adults contain **alcohol**, and it makes people drunk if they have too much.

alert *(a-lert)*
You're **alert** if you're watching very carefully, ready for action: *The guards always have to be alert in case someone tries to rob the bank.*

algae *(al-jee or alg-ee)*
seaweed and some other plants that grow in water.
Word use: Algae is the word we use for more than one. For one we use **alga**.

alien *(ay-lee-en)*
1. someone who is not a citizen of the country they live in.
2. a creature from another planet.

all
1. the whole of something: *Did you eat all the pie?*
2. every one of something: *I've lost all my marbles.*

allergy *(al-er-jee)*
a skin rash or sick feeling that some people get when they eat certain foods or go near certain plants.
Word building: Someone who has an allergy is **allergic** *(a-ler-jic)* to something.

alley *(al-ee)*
a narrow lane between buildings.
Word building: For more than one we use **alleys**.

alligator *(al-i-gay-tor)*
a large animal like a lizard which has sharp teeth and lives near water. It has a wider nose than a crocodile.

allow *(a-low; the last part rhymes with now)*
to let someone do something, or let something happen: *The principal doesn't allow people to walk their dogs on the school grounds.*

all right *(all rite)*
1. safe, and not hurt or sick: *Are you all right?* | *Val had a bad flu but she is all right now.*
2. good enough: *I suppose your school work is all right.*

ally *(al-lie)*
a person or country who is your friend or supporter: *My sister was my ally in the argument about which film we should see.*
Word building: For more than one we use **allies**.

almost *(all-most)*
nearly: *It's almost time for dinner!*

alone *(a-lone)*
You're **alone** if you're by yourself: *He sat alone in the empty playground.*

along
1. from one end to the other: *We walked along the beach.*
2. lined up with: *I placed my toys along the edge of the carpet.*

aloud *(a-loud)*
You are reading **aloud** when you speak the words, rather than just think them: *The poet read her poem aloud to the audience.*

alphabet *(alf-a-bet)*
all the letters of a language put in order: *The first letter of the alphabet is 'A'.*
Word building: When something has been arranged in the order of the alphabet, then it is in **alphabetical** order.

alps
high mountains.
Word building: People go to the alps for **alpine** sports such as skiing.

already *(all-red-ee)*
sooner than expected: *Have you finished with the computer already?*

altar *(**all**-tar)*

a special table in a church: *The bride and her father walked into the church and up towards the **altar**.*

Word use: Don't confuse this with **alter**.

alter *(**all**-ter)*

to change: *I will **alter** the painting by adding some bright yellow flowers. | Your appearance will **alter** as you get older.*

Word use: Don't confuse this with **altar**.

alternative *(al-**ter**-na-tiv)*

different or other: *She goes an **alternative** way to school. | We use **alternative** energy in our home.*

although *(all-**dhoh**)*

in spite of the fact that: ***Although** I had a big breakfast, I'm still hungry.*

altitude *(**al**-ti-chude)*

how high something is above the level of the sea: *Planes fly at a high **altitude**.*

altogether *(all-to-**gedther**)*

when everyone or everything is included: *If you count the baby then there are five people **altogether** living in our house.*

Word use: Don't confuse this with **all together**, which you use when a lot of things are grouped close to each other, as in *The workers were all together in the canteen.*

aluminium *(al-yu-**min**-ee-um)*

a metal that's silver-grey in colour, which is used to make things like drink cans.

always *(**all**-ways)*

all the time: *You are **always** on your computer playing games!*

amateur *(**am**-a-ter)*

someone who does something for fun and not for money: *In the past, only an **amateur** could go in the Olympic Games.*

Word use: The opposite of this is **professional**.

amaze *(a-**maze**)*

to surprise someone greatly: *It would **amaze** my friends if I changed the colour of my hair to green.*

Word building: I **amazed**, I am **amazing** | If you amaze someone, they might look at you in **amazement**.

ambassador *(am-**bass**-a-dor)*

someone who is sent by one country to represent it in another country.

ambition *(am-**bish**-on)*

something that you want for the future, such as to be successful, famous or rich: *My **ambition** is to be a rock star.*

Word building: If you have an ambition, then you are **ambitious**.

ambulance *(**am**-byu-lance)*

a special van that takes sick or injured people to hospital.

ambush *(**am**-bush)*

to hide and wait and then attack someone suddenly: *The bushrangers waited to **ambush** the wagon when it came around the bend.*

ammunition *(am-yu-**nish**-on)*

bullets or other things that you can fire from a gun or other weapon.

among *(a-**mung**)*

surrounded by: *Look at that beautiful rose **among** the thorns.*

amount *(a-**mount**)*

how much there is of something: *There is only a small **amount** of water left in the dam.*

amphibian *(am-fi-bee-an)*
an animal that begins life in the water and lives on land as an adult, such as a frog.

amuse *(a-muze)*
1. to make the time pass happily for somebody: *I wrote a short story to* **amuse** *myself while we sat in the waiting room.*
2. to make someone laugh or smile.
Word building: I **amused**, I am **amusing** | If something amuses you, what you feel is **amusement**.

ancestor *(an-sest-or)*
someone related to you who lived a long time ago.

anchor *(ang-kor)*
something heavy tied to a boat that you drop into the water so that it lands on the bottom and stops the boat floating away.

ancient *(ain-shent)*
very old: *This* **ancient** *vase is over 1000 years old.*

and
along with: *Use your pens* **and** *pencils to draw a picture.*

angel *(ain-jl)*
In some religions, an **angel** is a messenger of God. They are sometimes drawn as humans with wings.
Word use: Don't confuse this with **angle**.

angle *(ang-gl)*
the pointed shape that two straight lines make when they meet.
Word use: Don't confuse this with **angel**.

angry *(ang-gree)*
very cross.
Word building: You are angry when you have a feeling of **anger**.

animal *(an-i-mal)*
anything that's alive and can feel and move about. A plant is not an animal.

ankle *(ang-kl)*
the part of your body where your foot joins your leg.

anniversary *(ann-i-ver-sa-ree)*
the time each year when you remember something that happened at the same time in an earlier year: *Today is the second* **anniversary** *of the big fire.*

announce *(a-nounce)*
to let everyone know something: *They're going to* **announce** *the name of the winner.*
Word building: I **announced**, I am **announcing** | When you announce something, you make an **announcement**.

annoy *(a-noy)*
to make someone feel cross and cranky.
Word building: Something that annoys you is an **annoyance**.

annual *(an-yoo-al)*
Something is **annual** if it happens once a year: *We have our* **annual** *sports day in September.*
Word building: If the sports day is annual, then it happens **annually**.

another *(a-nudther)*
1. one more: *Can I please have* **another** *glass of juice?*
2. If you do something **another** way, you do it a different way.

answer *(an-ser or arn-ser)*
1. what you say if someone has asked you a question: *My* **answer** *is that I like roses best.*
2. to say something back when somebody asks a question: *Please* **answer** *when I speak to you.*

ant
a small insect that usually lives in a large group.

antelope (an-te-lope)
an animal like a deer, which can run very fast.

anthem (anth-em)
a song that you sing at important times or events: Australia's national **anthem** is 'Advance Australia Fair'.

antibiotic (an-tee-by-ot-ic)
a type of medicine that can cure infections and make you better.

anticlockwise (an-tee-clock-wize)
If something moves in an **anticlockwise** direction, it moves in the opposite direction to the hands moving on a clock: If you turn in a circle to the left, you are moving in an **anticlockwise** direction.

antique (an-teek)
something made a long time ago, like an old-fashioned chair or table.

anxious (ang-shus)
worried about what might happen: He was very **anxious** about his sick dog.
Word building: When you're anxious, you're full of **anxiety** (ang-zy-e-tee).

any (en-ee)
one or some: Have you got **any** lollies left in your packet?
Word building: Any kind of thing is **anything**. Any person is **anyone** or **anybody**.

anyway
in any case: I'm going to the shops **anyway**.

anywhere
any place: He could be **anywhere**.

Anzac (an-zak)
a soldier from Australia or New Zealand who fought during World War I.
Word use: This name was made by joining the first letters of the words **Australian** and **New Zealand Army Corps**.

apart
1. If you take something **apart**, you take it to pieces.
2. separated or not together: The two angry dogs were kept **apart**.

apartment
a home that is a group of rooms in a larger building: My best friend lives in the **apartment** right under ours.

ape
one of the large monkeys that don't have tails.

apologise (a-pol-o-jize)
to say you're sorry.
Word building: I **apologised**, I am **apologising** | When you apologise, you feel **apologetic** and you give someone an **apology**.

appeal (a-peel)
a call for help: They made an **appeal** for money to buy food for starving people.

appear (a-peer)
to come into sight: A comet is going to **appear** in the sky tonight.

appearance (a-peer-rance)
the way you look on the outside: You'd better do something about your **appearance** — your face is very dirty.

appendix (a-pen-dix)
1. a small part like a tube inside your body near your stomach. If it becomes swollen and sore, you could have **appendicitis** and need to have your appendix removed.
2. a section added at the back of a book to give extra information on things mentioned in the main part of the book.
Word building: For more than one we use **appendixes** or **appendices**.

appetite (ap-e-tite)
the feeling that you'd like to eat.

a
b
c
d
e
f
g
h
i
j
k
l
m
n
o
p
q
r
s
t
u
v
w
x
y
z

applaud *(a-**plord**)*
to show that you are pleased by clapping your hands.
Word building: If you applaud someone, then they get **applause**.

apple *(**app**-l)*
a crisp round fruit with thin red or green skin.

appointment *(a-**point**-ment)*
a special time you've made to do something: *I have an **appointment** to see the dentist at 3 o'clock this afternoon.*

approach *(a-**proach**)*
to come near to something: *The plane is about to **approach** the runway.*

approximately *(a-**prox**-i-mat-lee)*
about: *There are **approximately** thirty students in my class.* | *I have **approximately** $100 in my bank account.*

apricot *(**ay**-pri-cot)*
a small, round, yellow fruit. It is soft and juicy with one large seed inside.

apron *(**ay**-pron)*
a piece of clothing you wear in front to keep the clothes underneath it clean.

aquarium *(a-**kwair**-ree-um)*
a glass tank where you keep fish.

arch
a curved part which helps hold up a bridge or building, or forms the top of a doorway.
Word building: For more than one we use **arches**.

architect *(**ar**-ki-tect)*
someone whose job is to plan buildings.

area *(**air**-ree-a)*
1. a part or place: *That **area** of my back is itchy.* | *That **area** of Australia is very hot and dry.*
2. the size of a surface when you measure it: *The **area** of our school hall is 100 square metres.*

arena *(a-**ree**-na)*
a space that has been closed in for sports events and shows.

argue *(**arg**-yoo)*
to talk with someone who doesn't agree with you, in a noisy or cross way.
Word building: I **argued**, I am **arguing** | If you like to argue, then you are **argumentative**, and you keep having **arguments** with people.

arithmetic *(a-**rith**-me-tic)*
working things out using numbers: *I still use my fingers to count when I do **arithmetic**.*

arm
the part of your body from your shoulder to your hand.

armour *(**ar**-mor)*
1. the metal clothing that knights used to wear when they fought in battles.
2. the metal plates on planes and warships that protect them in a war.
Word building: Something that is covered with armour is **armoured**.

arms
the guns, knives and other weapons people use to fight with: *The soldiers were given **arms** before they went into battle.*

army *(**ar**-mee)*
a large number of people who are trained to fight on land.
Word building: For more than one we use **armies**.

around

1. on every side of: *We stood* ***around*** *the tree.*
2. in a circle: *We skipped* ***around***. | *The wheels go* ***around***.

arrange (a-**range**)

to put things in order: *We need to* ***arrange*** *the chess pieces on the board before we begin the game.*

Word building: I **arranged**, I am **arranging** | When you arrange something, you make an **arrangement**.

arrest (a-**rest**)

to take someone prisoner.

arrive (a-**rive**)

to come to the place you set out for.

Word building: I **arrived**, I am **arriving** | If you have arrived somewhere, you have made an **arrival**.

arrow (a-roe)

a thin pointed piece of wood that you shoot from a bow.

art

painting, drawing and sculpture.

artery (ar-te-ree)

one of the small tubes inside your body that carry blood from your heart.

Word building: For more than one we use **arteries**.

Word use: The tubes that carry blood to your heart are **veins**.

article

1. a particular thing: *She was so cold she put on every* ***article*** *of clothing she had in her suitcase.*
2. a piece of writing in a newspaper or magazine.
3. a word, such as 'a', 'an' or 'the', which comes before a noun to show if it relates to one particular person or thing.

artificial (art-i-**fish**-al)

Something is **artificial** if it has been made by humans: *That drink has* ***artificial*** *colouring in it.*

Word use: The opposite of this is **natural**.

artist (art-ist)

someone who makes beautiful things, especially paintings or drawings.

Word building: If you can make beautiful things like an artist, then you are **artistic**.

as

1. If something happens **as** something else is happening, it happens at the same time: ***As*** *she ran out of the house, her mobile phone rang.*
2. You use **as** to mean that something happens because of something else: *We're not going to the beach* ***as*** *it's too cold.*
3. as . . . as, You use this when you are comparing things that are the same in amount or value: *That tree has grown* ***as*** *high* ***as*** *the roof.* | *Sam can run* ***as*** *fast* ***as*** *Jack.*

ascend (a-**send**)

to climb or go up.

Word building: When you ascend, you make an **ascent**.

Word use: The opposite of this is **descend**.

ash

the powder left after something has been burnt: *You have spread* ***ash*** *from the fireplace all over the floor.*

ashamed (a-**shamed**)

very sorry about something wrong you have done: *I was* ***ashamed*** *when I realised how much I had upset Helena by gossiping about her.*

ask

to try to find something out: *We must* ***ask*** *how to get to the zoo.*

assemble (a-**sem**-bl)
1. to put together: *We watched in amazement as they began to **assemble** a spaceship.*
2. to come together: *The rest of the school will **assemble** to watch our play.*

assembly (a-**sem**-blee)
a group of people meeting for a special reason: *There was an **assembly** for everyone in the school to welcome the new principal.*
Word building: For more than one we use **assemblies**.

assist (a-**sist**)
to give someone help: *Please **assist** me with this experiment.*
Word building: If you assist someone, you give them your **assistance**, and you are their **assistant**.

asthma (**ass**-ma)
an illness that makes you cough a lot and sometimes makes it hard for you to breathe.

astonish (a-**ston**-ish)
to surprise someone very much.
Word building: When you astonish someone, they feel **astonishment**.

astronaut (**ast**-ro-nort)
someone trained to travel in a spaceship.

astronomy (a-**stron**-o-mee)
the study of the sun, moon, stars and planets.
Word building: Someone whose job is astronomy is an **astronomer**.

at
At is a very common word that is used in many ways. It usually has to do with where something is situated or is going, or with time: *He is **at** the station. | She aimed the ball **at** the goal. | Look **at** that huge dog. | She arrived **at** the airport just in time. | The plane leaves **at** four o'clock.*

athlete (**ath**-lete)
someone who trains to be good at sports such as running and jumping.
Word building: An athlete needs to be **athletic** to take part in **athletics**.

atlas (**at**-las)
a book of maps.

ATM (ay tee **em**)
a machine that you use to get money from a bank by using a coded plastic card and a PIN.
Word use: This stands for **Automatic Teller Machine**.

atmosphere (**at**-moss-fear)
the air all around the earth.

atom (**at**-om)
one of the very small bits that all things are made of.

attach (a-**tach**)
to fasten or join: *Please **attach** this label to my suitcase so that it won't come off.*
Word use: To **be attached to** someone is to like or love them very much.

attack (a-**tack**)
to begin to fight, often with weapons: *The army will **attack** the enemy at dawn.*

attempt (a-**tempt**)
to try to do something: *We will **attempt** to climb to the top of the mountain.*

attend (a-**tend**)
to be present at something: *Will your parents **attend** the meeting tonight?*
Word building: If you attend something, you are in **attendance**.

attention (a-**ten**-shon)
1. the fixing of your thoughts on something: *You need to give all your **attention** to solving this puzzle.*
2. a way of standing straight and still: *The soldiers stood at **attention**.*
Word building: If you pay attention, then you are being **attentive**.

attic *(at-ic)*
a room or a space inside the roof of a building: *We play hide-and-seek in our **attic**.*

attract *(a-tract)*
1. to pull or draw something nearer: *This magnet can **attract** steel pins.*
2. to interest or please someone by the way you look or behave: *Do you always **attract** people just by smiling at them?*

attractive *(a-trac-tiv)*
1. Someone is **attractive** if they are pleasing to look at: *Don't you think he is a very **attractive** man?*
2. Something is **attractive** if it makes you feel pleased and happy: *Spending the day at the beach is a very **attractive** idea.*

auction *(ok-shon)*
a sale at which things like houses or paintings are sold to the person who offers the most money.
Word building: Someone whose job is to sell things at an auction is an **auctioneer**.

audience *(or-dee-ence)*
a group of people who listen to or watch something like a concert or a play.

aunt *(arnt)*
1. the sister of your mother or father.
2. your uncle's wife.
Word use: You can also use **aunty**.

Australian Rules
a type of football played by teams of 18 players, which originated in Australia.
Word use: This is sometimes called **Aussie Rules** or **AFL**.

author *(or-thor)*
someone who writes books.

authority *(or-tho-ri-tee)*
the power to decide things, or to make people do as you think best: *The judge had the **authority** to send the thief to jail.*
Word building: If you have authority, then you are able to **authorise** things to happen.

autograph *(or-to-graf)*
someone's name in their own hand writing: *Justine has the Prime Minister's **autograph** in her collection.*

automatic *(or-tom-at-ic)*
1. Something is **automatic** if it can work or go all by itself: *Does your car have **automatic** windows or do you have to wind them?*
2. a car which has gears that change themselves.
Word building: If something is automatic, then it does things **automatically**.

autumn *(or-tum)*
the season of the year, after summer, when it starts to cool down and the leaves on some trees begin to change colour and fall.

available *(a-vail-a-bl)*
Something or someone is **available** if they are ready or able to be used: *There are three quiet horses **available** for you to ride.* | *Are you **available** to help put out the chairs?*

avalanche *(av-a-lanch)*
a large amount of ice and snow falling suddenly down a mountain.

avenue *(av-en-yoo)*
a street or road, often with trees on both sides of it.

average *(av-e-rij or av-rij)*
usual or ordinary: *It's just an **average** sort of bike — it doesn't do anything special.*

a
b
c
d
e
f
g
h
i
j
k
l
m
n
o
p
q
r
s
t
u
v
w
x
y
z

a
b
c
d
e
f
g
h
i
j
k
l
m
n
o
p
q
r
s
t
u
v
w
x
y
z

avocado *(av-o-car-doe)*
a green fruit with a tough skin and a large stone in the centre. It is shaped like a pear.

Word building: For more than one we use **avocados**.

avoid *(a-void)*
to keep away from something or someone.

awake *(a-wake)*
not asleep any more.

award *(a-ward; the last part rhymes with lord)*
a prize that you win for doing something well.

aware *(a-wair)*
If you are **aware** of something you know about it or have a feeling about it: *Are you aware that someone is creeping up behind you?*

away *(a-way)*
1. not in a place: *She is away from home. | Go away.*
2. not near: *Stand away from the door.*

awful *(or-ful)*
very bad or unpleasant.

awkward *(awk-ward)*
1. Someone who is **awkward** is clumsy in the way they move about: *That awkward person is always walking into things.*
2. Something that is **awkward** can cause you a lot of trouble: *This is an awkward room to paint because its walls are so bumpy.*

axe *(ax)*
a tool that has a sharp blade for chopping wood.

axle *(aks-l)*
the rod that goes through the middle of a wheel and which joins it to something: *My car has a broken axle — I'll have to call a tow truck.*

Bb

Ballerinas on bicycles balance basketballs.

baby *(bay-bee)*
a child or animal that's very young.
Word building: For more than one we use **babies**.

back
1. the part of something which is furthest away from the front.
2. the part of your body from the back of your neck to your bottom.

backwards *(back-wards)*
1. with the back part of something facing the front: *You've got your shirt on backwards.*
2. moving in the opposite direction to forwards: *We drove the car backwards into the garage.*

bacon *(bay-con)*
the meat which is taken from the back and sides of a pig, and is then salted.

bacteria *(bac-teer-ee-a)*
tiny living things that can cause disease and decay. They are so small, you need a microscope to see them.
Word use: Bacteria is the word we use for more than one. For one we use **bacterium**.

bad
1. Someone who is **bad** does things they know are wrong.
2. rotten or not good to eat: *You can tell that this apple is bad because it is brown and soft inside.*
Word building: more bad = **worse**, most bad = **worst** | If you are bad at doing something, you do it **badly**.

badge
a label you can pin or sew on to your clothes. It can tell people who you are, which group you belong to, or what sort of things you like.

badminton *(bad-min-ton)*
a game for two or four players who use racquets to hit a shuttlecock over a high net.

bag
a container for holding or carrying things: *Mum's wallet is in her bag.*

baggage
the suitcases and boxes which belong to a traveller: *I left my baggage at the hotel.*

bait
food you put on a hook or in a trap to catch fish or other animals.

bake
to cook something in an oven.

Word building: I **baked**, I am **baking**

baker *(bay-ker)*
someone whose job is to bake bread and cakes.

Word building: The place where the baker bakes the bread and cakes is a **bakery**.

balance *(bal-ance)*
to make or keep something steady: *I can balance a tennis ball on top of a ruler.*

Word building: I **balanced**, I am **balancing**

balcony *(bal-co-nee)*
a small verandah with rails, which comes out from the wall of a building.

Word building: For more than one we use **balconies**.

bald *(bawld)*
You are **bald** if you have only a little hair or no hair at all on your head.

Word building: Someone who is going bald is **balding**, and suffering from **baldness**.

ball[1]
a round object which you can bounce, kick, catch and use in games.

ball[2]
a dance held in the evening at which people wear formal suits and gowns.

ballerina *(bal-e-ree-na)*
a girl or woman who dances in a ballet.

ballet *(bal-ay)*
a sort of dancing, done by a group of dancers who act out a story on a stage.

balloon *(ba-loon)*
a small, coloured, rubber bag which you can fill with gas or air and use as a toy.

bamboo *(bam-boo)*
a plant which grows in hot countries and looks like very tall grass. Its hollow stems can be used for building huts or making furniture.

banana *(ba-nar-na)*
a long, curved fruit with a yellow skin that you peel off.

band[1]
a group of people who play music like rock or jazz.

band[2]
1. something you use for tying or fastening things: *I put a rubber band around my pencils to keep them all together.*
2. another word for **stripe**.

bandage *(ban-dij)*
a strip of material which you wrap around a sore part of your body.

bandaid *(band-aid)*
a cover that you stick over a sore to protect it.

bandicoot *(ban-dee-coot)*
a small Australian animal which has fur, a pointed nose, and sharp claws for digging. The female carries her babies in a pouch.

bang
1. a sudden, loud noise, like a balloon bursting.
2. to hit in a noisy way.

banish *(ban-ish)*
to send someone away because they've done something wrong.

banjo *(ban-jo)*
a musical instrument which you play by running your fingers across the strings and plucking them. It's smaller than a guitar, and looks a little bit like a frying pan.

Word building: For more than one we use **banjos**.

bank[1]
the sloping ground near the edge of a river or creek.

bank[2]
a place where people will look after your money until you need it again.

banksia *(bank-see-a)*
an Australian plant that has hundreds of tiny flowers crowded together in yellow or orange cylinder shapes.

Word use: It's named after Joseph Banks, who studied the plants of Australia when he visited with Captain Cook in 1770.

banquet *(bang-kwet)*
a big dinner party with many people.

baptism *(bap-tizm)*
the special time when someone is blessed and sprinkled with, or put under, water as a sign that they are new members of the Christian church.

bar
1. a long piece of wood or metal.
2. a long high table in a place like a hotel, where drinks are served.

barbecue *(bar-be-kyoo)*
1. a fireplace outdoors, for cooking meat over an open fire.
2. an outdoor party where the food is cooked over an open fire.

Word use: Another way of spelling this is **barbeque**.

barber *(bar-ber)*
someone whose job is to cut men's hair.

bare *(rhymes with care)*
without any covering: *We took off our shoes and ran in our bare feet.*

Word use: Don't confuse this with **bear**[1] or **bear**[2].

bargain *(bar-gan)*
something that you buy for less than you expect to pay for it: *My phone was a bargain at only $50.*

bark[1]
the loud, sharp noise a dog makes.

bark[2]
the outer covering on the trunk and branches of a tree.

bar mitzvah *(bar mits-va)*
the special time when a Jewish boy turns thirteen, and becomes an adult member of the Jewish community.

barn
a large shed on a farm, used to store hay or as a shelter for animals.

barramundi *(barra-mun-dee)*
a large, silver-grey coloured fish, which is good to eat.

Word use: This word comes from an Aboriginal language of Queensland. See the map of Australian Aboriginal languages at the end of this book.

barrel *(ba-rel)*
a large, rounded container made of strips of wood held in place by iron bands. Beer and wine are often kept in barrels.

barrier *(ba-ree-er)*
something that blocks the way.

base
1. the bottom part of anything.
2. the main place from where things are organised: *The explorers went back to base to get more food.*
3. one of the four fixed positions on a softball or baseball field that a runner tries to run around.

baseball *(base-ball)*
a ball game played by two teams in which a long, thin bat is used to hit a hard ball. The batter must run around the three bases on the field and return home to score a point.

basement *(base-ment)*
a room or space below the ground floor.

bash
to hit hard.

basic
main or most important: *The basic ingredient of a sandwich is bread.*

basin *(bay-sin)*
1. a small sink or shallow container that holds water for washing.
2. a bowl that you use to mix or cook food in.

basket *(bar-sket)*
a container to carry or keep things in, usually made of cane or straw.

basketball *(bask-et-ball)*
a ball game played by two teams of five people. Players can bounce the ball and they must try to score a goal by throwing the ball into the ring on top of a tall post.

bat¹
a stick that you use to hit the ball in games like cricket.
Word building: I **batted**, I am **batting**

bat²
a small animal with fur and wings. It flies about at night to feed on fruit and insects, and in the daytime it sleeps hanging upside down.

bath
a container for washing yourself in, large enough for you to sit or lie in.
Word building: When you wash yourself in a bath of warm water, you **bathe** *(baydh)*.

bathroom
a room with a basin, a bath or a shower, and often a toilet.

bat mitzvah *(bat mits-va)*
the special time when a Jewish girl turns twelve, and becomes an adult member of the Jewish community.

battery *(bat-e-ree)*
a container which stores electricity.
Word building: For more than one we use **batteries**.

battle *(bat-l)*
1. a big and serious fight.
2. to struggle: *We had to battle against the strong current for more than an hour.*
Word building: I **battled**, I am **battling** | Someone who battles is a **battler**.

bay
a curve in the shore of a sea, harbour or lake. The water inside the curve is usually calm.

be
You can use **be** or one of its different forms in several ways, for example:
1. if you are describing someone or something: *She is beautiful.* | *I am tired.* | *My father is a cook.* | *Yesterday was Sunday.* | *The children were very noisy.* | *Are they here?*
2. as a helping word with another word: *I am shopping.* | *She was walking.* | *They are coming.*
Word building: I **am**, you **are**, he **is**, we **are**, they **are**; I **was**, you **were**, he **was**, we **were**, they **were**; I have **been**, I am **being**

beach
a sandy place on the edge of a sea, lake or river where you can usually play and swim.

bead
a small, hard ball which has a hole through the middle so that you can thread it onto a string.

beak
the hard pointed part of a bird's mouth.
Word use: Another word that means nearly the same is **bill**.

beam
1. a long, strong piece of wood, concrete or metal.
2. a long line of light, like one from a torch or a lighthouse.

bean
a plant with small, smooth seeds growing in long pods. You eat the seeds and the pods as a vegetable.

bear¹ *(bair)*
1. to carry or hold up something: *Will the wooden bridge **bear** the weight of the elephant?*
2. to put up with: *When I broke my leg the pain was almost too much to **bear**.*
3. to produce or grow something: *I hope the peach tree will **bear** fruit.*

Word building: I **bore**, I have **borne**, I am **bearing**

Word use: Don't confuse this with **bare** or **bear²**.

bear² *(bair)*
a large animal with short, rough fur, long, sharp claws, and a very short tail.

Word use: Don't confuse this with **bare** or **bear¹**.

beard
the hair that grows on a man's chin and cheeks.

beast
1. any animal with four legs, like a cow or a dog.
2. a rough cruel person.

beat *(beet)*
1. to hit something again and again.
2. to make a movement again and again: *There was a scream as the lights went out and my heart began to **beat** quickly.*
3. a sound made again and again: *We could hear the **beat** of the drum.*

Word building: I **beat**, I have **beaten**, I am **beating**

beautiful *(**byoo**-ti-ful)*
things are beautiful if they are pleasing to look at.

Word building: If something is beautiful, it has **beauty**.

because *(be-**corze** or be-**coz**)*
for the reason that: *We have to save water **because** there is a drought.*

become *(be-**cum**)*
to come or grow to be: *If you spend too much time in front of that computer screen, your eyes will **become** sore.*

bed
1. a piece of furniture to sleep on, with a mattress, pillow and covers.
2. a plot of earth in a garden: *I planted roses in that flower **bed**.*
3. the ground under a sea or river.

bedroom
a room for sleeping in: *I will have my own **bedroom** in the new house.*

bee
a flying insect which makes honey and which can sting you.

beef
the meat from a cow or bull.

beer *(rhymes with **ear**)*
a drink with alcohol in it that some adults drink.

beetle *(**beet**-l)*
a flying insect which has a hard covering over its wings.

before *(be-**for**)*
1. at a time earlier than: *You must have your bath **before** you go to bed.*
2. in front of: *You were **before** me in the line at the cinema, and you got the last movie ticket.*

before-school care
a place where you can go in the mornings, where people look after you before school starts.

a
b
c
d
e
f
g
h
i
j
k
l
m
n
o
p
q
r
s
t
u
v
w
x
y
z

beg
to ask for something that you need badly: *They were so poor they had to **beg** for food.*
Word building: I **begged**, I am **begging** | Somebody who needs to beg for money, clothes or food is a **beggar**.

begin *(be-**gin**)*
to start.
Word building: I **began**, I have **begun**, I am **beginning** | When you are just beginning to learn to do something, you are a **beginner**.

beginning
the start, or first part, of something: *January is at the **beginning** of the year.*

behave *(be-**have**)*
1. to act in a particular way: *If you don't **behave** properly, you will be sent home from camp.*
2. To **behave** yourself is to be good: *Our teacher told us to **behave** ourselves and work quietly.*
Word building: I **behaved**, I am **behaving** | The way you behave is your **behaviour**, whether it's good or bad.

behind *(be-**hind**)*
at the back of: *We keep the broom **behind** the kitchen door.*

believe *(be-**leev**)*
to think that something is true or right: *Do you **believe** that he is telling the truth?*
Word building: I **believed**, I am **believing** | Something that you believe is a **belief**.

bell
a piece of metal shaped like a cup upside down, which makes a ringing sound when you hit it.

bellow *(**bell**-oe)*
to roar or cry out loudly.

belly *(**bell**-ee)*
the front part of your body that has your stomach inside it.
Word use: Another word that means nearly the same is **abdomen**.

belong *(be-**long**)*
1. to be owned by someone: *This pen must **belong** to you, because mine is still in my bag.*
2. to be part of: *I **belong** to a swimming club.*
3. to be in the right place: *Does this cup **belong** on the top shelf?*

below *(be-**lo**)*
1. underneath: *Please write your address **below** your name on the form.*
2. lower than: *My brother is in the class **below** me at school.*

belt
a strip of strong material worn around your waist to keep your pants up.

bench
1. a long seat.
2. a strong table to work at.
Word building: For more than one we use **benches**.

bend
1. to curve or turn.
2. to lean down.
3. a curve.
Word building: I **bent**, I am **bending**

beneath *(be-**neeth**)*
under: *The treasure is hidden somewhere **beneath** the sand.*

bent
crooked or curved: *The wire is **bent**.*

beret *(be-ray)*
a soft round cap.

berry *(be-ree)*
a small fruit, often brightly coloured.
Word building: For more than one we use **berries**.
Word use: Don't confuse this with **bury**.

beside *(be-side)*
next to: *If I sit beside you, we can read the book together.*

besides
1. in addition to: *Is anyone coming to the movie besides you?*
2. other than: *We have two other dogs besides this one.*

best
as good as possible and better than anything or anyone else: *She's pretty good at swimming and tennis, but she's best at running.*

betray *(be-tray)*
to hurt somebody by telling their secret when you're not supposed to.
Word building: When you betray somebody, your action is a **betrayal**.

better *(bett-er)*
1. more than just good, but not the best: *One biscuit would be good, but two would be better.*
2. well again, or getting well: *Yesterday I was sick, but today I am better.*

bettong *(bett-ong)*
a very small kangaroo that looks like a small wallaby with a short nose. It is endangered. See the table at the end of this book.
Word use: This word comes from the Dharug language of New South Wales. See the map of Australian Aboriginal languages at the end of this book.

between *(bee-tween)*
in the middle of one thing and another: *Six is between five and seven. | Our house is between the red house and the blue house.*

beware *(be-wair)*
to be careful of something or someone: *The sign said 'Beware of the dog'.*

bewilder *(be-wil-der)*
to puzzle someone.

beyond *(be-yond or bee-yond)*
further than: *I would like to travel beyond the moon!*

bicentenary *(by-sen-teen-a-ree)*
a 200th anniversary.
Word building: For more than one we use **bicentenaries**.

bicycle *(by-sik-l)*
a thing that you can ride, which has two wheels, pedals and handlebars for steering it.
Word building: This word is often shortened to **bike**.

big
1. large in size or amount: *Australia is a big island.*
2. elder: *I have two big sisters.*
Word building: more big = **bigger**, most big = **biggest**

bike rack
a structure that you can lock bikes onto for safety.

bilby *(bil-bee)*
a type of bandicoot that is vulnerable. See the table at the end of this book.
Word use: This word comes from the Yuwaalaraay language of New South Wales. See the map of Australian Aboriginal languages at the end of this book.

bill¹
a written note saying how much you owe for something: *We finished our meal and asked the waiter for our bill.*

bill²
the hard part of a bird's mouth, broader and flatter than a beak.

billabong *(bill-a-bong)*
a waterhole that was once part of a river.
Word use: This word comes from the Wiradjuri language of New South Wales. See the map of Australian Aboriginal languages at the end of this book.

a
b
c
d
e
f
g
h
i
j
k
l
m
n
o
p
q
r
s
t
u
v
w
x
y
z

billion
a thousand times a million (1 000 000 000).

billy *(bill-ee)*
a tin with a lid, that you use to boil water in over an open fire.
Word use: This is also known as a **billy can**.

billy goat
a male goat.

bin
a box or container used to store rubbish or other things: *Put the papers in the recycling* **bin**.

bind *(rhymes with* **find***)*
to tie up.
Word building: I **bound**, I am **binding**

bindi-eye *(bin-dee-eye)*
a small plant that sometimes grows in grass. It has tiny, sharp thorns.
Word use: This word comes from the Yuwaalaraay and Kamilaroi languages of New South Wales. See the map of Australian Aboriginal languages at the end of this book.

binoculars *(bin-**ok**-yu-lars)*
special glasses that you look through, which make faraway things seem much nearer.

biodegradable *(by-o-de-**grade**-a-bl)*
able to decay, especially in soil: **Biodegradable** *packaging is not harmful to the environment.*

biology
the science or study of all living things.

bird
an animal with two legs, two wings, and feathers.

birth
1. the start of a life.
2. any beginning.

birthday
the date of your birth.

birthplace
the place where someone was born or where something came from.

biscuit *(bis-kit)*
a small, thin, dry cake.

bistro *(biss-tro)*
a small, casual restaurant.

bit[1]
a small piece of something.

bit[2]
a small metal bar which goes into a horse's mouth and is attached to the reins.

bite
to grab or take a piece out of something with your teeth.
Word building: I **bit**, I have **bitten**, I am **biting** | When you bite something, you take a **bite** out of it.
Word use: Don't confuse **bite** with **byte**.

bitter
1. having a sharp unpleasant taste: *This food is very* **bitter**.
2. angry and hurt: *Don't feel* **bitter** *if you don't win.*

black
Something is **black** if it is completely dark in colour.

blackboard *(black-bord)*
a large, dark-coloured board used for writing or drawing on with chalk.

blade
1. the flat part of a knife set into the handle.
2. something that has the same shape as a knife blade, like a leaf of grass.

blame
to say that someone made something bad happen: *Don't **blame** me — I didn't break your phone.*
Word building: I **blamed**, I am **blaming**

blank
Something is **blank** if it hasn't been written or printed on.

blanket *(blang-ket)*
a large woollen cover that you use to keep warm in bed.

blast *(rhymes with last)*
1. a sudden, strong rush of wind or air.
2. to blow something up into pieces.

blaze
to burn with a lot of flame: *I like to see a good fire **blaze** in the fireplace.*
Word building: it **blazed**, it is **blazing**

blazer *(blay-zer)*
a jacket, often with a sports badge sewn on the pocket.

bleach
to make something white or pale: *I will have to **bleach** my white shirt to get rid of the stains on it.*

bleak
so cold that it makes you feel miserable.

bleat
to make the cry that a sheep or goat makes.

bleed
to have blood coming out: *I bumped my nose and it began to **bleed**.*
Word building: I **bled**, I am **bleeding**

blend
to mix together.
Word building: A small machine you use in the kitchen to blend things is a **blender**.

bless
to pray that God will keep someone safe and happy: *The priest went to the hospital to **bless** the sick child.*

blind *(rhymes with dined)*
1. You're **blind** if you can't see because there is something wrong with your eyes.
2. a cover over a window, which keeps out the light.
Word building: If you are blind, then you suffer from **blindness**.

blink
to shut and open your eyes quickly and often: *Try not to **blink** while the doctor examines your eyes.*

blister *(bliss-ter)*
a small swelling on your skin filled with watery liquid.

block
1. a hard piece of wood, stone, metal or anything like this: *Can you help me carry this **block** of wood?*
2. a piece of land you can build a house on.
3. a building with many flats, offices, and things like that.
4. to be in the way of something: *Some accidents **block** the traffic.*

blog
a diary you write on the internet: *I'm going to write about this movie in my **blog**.*
Word building: If you write a blog, you are a **blogger**.

blond
You are **blond** if you have fair hair and skin.
Word building: A woman or girl with blond hair is a **blonde**.

blood *(blud)*
the red liquid that flows through your body.

Word building: If something has blood on it, then it is **bloody**.

bloom
to grow flowers: *Our rose bush will bloom in summer.*

blossom *(bloss-om)*
the flower of a fruit tree.

blouse
a loosely fitting shirt for a woman or girl, usually tucked in at the waist.

blow¹
1. a sudden hard hit or knock.
2. the sudden shock you feel when something bad happens without warning.

blow²
1. to be moving along: *The wind will blow and there will be heavy rain for three more days.*
2. to make a stream of air come out of your mouth: *The wolf had to blow very hard to make the straw house fall down.*

Word building: I **blew**, I have **blown**, I am **blowing**

blue
Something is **blue** if it is the colour of a clear sky.

Word building: more blue = **bluer**, most blue = **bluest**

bluebottle *(blu-bott-l)*
a small, blue, sea animal. It has long tentacles which can sting you.

blue-tongue *(blu-tung)*
a large Australian lizard with a blue tongue.

blunder *(blun-der)*
1. a silly mistake.
2. to move in a clumsy way.

blunt
not sharp: *I can't cut the meat with this blunt knife.*

blush
to go red in the face when you're ashamed or shy.

BMX bike *(bee-em-ex bike)*
a strongly built bicycle with smaller wheels and thicker tyres than other bikes. It is good for riding on dirt tracks.

board *(bord)*
1. a long, thin piece of wood.
2. a flat piece of wood or card made for a special reason: *You get out the chess board, and I'll find the lost chess pieces.*
3. to get on something: *Passengers flying to Brisbane should board the plane now.*
4. to pay for a room and meals somewhere: *My sister is going to board at school this year.*

Word building: Someone who boards somewhere is a **boarder**.

Word use: Don't confuse **board** with **bored**, which describes someone who is tired of something.

boast
to speak in a way that shows you are too proud of yourself or things that belong to you.

Word building: Someone who likes to boast is a **boaster** and says **boastful** things.

boat
something that floats, smaller than a ship but big enough to carry people or things over water.

body *(bod-ee)*
1. all of a living person or animal: *Your body is not the same shape as mine.*
2. a dead person or animal: *I found the body of a dead bird in the bush.*

Word building: For more than one we use **bodies**.

boil

1. to heat water, or something like it, until it bubbles and steam comes off.
2. to cook food by putting it in boiling water.

bold

so brave that you aren't afraid to take risks.

Word building: A bold person shows **boldness** and acts **boldly**.

bolt

1. a bar which you slide to hold a door or gate shut.
2. a thick metal pin which you use to hold pieces of wood or metal together.

bomb *(bom)*

something made so that it will blow up and cause a lot of damage.

bone

one of the hard parts of your body that make up your skeleton.

Word building: If something is made of bone, then it is **bony**.

bonfire *(bon-fire)*

a large fire that you light outside in an open place to have a party around.

boogie board *(boog-ee bord)*

a small, light and slightly curved board that you take into the surf so that you can lie on it and let the waves take you back to the shore.

book

1. a lot of pages fastened together with a cover, with words written or printed in it for you to read.
2. to order something ahead of time or before you need it: *I'll **book** the tickets for tomorrow's play.*

Word building: If you book your tickets ahead of time, you make a **booking**.

bookcase

a set of shelves for books.

bookmark

1. a strip of paper, cloth, or something similar placed between the pages of a book to mark a place.
2. a website's address that you save in your computer because you want to be able to return to the website easily.

boomerang *(boom-e-rang)*

a curved stick traditionally used as a weapon by Aboriginal people. One kind comes back to you when you throw it.

Word use: This word comes from the Dharug language of New South Wales. See the map of Australian Aboriginal languages at the end of this book.

boot[1]

1. a kind of shoe which covers the lower part of your leg.
2. a separate part for bags and other luggage at the back of a car.

boot[2]

to start up a computer by loading its memory system.

Word use: You can also use **boot up**.

border *(bord-er)*

1. the edge or side of anything.
2. a line that separates or divides one country or State from another.

Word use: Don't confuse this with **boarder**, which is someone who pays for meals and somewhere to sleep.

bore[1]

1. to make a round hole with a drill or with something like that.
2. a deep hole you drill in dry parts of a country to reach water that is under the ground.

Word building: I **bored**, I am **boring**

bore²

1. to make someone tired or weary: *These cartoons **bore** me — I've seen them before.*
2. a dull person.

Word building: he **bored**, he is **boring** | Things that bore you are **boring** and fill you with feelings of **boredom**.

born

brought into life as a baby: *My brother was **born** yesterday.*

borrow *(bo-roe)*

to take or get something, knowing that you have to give it back: *I **borrow** books each week from the school library.*

Word use: Compare this with **lend**.

boss

the person who gives other people work and tells them what to do.

Word building: If you act too much like a boss, then you are **bossy**.

both

the two together: ***Both** children went to the circus.*

bother *(bodh-er)*

to annoy or pester someone.

Word building: Things that bother you are **bothersome**.

bottle *(bot-l)*

a container, usually made of glass, that's narrow at the top and has no handle. We often use bottles to put water, milk and other drinks in.

bottlebrush *(bott-l-brush)*

an Australian plant with red or pink flowers like brushes.

bottom *(bott-om)*

1. the lowest part of anything.
2. the round part of the body at the base of your back.

bough *(rhymes with **cow**)*

one of the large branches of a tree.

Word use: Don't confuse this with **bow**¹ or **bow**².

boulder *(bold-er)*

a large, smooth rock.

bounce

1. to hit against something and return: *The ball should **bounce** on this wooden floor.*
2. to throw one thing against another and make it return: *They like to **bounce** their balls along the footpath.*

Word building: I **bounced**, I am **bouncing**

bound

a jump or leap: *With a mighty **bound** the kangaroo escaped over the fence.*

boundary *(bownd-ree)*

a line that divides one thing from another, or marks a limit: *Here's the **boundary** between your land and mine.*

Word building: For more than one we use **boundaries**.

bouquet *(boo-**kay** or boh-**kay**)*

a bunch of flowers.

bow¹ *(rhymes with **cow**)*

to bend or stoop down to show respect for someone: *The karate champion will **bow** to her opponent.*

Word use: Don't confuse this with **bough** or **bow**².

bow² *(boe)*

1. a piece of wood bent by a string stretched from one end of it to the other. It is used to shoot arrows.
2. a knot you make with two loops and two ends: *I'll tie this ribbon in a **bow** for your hair.*
3. the special stick you use to play a musical instrument with strings like a violin.

Word use: Don't confuse this with **bough** or **bow**¹.

bowl[1] *(bole)*
a deep, round dish.

bowl[2] *(bole)*
to throw a cricket ball towards the person batting.

Word building: If it's your turn to bowl in cricket, you are the **bowler**.

box[1] *(boks)*
a container with a lid.

Word building: For more than one we use **boxes**.

box[2] *(boks)*
to fight with your hands or fists.

Word building: If you box using special gloves, then you are a **boxer** and take part in the sport of **boxing**.

boy
a male child.

bracelet *(brace-let)*
a chain or band worn around your wrist for decoration.

brain
1. the soft, grey mass inside the top of your head. It controls your body's ability to feel, think and move.
2. a very clever person who knows many things: *She's the real brain in our family.*

Word building: Someone who is a brain is **brainy**.

brake
the part of a car, or bike or any other machine like this, which stops it or slows it down.

Word use: Don't confuse this with **break**.

branch
1. one of the large arm-like parts of a tree or shrub.
2. one of a group of shops, offices or banks with the same name, or run by the same people: *Our bank once had a branch in every suburb.*

Word building: For more than one we use **branches**.

brand
1. the mark or label which shows where something comes from or who makes it.
2. a kind or make of something: *Please buy my favourite brand of ice-cream.*

brass *(rhymes with class)*
a yellow metal made when copper and zinc are mixed together: *My new trumpet is made of brass.*

brave
You are **brave** if you are able to do something that frightens you: *The brave girl saved her brother from drowning in the wild surf.*

Word building: If you are brave, then you do things **bravely** with a lot of **bravery**.

Word use: Another word that means nearly the same is **courageous**.

bread *(bred)*
a food made when you bake a dough of flour and water, usually adding yeast to make it rise or swell up.

breadth *(bredth)*
how far something is from one side to the other: *What's the breadth of this creek?*

Word use: Another word that means nearly the same is **width**.

break *(brake)*
1. to split into bits in a rough or sudden way.
2. to not keep something like a rule or a promise: *They often break their word and don't do what they say they will.*
3. a short rest.

Word building: I **broke**, I have **broken**, I am **breaking** | If something can break, then it's **breakable**.

Word use: Don't confuse **break** with **brake**.

breakfast *(brek-fast)*
the first meal of the day.

a
b
c
d
e
f
g
h
i
j
k
l
m
n
o
p
q
r
s
t
u
v
w
x
y
z

a
b
c
d
e
f
g
h
i
j
k
l
m
n
o
p
q
r
s
t
u
v
w
x
y
z

breast *(brest)*
1. an old-fashioned word for your chest.
2. a part of a woman's body that makes milk to feed babies.

breath *(breth)*
the air that you take into your lungs and let out again.
Word building: If you are short of breath, then you are **breathless**. When you take a breath, you **breathe** *(breedh)*.

breed
1. to keep animals so that they can produce young ones.
2. a special sort or kind: *Those sheep with the black faces are my favourite breed*.
Word building: I **bred**, I am **breeding**

breeze
a light or gentle wind.

brick
a hard block of baked clay, used for building.
Word building: Someone who builds with bricks is a **bricklayer**.

bride
a woman who is being married.

bridegroom *(bride-groom)*
a man who is being married.

bridesmaid *(brides-maid)*
a woman whose job is to help a bride on the day of her wedding.

bridge
something built over a river, road or railway line. It is a way of getting from one side to the other.

brief *(breef)*
short: *I'm making a brief visit to the library — just long enough to return my books.*

brigade *(bri-gade)*
a group of people trained to do a special job. These people usually wear a uniform: *Quick, call the fire brigade to put out the fire!*

bright *(brite)*
1. Something is **bright** if it shines or gives out a strong light.
2. clever.
3. happy.
Word building: If something is bright, it shines **brightly** and **brightens** things up with its **brightness**.

brilliant *(brill-yant)*
1. Something is **brilliant** if it shines with a very bright light.
2. very, very clever.
3. so good that it stands out from all the rest: *The film I saw last night was brilliant*.
Word building: If something or someone is brilliant, they have **brilliance**.

brim
1. the top edge of something hollow like a cup or bowl: *He filled my mug to the brim with soup.*
2. the outer edge of a hat: *She pulled down the brim to protect her face from the sun.*

bring
to carry something with you: *Remember to bring your towel to the beach.*
Word building: I **brought**, I am **bringing**

bristle *(briss-l)*
a short, stiff hair or something like this.

brittle *(britt-l)*
Something is **brittle** if it is likely to break easily: *That shell was so brittle that it cracked when I picked it up.*

broad (brawd)
very wide.

Word building: If you make something broad you **broaden** it and increase its **breadth**.

broadcast (brawd-cast)
to send information by radio or television: *They will **broadcast** the program this afternoon.*

Word building: I **broadcast**, I have **broadcast**, I am **broadcasting**

broccoli (brok-o-lee or brok-o-lie)
a green vegetable with small, hard flowers like a cauliflower.

broken (broke-n)
1. Something is **broken** if it is smashed into pieces.
2. not able to work properly because something is wrong with one of the parts: *Can you fix my **broken** watch?*

Word use: You can also find this word at **break**.

brolga (brol-ga)
a large, silvery-grey bird. It has long legs and it dances.

Word use: This word comes from the Kamilaroi language of New South Wales. See the map of Australian Aboriginal languages at the end of this book.

bronze (bronz)
a brown metal which is made by mixing copper and tin.

brooch (broach)
an ornament made so that you can fasten it to your clothes with a pin: *My mother is wearing a beautiful opal **brooch** on her coat.*

Word building: For more than one we use **brooches**.

broom
a brush with a long handle. It is used for sweeping.

brother (rhymes with mother)
a man or boy who has the same parents as you.

brown
Something is **brown** if it is the colour of earth. You mix red, yellow and black together to make brown.

browser
computer software that helps you search for things on the internet.

bruise (bruze)
a mark that comes on your skin if you have had a fall or been hit.

brush
a tool made of hair or bristles fastened to a handle, like a paintbrush, a hairbrush or a scrubbing-brush.

Word building: For more than one we use **brushes**.

bubble (bubb-l)
a small ball of air or gas: *A **bubble** from the lemonade went up my nose. | The **bubble** I blew with the soapy water floated away.*

bubblegum
chewing gum which can be blown into bubbles.

bucket (buck-et)
a round container with a flat bottom and a handle. It is used for carrying things such as water or sand.

buckle (buck-l)
something you use to fasten a belt or strap. Some shoes have buckles on them.

Buddhism *(bood-izm; the first part rhymes with **wood**)*

a religion started by a special teacher called the Buddha who lived in India a very long time ago. This religion teaches that we can be happy if we destroy greed and hatred in ourselves.

Word building: Someone who follows Buddhism is called a **Buddhist**.

budge

to move: *I won't **budge** from this chair until you chase away that spider! | We can't **budge** this heavy table.*

Word building: I **budged**, I am **budging**

Word use: This word is usually used with the word 'not'.

budgerigar *(budge-e-ree-gar)*

a kind of small yellow and green parrot. It is found in parts of Australia away from the coast but can be kept in a cage. Some people breed them in other colours such as blue.

Word building: This word is often shortened to **budgie**.

Word use: This word comes from the Kamilaroi language of New South Wales. See the map of Australian Aboriginal languages at the end of this book.

buffalo *(buff-a-lo)*

a sort of wild cattle, sometimes tamed and used for pulling heavy loads.

Word building: For more than one we use **buffaloes** or **buffalos**.

buffet *(buff-ay)*

a table or counter in a restaurant holding food that you can help yourself to.

build *(bild)*

to make something by joining parts together: *They have started to **build** our new house.*

Word building: I **built**, I am **building** | Someone whose job is to build houses and other buildings is a **builder**.

building *(bild-ing)*

something you build for people to live or work in, such as a house or an office block.

bulb

1. the round, white underground part of some plants, such as the onion.
2. anything with a shape rather like that of an onion: *Please get me a new electric light **bulb** out of the box.*

bulge

to swell out.

Word building: I **bulged**, I am **bulging**

bull *(rhymes with **wool**)*

1. the male of cattle.
2. a male elephant, whale or seal.

Word use: The female is a **cow**.

bulldozer *(bull-dozer)*

a strong tractor with a blade in front. It is used to move trees and rocks and to make land flat.

bullet *(bull-et)*

a small piece of metal made to be shot from a small gun.

bully

someone who hurts or frightens people smaller or weaker than themselves.

Word building: For more than one we use **bullies**.

bump

1. to knock against something by mistake: *I'm trying not to **bump** the table.*
2. a small swollen lump on your body caused by a knock or hit.
3. a small part raised higher than what is all around it: *Don't drive your car over that **bump** in the road.*

Word building: Something that has many bumps is **bumpy**.

bun

1. a kind of round bread roll which can be plain or sweetened.
2. hair arranged at the back of your head in the shape of a bun.

bunch

a group of things that are joined or have been gathered together.

Word building: For more than one we use **bunches**.

bundle *(bund-l)*

a group of things held together in a loose way: *I took my **bundle** of sticks back to the camp.*

bungee jumping *(bun-jee jump-ing)*

a sport in which you jump from a high place to which you are attached by a long, thick elastic cord around your feet.

bunk *(bungk)*

1. a narrow bed built like a shelf, such as one on a ship.
2. one of two matching beds built one above the other.

bunyip *(bun-yip)*

a make-believe creature from Aboriginal stories. It is said to live in swamps and billabongs.

Word use: This word comes from the Wembawemba language of Victoria. See the map of Australian Aboriginal languages at the end of this book.

buoy *(boy)*

something that's made to float in one spot in the sea so that it can guide ships.

burden *(berd-n)*

a load that is very heavy to carry.

burger

a bread roll containing a flat, round piece of minced beef, chicken, fish or vegetables and often other things like cheese, lettuce, tomato and sauce.

burglar *(berg-lar)*

someone who breaks into a building to steal things.

Word building: If burglars steal things from buildings, they **burgle** them and they commit the crime of **burglary**.

burn *(bern)*

1. to be on fire.
2. to hurt by heat or fire: *You'll **burn** your mouth on that hot sausage.*
3. a sore made by something hot.

Word building: it **burnt** or it **burned**, it is **burning**

burrow *(bu-roe)*

a hole in the ground that an animal digs to live in.

burst *(berst)*

1. to split or break open without warning.
2. to rush all at once: *The children **burst** into the room before I could stop them.*

Word building: it **burst**, it is **bursting**

bury *(rhymes with **merry**)*

to put something in the ground and cover it over with earth.

Word building: I **buried**, I am **burying** | If you bury a dead person in a coffin, then you give them a **burial**.

Word use: Don't confuse **bury** with **berry**.

bus

a very long vehicle with many seats for carrying passengers from one place to another.

bush

1. a plant with lots of branches coming out from the bottom of its trunk.
2. land which has its natural growth of trees: *I'm going for a walk in the **bush** behind the school.*

Word building: Something that is thick and looks like a bush is **bushy**.

bushcare *(bush-care)*
caring for nature by looking after native plants.

bushfire
a fire in the bush or forest.

bushranger *(bush-rain-jer)*
someone who hid in the bush and got their money and food by robbing travellers: *Ned Kelly was a famous **bushranger**.*

business *(biz-ness)*
1. someone's work or job.
2. a place or activity that makes money: *My cousin took over this furniture **business** from my uncle.*

busy *(biz-ee)*
1. You are **busy** if you have plenty to do.
2. with many things happening: *Christmas is a **busy** time of year at our shop.*
Word building: more busy = **busier**, most busy = **busiest** | If you are busy doing something, then you do it **busily**.

but
1. You use **but** if you want to add something different to something you have just said: *We chased the cat across the park, **but** we had to stop when it climbed to the top of a tree.*
2. except: *I have had nothing **but** water all day.*

butcher *(butch-er)*
someone whose job it is to cut up meat and get it ready to sell.
Word building: The shop where a butcher sells meat is a **butchery**.

butter *(butt-er)*
a soft, yellow food made from cream. You can spread it on things like bread, or use it for cooking.

butterfly *(butt-er-fly)*
an insect with large wings which are often brightly coloured.
Word building: For more than one we use **butterflies**.

button *(butt-n)*
1. a small, round object sewn onto your clothes to join two parts together.
2. a small, round object, such as a knob you press to ring a bell.

buy *(by)*
to get something by paying money for it.
Word building: I **bought**, I am **buying**
Word use: Don't confuse this with **by**.

buzz
a low hum like the sound a bee makes.

by
1. near: *We live **by** the beach.*
2. using as a way: *I will come **by** bus.*
Word use: Don't confuse this with **buy**.

byte *(bite)*
a unit of information stored by a computer.
Word use: Don't confuse this with **bite**.

Cc

Caterpillars on cushions chew cactus.

cab
1. a taxi.
2. the covered part of a truck where the driver sits.

cabbage *(cabb-ij)*
a vegetable with large, green leaves.

cabin *(cab-in)*
1. a small house or hut.
2. a room in a ship where people sleep.
3. the space inside a plane where people sit.

cable *(cay-bl)*
thick, strong rope, or several bits of wire twisted together.

cactus *(cac-tus)*
a plant with spikes, which grows in hot, dry places. It can store water in its thick stem.
Word building: For more than one we use **cacti**.

cafe *(caf-ay)*
a shop where you can buy coffee and other drinks, or eat a small meal.

cage
a box or room made with wire or bars, for keeping animals or birds in.

cake
a sweet food made with butter, flour, sugar and eggs. You bake it in an oven.

calculate *(cal-kyoo-layt)*
to work out using maths or by thinking carefully: *I will* **calculate** *the answer to this homework question.* | *Can you please help me* **calculate** *the distance to the park from the school?*
Word building: I **calculated**, I am **calculating**

calculation *(cal-kyoo-lay-shun)*
1. the act of calculating: *I need some help with this* **calculation**.
2. the answer or result you get from calculating: *According to my* **calculations**, *my brother is three times as lazy as I am.*

calculator *(cal-kyu-lay-tor)*
a small machine that you can use to do sums.

calendar *(cal-en-dar)*
a chart that shows you the days and weeks of each month of the year.

calf[1] *(carf)*
1. a young cow or bull.
2. a young whale, elephant or seal.
Word building: For more than one we use **calves**.

calf² *(carf)*
the back part of your leg, below the knee.
Word building: For more than one we use **calves**.

call
1. to shout out to someone.
2. to ask someone or something to come: *I'd better call a doctor.*
3. to telephone someone.
4. to give a name to someone or something: *Her parents decided to call her Sue. | What do you call that strange red fruit?*

calm *(carm)*
1. still, with no bumpy movements: *The boat hardly rocked on the calm sea.*
2. You are **calm** if you don't get upset or excited.
Word building: If someone is calm, then they are able to do things **calmly**.

camel *(cam-el)*
a large, four-footed animal with humps on its back. It is used to carry people and loads across the desert.

camera *(cam-ra)*
a machine which you use to take photographs.

camouflage *(cam-o-flarzh)*
to hide something by changing the way it looks: *You need to use brown mud to camouflage your pale face so you can hide in the jungle.*
Word building: I **camouflaged**, I am **camouflaging**

camp
1. a group of tents or caravans where you can live outdoors for a while.
2. to live for a while in a tent.
Word building: If you camp at a place, then you are a **camper**.

can¹
a metal container for holding food and drink.

can²
to be able to do something.
Word use: This word is a helping word. It is always used with another one in the form I **can** or I **could** do something.

canal *(ca-nal)*
a waterway made for boats to carry people and cargo to places where there is no river.

canary *(ca-nair-ree)*
a small, yellow bird that sings sweetly. You can keep it as a pet.
Word building: For more than one we use **canaries**.

cancel *(can-sel)*
to stop something that you have arranged from happening: *We had to cancel the festival because of the rain.*
Word building: I **cancelled**, I am **cancelling** | If you have to cancel something, you make a **cancellation**.

cancer *(can-ser)*
a bad illness that can make a lump grow in one part of your body and spread to other parts as well.

candle *(cand-l)*
a piece of wax with a wick in it which burns to give light.

cane
the thin hard stem of some plants, such as bamboo.

cannibal *(can-i-bl)*
someone who eats other people.

cannon *(can-on)*
a large gun on wheels.

cannot *(ca-not)*
can not: *You can have cake, but you **cannot** have ice-cream with it.*

canoe *(ca-noo)*
a light narrow boat that you move by using paddles.
Word building: Someone who paddles a canoe is a **canoeist**.

canteen *(can-teen)*
a place in a school, factory or office that sells food.

canvas *(can-vas)*
strong cotton cloth used to make things like sails and tents.

canyon *(can-yon)*
a long deep valley with very steep sides.

cap
1. a soft hat with a stiff piece sticking out at the front to shade your face.
2. a lid or top.

capital *(cap-i-tl)*
1. the most important city of a country or State.
2. a large letter: *My name, Aminata, starts with a **capital** 'A'.*

capsize *(cap-size)*
to turn over: *Look out! The boat is going to **capsize**.*
Word building: it **capsized**, it is **capsizing**

capsule *(cap-shool)*
1. a very small container that has medicine powder inside it.
2. the part of a spaceship where the astronauts sit at the controls.

captain *(cap-tn)*
1. someone who is in charge of a ship or plane.
2. someone who is in charge of a group of soldiers.
3. any person who is in charge of other people, especially a sports team.

capture *(cap-cher)*
to grab someone or take control of something in a rough way.
Word building: I **captured**, I am **capturing** | Someone you capture is your **captive**.

car
a vehicle with wheels that travels on land.
Word building: This word is a short way of saying **motor car**.

caramel *(ca-ra-ml)*
a light-brown sweet, made from sugar, butter and milk.

caravan *(ca-ra-van)*
a van with windows and a door, that can be pulled along by a car. You can live in it when you are on holidays.

carbon footprint
Your **carbon footprint** is a measure of how much you hurt the environment by using things whose production gives off carbon dioxide and other gases that can be harmful to the environment. These gases are produced when natural resources, such as coal and oil, are burnt to make electricity or to make cars go: *Let's reduce our **carbon footprint** by turning off the lights when we don't need them.*

card
1. a piece of folded stiff paper or cardboard, with a picture on the front and writing inside, such as a birthday card or a Christmas card.
2. one of a set of oblong pieces of cardboard with pictures on them. You use them for playing card games such as snap.

cardboard *(card-bord)*
a thick stiff sort of paper.

cardigan *(card-i-gan)*
a knitted jacket with buttons down the front.

care
1. You **care** about something if it's important to you.
2. You do something with **care** when you fix all your thoughts on it and give it your complete attention.
3. care for, If you **care for** someone or something, you look after them.
Word building: I **cared**, I am **caring** | If you do things with care, then you are **careful**. If you don't do things with care and don't bother to think first, then you are **careless**.

cargo *(car-go)*
the goods carried on a ship, plane, truck, and so on, from one place to another.
Word building: For more than one we use **cargoes**.

carnival *(carn-i-val)*
1. sporting events held one after the other on a certain day: *I'm going to watch my sister race at the surf **carnival** on Saturday.*
2. a special time when there are processions in the streets and people like to join in with dancing and singing.

carol *(ca-rol)*
a happy Christmas song or hymn.

carpenter *(car-pen-ter)*
someone who makes things out of wood and puts up wooden parts of a building.
Word building: The work a carpenter does is **carpentry**.

carpet *(car-pet)*
a thick cover for a floor. You weave it from wool, or something like this.

carriage *(ca-rij)*
1. one of the cars on a train, for carrying passengers.
2. a thing which looks like a box on wheels, for carrying people about. It is pulled by a horse or horses.

carrot *(ca-rot)*
a vegetable. You eat the orange-coloured root which grows under the ground.

carry *(ca-ree)*
to take someone or something from one place to another.
Word building: I **carried**, I am **carrying**

cart
a small box on wheels that you use to move something heavy. Some have two wheels and are pulled by a horse.

carton *(cart-on)*
a box made of cardboard or plastic. It is often used to hold food or drink before it is sold: *Can you please buy a **carton** of milk?*

cartoon *(car-toon)*
1. a funny drawing: *Did you see that **cartoon** in the paper?*
2. a film or television program made with drawings instead of with real people: *Dad watches **cartoons** with us on Saturday morning.*
Word building: Someone whose job is to draw cartoons is a **cartoonist**.

carve
1. to cut something hard to give it a certain shape.
2. to cut meat into pieces or slices.
Word building: I **carved**, I am **carving**

car wash *(car wash)*
a large machine that washes your car for you automatically.

case
1. a container: *I'll put my pens into my pencil **case**. | Help me unpack this **case** of apples.*
2. an oblong bag for carrying clothes.

cash
money in paper notes or coins.
Word use: In a shop, the cash is stored and counted in a **cash register**.

casino (ca-**see**-no)
a building or large room where people play special games to gamble.
Word building: For more than one we use **casinos**.

cassette (cass-**ett**)
the plastic container that holds the tape you use to record film for a video or sound for a tape-recorder.

cassette recorder (ca-**set** re-**cord**-er)
a machine that plays or records cassettes.

cast (rhymes with **last**)
1. to throw out something or fling it somewhere.
2. all the actors in a play, film or television show.
3. the plaster that has set hard around a broken arm or leg.
Word building: I **cast**, I have **cast**, I am **casting**

castle (**car**-sel or **cass**-el)
a large building made of thick stone, often with towers and a strong wall: *Kings and queens used to live in* **castles**.

casual (**ca**-zhoo-al)
1. Something is **casual** if it happens by chance: *They became friends after a* **casual** *meeting.*
2. without thinking: *My father got upset when I made a* **casual** *remark about the nasty smell in the kitchen.*
3. not meant for important occasions: *I wore my* **casual** *clothes to the beach.*
Word building: If you say or do something in a casual way, then you say or do it **casually**.

casualty (ca-zhoo-al-tee)
someone hurt or killed in an accident or war.
Word building: For more than one we use **casualties**.

cat
1. a small furry animal often kept as a pet.
2. a member of the cat family, which includes lions, tigers and other similar animals.

catch (cach)
1. to grab someone or something you've been chasing.
2. to take in your hands: *Can you* **catch** *this ball?*
3. to be in time for something: *You'll have to run if you want to* **catch** *the bus.*
4. to get or receive something: *You will* **catch** *a cold if you wear your wet shoes all day.*
Word building: I **caught**, I am **catching**

caterpillar (**cat**-er-pill-ar)
a grub that turns into a moth or a butterfly.

cathedral (ca-**thee**-dral)
a very big and important church.

cattle (**catt**-l)
cows and bulls kept on a farm.

cauliflower (**col**-ee-flower; the last part rhymes with **power**)
a vegetable with a large round part at the top of its stem, made up of hard white flowers.

cause
to make something happen.
Word building: I **caused**, I am **causing**

cautious (**caw**-shus)
You are **cautious** if you take great care when there is danger.
Word building: If you are cautious, then you do things with **caution**.

cave
a hollow place in the side of a hill.

a
b
c
d
e
f
g
h
i
j
k
l
m
n
o
p
q
r
s
t
u
v
w
x
y
z

CD (see-**dee**)

a round piece of flat, shiny metal on which music is recorded and played on a special machine.

Word building: This word is a short way of saying **compact disc**.

Word use: A machine that you play CDs on is called a **CD player**.

CD-ROM (see-dee-**rom**)

a compact disc containing writing, sound and pictures that can be displayed on a computer.

cease

to stop.

Word building: I **ceased**, I am **ceasing**

ceiling (**seel**-ing)

the inside part that covers the top of a room.

celebrant (**sel**-e-brant)

a special person who leads a ceremony such as a wedding.

celebrate (**sel**-e-brate)

to have a party to show that you are happy about something.

Word building: I **celebrated**, I am **celebrating** | If you celebrate something, then you have a **celebration**.

celery (**sel**-e-ree)

a vegetable with long, green stalks that are good to eat.

cell (sel)

1. a small room in a prison.
2. one of the very tiny parts of everything that is alive. A cell is so small that you need a microscope to see one.

cellar (**sell**-ar)

a room under the ground, for keeping things like wine.

Celsius (**sel**-see-us)

a way to measure how hot something is, using 0° as the point where ice melts and 100° as the point where water boils.

Word use: The sign for **Celsius** is **C**, so *30°C* means *30 degrees Celsius*.

cement (se-**ment**)

the grey powder you use for making concrete.

cemetery (**sem**-e-tree)

a place for burying dead people.

Word building: For more than one we use **cemeteries**.

cent (sent)

a small amount of money. You need 100 cents to make one dollar.

Word use: Don't confuse this with **scent** or **sent**, which is a form of the word **send** (*I sent the letter yesterday*).

centenary (sen-**teen**-a-ree or sen-**ten**-a-ree)

a 100th anniversary.

Word building: For more than one we use **centenaries**.

centimetre (**sent**-i-meet-er)

You measure something in **centimetres** when you are using a metric ruler. There are 100 centimetres in a metre.

centipede (**sent**-i-peed)

a small animal that is rather like an insect. It has a long, thin body and many pairs of legs.

centre (**sent**-er)

the middle point: *Go and stand at the centre of the circle.*

Word building: If something is at or in the centre, then it is **central**.

century (**sen**-cha-ree)

a hundred years.

Word building: For more than one we use **centuries**.

cereal (**sear**-ree-al)

1. wheat, maize, rice or other grain plants that a farmer grows for food.
2. a food made from grain, especially the food you eat at breakfast with milk.

Word use: Don't confuse this with **serial**.

cerebral palsy *(serra-bral **porl**-zee)*
a kind of paralysis caused by injury to your brain, resulting in jerky movement of your arms and legs.

ceremony *(**se**-re-mo-nee)*
the things you do to mark an important event in your life, often with other people there to watch.
Word building: For more than one we use **ceremonies**.

certain *(**sert**-n)*
sure: *Are you **certain** they'll come?*
Word building: If you're certain about something, you think it will **certainly** happen.

certificate *(se-**tif**-i-ket)*
a piece of paper that says in writing some important things about you: *I had to show the principal my birth **certificate**.*

chain
1. metal rings joined together in a row.
2. any series of things linked together.

chair
a seat with a back, for one person to sit on.

chalk *(chork)*
1. a soft, white rock.
2. a stick of soft, light-coloured rock for drawing or writing on something dark-coloured.

challenge *(**chall**-enj)*
to ask someone to see if they can do better than you at something: *I'll **challenge** you to a game of chess.*
Word building: I **challenged**, I am **challenging** | If you challenge someone, then you are the **challenger**.

champion *(**champ**-pee-on)*
someone who is the best at a sport or in a contest.

chance *(rhymes with **dance**)*
1. Something happens by **chance** if you haven't planned it.
2. a good time for something: *This is your **chance** to show us your new skills.*

change
1. to make something different.
2. to become different.
3. the money you get back when you buy something that costs less than the money you gave for it.
Word building: I **changed**, I am **changing** | If something changes often, then it is **changeable**.

channel *(**chan**-el)*
1. a narrow way in the ground for water to flow along.
2. a narrow piece of water joining two seas.
3. a television station.

chant
to say words over and over again so that they sound like music.

chapter *(**chap**-ter)*
a part of a book, usually with a number and a title.

character *(**ca**-reck-ter)*
1. someone in a story.
2. the special things about you that make you different from other people: *He's quiet and thoughtful, with a **character** not at all like his noisy cousin.*

charge *(rhymes with **large**)*
1. to ask an amount of money for something: *How much do you **charge** for mowing the lawn?*
2. to accuse someone of doing something wrong: *If you drive too fast, the police will **charge** you with speeding.*
3. to rush forwards.
Word building: I **charged**, I am **charging**
Word use: If you are **in charge**, you are the boss or leader.

charity (*cha*-ri-tee)
1. the help or money you give to people who need it.
2. a group which gives money, clothes and food to people who need it.

Word building: For more than one we use **charities**. | When a person or group gives charity to somebody who needs help, then they are doing a **charitable** thing.

charm
1. to please or put in a good mood: *My baby brother's smile can **charm** even our cranky old neighbour.*
2. something which pleases and attracts you: *We were delighted with the **charm** of the old stone cottage.*

Word building: Someone or something with the ability to charm is **charming**.

chart
a map or plan.

chase (*rhymes with **face***)
to follow something or someone quickly and try to catch them: *I kicked the ball down the hill so that my dog could **chase** it.*

Word building: I **chased**, I am **chasing**

chat
1. to talk in a friendly way: *The two friends can **chat** on the phone for hours.*
2. a friendly talk: *I had a **chat** with my neighbour over the fence.*

Word building: I **chatted**, I am **chatting** | If someone likes to chat, they are **chatty**.

chatter (*chatt*-er)
to talk quickly and noisily.

Word building: An everyday word for someone who talks a lot is **chatterbox**.

cheap (*cheep*)
Something is **cheap** if it costs less to buy than usual.

cheat
1. to break the rules in a sneaky way: *Did you try to **cheat** in the test by looking at my work?*
2. to trick: *Don't let anyone **cheat** you out of your money.*
3. somebody who breaks the rules or tries to trick you in a sneaky way.

check
1. to look into something to make sure that it is correct: *I think the concert is next Friday, but I'll **check** with my friend.*
2. decorated with a pattern of squares: *He wore a blue-and-white **check** shirt.*

Word use: Don't confuse this with **cheque**.

cheek
the side of your face, below your eye. When you fill your mouth with air, both your cheeks puff out.

cheeky (*cheek*-ee)
rude, and without respect.

Word building: more cheeky = **cheekier**, most cheeky = **cheekiest** | You are cheeky if you behave **cheekily**, and your **cheekiness** might annoy your teacher.

cheer
1. to shout or show that you approve of something, or that you want something to happen: *We will **cheer** for our team, because we want them to win.*
2. a shout which shows that you approve.
3. a feeling of happiness.

Word building: If you **cheer up** someone, then you make them feel happier. Someone who is full of cheer is a **cheerful** person.

cheer squad (*cheer* skwod)
a small group of people who cheer a competitor or team, usually a sports team.

cheese (*cheeze*)
a firm, yellow food made from milk.

chemist *(kem-ist)*
1. a shop where medicines are made and sold.
2. someone whose job is to make and sell medicines.

chemistry
the science of what things are made of and the ways they react with each other.

cheque *(chek)*
an order that you write to your bank asking them to pay an amount of money to someone. It is usually written on a special form and you must sign it.
Word use: Don't confuse this with **check**.

cherry *(che-ree)*
a small, round, red fruit with a hard stone in the centre.

chess
a board game played by two people using sixteen small pieces on a board marked with black and white squares.

chest
1. the front part of your body between your neck and waist.
2. a large, strong box with a lid.

chew *(choo)*
to bite and crush something with your teeth.

chewing gum
a lolly that you only chew and do not swallow.

chicken *(chik-en)*
1. a hen or rooster, especially a young one.
2. the meat of a hen or rooster.

chickenpox *(chik-en-pox)*
an illness that makes you feel hot and gives you red spots that itch.

chickpea *(chik-pee)*
a small, round, yellow vegetable, like a pea.

chief *(cheef)*
1. the leader or person in charge.
2. main or most important.

child *(rhymes with **wild**)*
1. a boy or girl.
2. a son or daughter.
Word building: For more than one we use **children**. | The time you spend as a child is your **childhood**. Someone who behaves like a silly child is behaving in a **childish** way.

chill
1. to make colder: *Put these drinks in the fridge to **chill** them for the party.*
2. a feeling of cold: *Winter must be on the way — there's a **chill** in the air.*
3. an illness that makes you shiver and sneeze.
Word building: When there is a chill in the air, the day feels **chilly**.

chilli *(chill-ee)*
a small green or red vegetable that tastes hot, and is used in cooking.

chimney *(chim-nee)*
a long pipe which runs from the fireplace to the roof and takes smoke to the outside of the building.
Word building: For more than one we use **chimneys**.

chimpanzee *(chim-pan-zee)*
a small African ape.

chin *(chin)*
the part of your face below your mouth.

china *(chine-a)*
delicate plates, cups and ornaments made out of a special fine clay: *We use the good **china** when we have guests over for dinner.*

chip
1. a small piece chopped or split off something larger: *Dad cut the potatoes into **chips** and cooked them for dinner.*
2. to chop, cut or break a small piece off something larger.
Word building: I **chipped**, I am **chipping**

a
b
c
d
e
f
g
h
i
j
k
l
m
n
o
p
q
r
s
t
u
v
w
x
y
z

chocolate (*choc*-let)
a sweet brown food made from sugar and the crushed seeds of a tropical tree.

choice
1. the act of choosing something.
2. the thing that is chosen: *The green one is my choice.*
3. a number of things to choose from: *The library has a wide choice of books to read.*

choir (*kwire; rhymes with fire*)
a group of people who sing together.

choose (*rhymes with news*)
1. to pick out or select.
2. to decide to do one thing instead of something else.

Word building: I **chose**, I have **chosen**, I am **choosing**

chop
1. a slice of meat with the bone in it.
2. to cut up something by hitting it hard and quickly with a sharp tool: *I used a small axe to chop the wood for the fire.*

Word building: I **chopped**, I am **chopping**

chopsticks (*chop*-sticks)
a pair of thin sticks, usually made of wood, ivory or plastic, used to lift food when you are eating. They are especially used with Asian food.

chorus (*cor*-rus)
the words that are repeated after each verse of some songs or poems.

christen (*kriss*-en)
to give a name to somebody in a Christian ceremony, especially to a baby: *The family took their new daughter to the church for the minister to christen.*

Word building: When a baby is christened the priest or minister performs a **christening**.

Christianity (*kris-tee-an-i-tee*)
a religion started by a special teacher called Jesus Christ who lived a long time ago. This religion teaches that Jesus Christ is the Son of God.

Word building: Someone who follows Christianity is called a **Christian**.

Christmas (*kriss*-mas)
the birthday of Jesus Christ, celebrated on 25 December. It is a special day when people usually give presents to each other.

chuckle (*chuck*-l)
1. to laugh quietly: *I enjoy a book that can make me chuckle.*
2. a quiet laugh.

Word building: I **chuckled**, I am **chuckling**

church (*cherch*)
a building where people meet to pray and to learn about God.

churinga (*choo*-ring-ga)
a sacred wooden object important in Aboriginal culture.

Word use: This word comes from the Arrernte language of the Northern Territory. See the map of Australian Aboriginal languages at the end of this book.

cicada (*si-car*-da or *si-cay*-da)
a large flying insect which is found in the trees in summer. It makes a loud high noise that goes on and on.

cigar (*si-gar*)
tobacco leaves rolled tightly together, which some people smoke.

cigarette (*sig-a-ret*)
tobacco leaves chopped up and put inside a tube of thin paper which some people smoke.

cinema
a theatre where films are shown.

circle *(serk-l)*
1. a perfectly round shape, like a wheel. See the picture at the end of this book.
2. anything that has a round shape: *We all joined hands and danced around in a circle.*
3. to go around and around something: *The plane had to circle the airport for half an hour until the fog had cleared.*
Word building: I **circled**, I am **circling** | If something is like a circle, then it is **circular**.

circus *(serk-us)*
a show in a big tent with clowns, acrobats, jugglers and sometimes animals.

citizen *(sit-i-zen)*
a person who belongs to a nation.
Word building: A person who is a citizen is said to hold **citizenship**.

citizenship ceremony *(sit-i-zen-ship se-re-mo-nee)*
the special time when someone becomes a citizen of a country that they were not born in.

city *(sit-ee)*
a big and important town with lots of tall buildings. Many people live and work in a city.
Word building: For more than one we use **cities**.

claim
to say that something belongs to you.

clamp
1. to hold something tightly: *Put glue on both pieces, and then clamp them together while it sets.*
2. a tool which holds something tightly.

clap
1. to hit your hands together to show that something pleases you: *The crowd began to clap as soon as she had finished her speech.*
2. a sudden loud noise: *We were all frightened by the clap of thunder.*
Word building: I **clapped**, I am **clapping**

class
a group of pupils who are taught together.

classmate
a member of the same class: *Please welcome our new classmate, Anna.*

classroom
a room in a school where students are taught.

claw
the hard, sharp, curved nail on the foot of a bird or animal.

clay
thick, sticky mud which is used to make pots and bricks. You make it into the shape you want and then dry or bake it until it is hard.

clean
1. without dirt or stains.
2. to wash, sweep or remove the dirt from something.
Word building: If something is clean you can often see and smell its **cleanliness**. Somebody whose job is to clean is a **cleaner**.

clear
1. light or bright: *The wind blew the clouds away, so that the day was clear when we set off for our walk.*
2. free from things which get in the way: *If the road is clear it will take you only five minutes to get to the station.*
3. to take away the things you don't want: *You clear the table and I'll do the washing-up.*
Word building: When something is clear and easy to see, then you can see it **clearly**.

clerk *(clark)*
somebody who works in an office, doing things like opening the mail, sending out bills, and keeping a list of money that has been spent.
Word building: A clerk does the **clerical** jobs in an office.

a
b
c
d
e
f
g
h
i
j
k
l
m
n
o
p
q
r
s
t
u
v
w
x
y
z

clever *(clev-er)*
1. good at thinking: *You have to be clever to beat Mum at chess.*
2. very good at doing something.
Word building: If you are clever at something, you do it **cleverly**.

click
1. a short, sharp noise, sometimes made with your fingers.
2. to press the button on a computer mouse.

cliff
a very steep, rocky slope, sometimes at the edge of the sea.

climate *(clime-at)*
the usual weather in a place.

climate change *(clime-at change)*
an unusual change in climate that lasts for a long time.

climax *(cli-max)*
the highest or most exciting part of something: *The climax of the movie was when the girl discovered the treasure.*

climb *(clime)*
1. to move upwards: *We watched the plane climb slowly towards the clouds.*
2. a movement to a higher place: *It's a hard climb to the top.*

cling
to hold onto something very tightly.
Word building: I **clung**, I am **clinging**

clinic *(clin-ic)*
a medical centre where you can go to see a doctor or have something special done, like an X-ray.

clock
a machine that shows you what the time is.

clockwise *(clock-wize)*
If something moves in a **clockwise** direction, it moves in the same direction as the hands move on a clock: *If you turn in a circle to the right, you are moving in a clockwise direction.*

close[1] *(cloze)*
1. to shut.
2. to end: *The concert will close with the school song.*
Word building: I **closed**, I am **closing**

close[2] *(cloce)*
near: *We live so close to the railway line that we can see the trains from our window.*

cloth
woollen or cotton stuff that you can use to make clothes out of, or clean up with.

clothes *(clodhz)*
things you wear to cover your body and keep you warm.
Word building: When you put on your clothes, you **clothe** yourself with **clothing**.

cloud *(clowd)*
a mass of water drops floating in the air, usually white or grey and fluffy-looking. Sometimes it turns into rain, which falls to the ground.
Word building: If there are clouds in the sky, then the sky is **cloudy**.

clover *(rhymes with over)*
a small plant which has leaves with three round parts. Some people say that if you find a clover leaf with four round parts, you will have good luck.

clown
someone in a circus who wears funny clothes, who has a painted face and who makes people laugh.

club

1. a group of people who meet together because they have the same hobby or they like the same things.
2. a shape like a black clover leaf on some playing cards.
3. a heavy stick used as a weapon.

clue *(cloo)*

something that might give you the answer to a puzzle.

clumsy *(**clum**-zee)*

You are **clumsy** if you often drop, spill or bump into things.

Word building: more clumsy = **clumsier**, most clumsy = **clumsiest**

clutch *(cluch)*

to grab something and hold it tightly.

coach

1. a carriage pulled by horses.
2. a large bus with comfortable seats.
3. someone whose job is to train people in a sport, such as swimming or football.

coal *(cole)*

a shiny, black rock that you burn to make heat.

coast *(rhymes with **most**)*

the land next to the sea.

Word building: If a town is on the coast, then it is a **coastal** town.

coat

something you wear over your other clothes to keep you warm and dry. It usually has long sleeves and buttons down the front.

cobweb *(**cob**-web)*

a thin, sticky thread which a spider uses to catch insects.

cock

a rooster or male bird.

cockatiel *(cok-a-**teel**)*

a small parrot with a long tail and a crest on top of its head like a cockatoo.

cockatoo *(cock-a-**too**)*

a parrot that can make the feathers on the top of its head stand up.

coconut *(**co**-co-nut)*

a large, round nut that grows on a palm tree.

cocoon *(co-**coon**)*

the soft shell that grubs like silkworms spin from thin threads. They make it to cover themselves before they begin to grow and change into adult insects.

code

the special signs, letters or words you use to send messages: *The spy wrote the letter in a secret **code**.*

coffee *(**coff**-ee)*

a hot drink made from the crushed roasted beans of a special plant.

coffin *(**coff**-in)*

a long box in which a dead body is put.

coin *(coyn)*

a piece of money made from metal.

cold

1. You're **cold** if you shiver and need to put on warm clothes.
2. Something is **cold** if it makes you feel cold: *The weather is **cold** today.*
3. an illness which makes you sneeze and makes your nose run.

collapse *(co-**laps**)*

to fall down suddenly.

Word building: I **collapsed**, I am **collapsing**

a
b
c
d
e
f
g
h
i
j
k
l
m
n
o
p
q
r
s
t
u
v
w
x
y
z

collar (coll-ar)
1. the part of your shirt or coat which goes around your neck.
2. a leather band you put around the neck of a dog or cat.

collect (co-lect)
1. to bring things together: *I like to collect autographs.*
2. to go and get someone or something.

Word building: If you collect things, then you have a **collection**.

college
1. a place for learning, like a university, that you can go to after you finish high school.
2. a large school.

collision (co-lizh-on)
a crashing together of two things.

Word building: If two things have a collision, then they **collide**.

colony (col-o-nee)
1. a group of people who live in a country, away from their home country, and who control the people already living there.
2. a place which has been taken over by people from another country.

Word building: For more than one we use **colonies**.

colour (cul-or)
1. Colour is one reason that some things look different from others, because different things can have different colours. A rainbow has seven different colours — red, orange, yellow, green, blue, indigo and violet.
2. to use your pencils or paints to fill in the blank parts of a picture.

comb (rhymes with roam)
a piece of plastic or metal with thin points sticking out. You use it to part your hair and to keep it tidy.

come (cum)
1. to move towards someone or something: *The dog will come to me if I call it.*
2. to travel somewhere with someone: *Can you come to the beach with us?*
3. to arrive or happen: *Your turn will come soon.*

Word building: I **came**, I have **come**, I am **coming**

Word use: The opposite of this is **go**.

comet (com-et)
an object in space that moves around the sun. It is much smaller than a planet and has a bright centre with a long misty part behind it like a tail.

comfort (cum-fet)
to make someone feel less sad or worried: *If the baby cries I will comfort her.*

comfortable (cumf-ta-bl)
pleasant for your body: *Sometimes I fall asleep if I do my homework in a comfortable chair.*

comic (com-ic)
a magazine or newspaper with funny or exciting stories told in pictures.

command (co-mand or co-marnd)
to tell someone that they have to do something: *'I command you to attack the enemy', said the general.*

commercial (co-mer-shal)
words or pictures on radio or television, that are supposed to make you notice something and then go and buy it.

Word use: Another word that means nearly the same is **advertisement**.

common (com-on)
1. Something is **common** if there is lots of it around: *This is a common weed — you find it everywhere.*
2. Something is **common** if people usually do it: *It's common for people to go to the beach in summer.*

commonwealth (*com*-on-welth)
a country made up of several States. There is one government for the whole country and each State has its own government as well: *Who is the Prime Minister of the* **Commonwealth** *of Australia?*

communication (co-mune-i-*cay*-shon)
the sharing of thoughts, ideas or information with someone.

community
a group of people who live near each other and share common interests.
Word building: For more than one we use **communities**.

compact disc
a disc for storing recorded music or information which can be read by a machine such as a computer.
Word building: This is sometimes shortened to **CD**, especially for music, and **CD-ROM**, especially for computer information.

companion
someone who travels or spends time with someone else: *Are you taking a* **companion** *on your holiday?*
Word building: If you have a companion, you have **companionship** with them. If someone is a good companion, they are **companionable**.

company (*cum*-pa-nee)
a group of people who run a business: *That* **company** *makes computers.*
Word building: For more than one we use **companies**.

compare (com-*pair*)
to look at things to see if they are the same or different, or to see if one is better than another.
Word building: I **compared**, I am **comparing** | If you compare things, then you make a **comparison**.

compass (*cum*-pass)
an instrument with a needle that points to the north. You use it to find out which way to go.

competition (com-pe-*tish*-on)
a test between two or more people to see who is the best or who will win.
Word building: If you take part in a competition, then you **compete** with the other **competitors**.

complain (com-*plain*)
to tell someone about all the things you don't like, or that make you unhappy.
Word building: If you complain about something, then you make a **complaint**.

complete (com-*pleet*)
1. Something is **complete** if all its parts are there: *Are you sure you still have a* **complete** *set of crayons?*
2. to finish something.
Word building: I **completed**, I am **completing** | If something is done in a complete way, it is done **completely**.

complicated (*com*-pli-cayt-ed)
Something is **complicated** if it's tricky and hard to understand.

complication
1. something that makes things complicated: *I've written clear directions to get to my house — but just call me if you come across a* **complication**.
2. something exciting or interesting that happens in a story and makes the reader want to know what happens next: *The* **complication** *of the story was when a spaceship suddenly appeared in the sky.*

compliment (*com*-pli-ment)
something nice you say to someone: *The teacher paid me a* **compliment** *by saying my story was the best in the class.*

composer *(com-**pose**-er)*
someone who writes music.

composition *(com-po-**zish**-on)*
a piece of writing or music that you make up.

compost *(**com**-post; the last part rhymes with **lost**)*
a mixture of food scraps, leaves and other things that rot. It is often added to the soil in the garden to help the plants grow.

computer *(com-**pute**-er)*
a machine which can be used to store and give out information and facts very quickly.

computer game
a game that is played on a computer.

computer program
a set of stored instructions inside a computer that tells the computer how to do things.

concentrate *(con-sen-trate)*
to think very hard about one thing: *Just **concentrate** on watching the ball and you'll be able to catch it.*
Word building: I **concentrated**, I am **concentrating** | If you concentrate on something, you give it your **concentration**.

concert *(**con**-sert)*
a performance of music for people to come and listen to.

concrete *(con-creet)*
cement, sand, water and gravel mixed together and used for building. It goes hard as it dries.

condition *(con-**dish**-on)*
the way something or someone is: *That bike is in poor **condition** because you left it out in the rain and now it's rusty.*

conduct *(**con**-duct)*
1. the way you behave or act.
2. *(con-**duct**)* to lead an orchestra or a choir: *It's your turn to **conduct** the band, so don't forget to show the flutes when to start.*

conductor *(con-**duk**-tor)*
1. someone who collects tickets on a tram, bus or train.
2. someone who keeps the players in an orchestra together and shows them when to play.

cone
1. a shape with a flat round bottom and sides that meet in a point at the top. The top of a wizard's hat is a cone. See the picture at the end of this book.
2. the hard, bumpy fruit of pine and fir trees.

confess *(con-**fess**)*
to say that you have done something wrong: *I **confess** that I ate your lollies.*
Word building: If you confess to something, then you make a **confession**.

confetti *(con-**fet**-ee)*
small bits of coloured paper that people sometimes throw at weddings.

confident *(con-fi-dent)*
You're **confident** if you feel sure about something.
Word building: If you're confident, then you have a feeling of **confidence**.

confuse *(con-**fuze**)*
to mix someone up: *You will **confuse** me if you don't speak more slowly.*
Word building: I **confused**, I am **confusing** | If something confuses you, then you're filled with **confusion**.

congratulate *(con-**grat**-yu-late)*
to tell someone you're happy that something good has happened to them.
Word building: When you congratulate someone, you give them your **congratulations**.

conjunction (con-**junk**-shon)
a word, such as 'and' or 'because', used to join parts of a sentence.

connect (co-**nect**)
to join one thing to another thing.
Word building: If you connect things, you make a **connection**.

conquer (**cong**-ker)
to beat an enemy.
Word building: If you conquer an enemy, then you are the **conqueror** and you have made a **conquest**.

conscious (**con**-shus)
You're **conscious** if you know what is happening around you: *Luckily, the person who was hurt in the accident is still conscious.*
Word use: The opposite of this is **unconscious**.

conservation (con-ser-**vay**-shon)
taking care of the air we breathe, our water, our plants and our animals, so that no-one spoils them or hurts them.
Word building: Someone who believes conservation is important is called a **conservationist**.
Word use: Don't confuse **conservation** with **conversation**.

consider (con-**sid**-er)
to think about something with care.
Word building: When you consider something, you give it **consideration**.

consist (con-**sist**)
to be made up of: *These cakes consist of flour, milk, eggs, butter and sugar.*

consonant (**con**-so-nant)
any letter of the alphabet which isn't **a**, **e**, **i**, **o** or **u**.
Word use: Look at **vowel**.

construct (con-**struct**)
to build something.
Word building: Something you construct is a **construction**.

contain (con-**tain**)
to have something within: *These tanks contain water. | This book will contain a list of all the words I need to learn to spell.*

container (con-**tain**-er)
anything that can hold things inside itself or that you can put things in: *I use this box as a container for my blank CDs.*

container ship
a ship that carries cargo in large containers.

contaminate (con-**tam**-i-nate)
to make something dirty: *The pollution from the factory will contaminate the water.*
Word building: it **contaminated**, it is **contaminating**

content (con-**tent**)
pleased or happy.
Word building: If you are content, then you have a feeling of **contentment**.

contents (**con**-tents)
whatever is inside or held in something: *She slowly opened the lid and revealed the contents of the box.*

contest (**con**-test)
a fight or competition.
Word building: If you enter a contest, then you are a **contestant**.

continent (**con**-ti-nent)
one of the large areas of land in the world: *Australia is an island continent.*

continue (con-**tin**-yoo)
to keep on doing something.
Word building: I **continued**, I am **continuing**

contract (**con**-tract)
a piece of paper you sign, which says you have to do something: *They signed a contract when they bought a new house.*

contrast *(con-trarst)*

1. to look different alongside something else: *The white flowers **contrast** with the green leaves.*
2. *(con-trast)* a strong difference: *There is a **contrast** in the way we do things.*

contribute *(con-trib-yute)*

to give your share to something: *Will you **contribute** to Sally's birthday present?*

Word building: I **contributed**, I am **contributing** | If you contribute something, then you make a **contribution**.

control *(con-trol)*

1. to be in charge of something.
2. to keep something held back: *You must learn to **control** your temper and not shout at people who annoy you.*

Word building: I **controlled**, I am **controlling**

convenient

suited to your needs: *It is **convenient** that the school is so close to our house.*

Word building: If something is convenient, you talk about its **convenience**.

conversation *(con-ve-say-shon)*

a friendly talk you have with someone.

Word use: Don't confuse this with **conservation**.

convict *(con-vict)*

someone who has done something wrong and is in prison.

cooee *(coo-ee)*

a long, loud call used to signal someone, especially when you are in the bush.

Word use: This word comes from the Dharug language of New South Wales. See the map of Australian Aboriginal languages at the end of this book.

cook

1. to heat food until it's ready to eat.
2. someone who gets food ready to eat.

Word building: If you learn how to cook food, then you learn **cookery**.

cool

1. not too cold.
2. an everyday word used to describe something excellent: *This new computer game is really **cool**!*

coolibah *(cool-i-ba)*

a sort of gum tree with short twisted branches.

Word use: This word comes from the Yuwaalaraay language of New South Wales. See the map of Australian Aboriginal languages at the end of this book.

copper

a fairly soft reddish-brown metal.

copy *(cop-ee)*

1. something you can make the same as something else: *I'll make a **copy** of that letter for you.*
2. to do or make something the same as something else: ***Copy** the way I do the dance.* | *I have to **copy** the word list on the whiteboard.*

Word building: I **copied**, I am **copying** | For more than one we use **copies**.

copyright *(cop-ee-rite)*

a law that stops you from using other people's writing, drawings or music without permission.

coral *(co-ral)*

the hard stuff in many different shapes that's formed from the bones of small sea animals. You can find it in many beautiful colours in places like the Great Barrier Reef.

core *(cor)*

1. the middle part of a piece of fruit, containing the seeds.
2. the middle part of the earth.

corn

a plant with small, hard seeds which you can eat as a vegetable or grind to make flour.

corner (*cor*-ner)
the place where two edges meet: *There's a light at the **corner** of those two streets.* | *Put it in the **corner** of the room.*

corpse (*corps*)
the body of a dead person.

correct (co-**rect**)
1. to put something right: ***Correct** your spelling as you read through your work.*
2. Something is **correct** if it has no mistakes: *Well done! Your work is **correct**.*
Word building: If you correct something, then you make a **correction**.

corridor (**co**-ri-dor)
a part of a building that is long and narrow and leads from one room to another.

corroboree (co-**rob**-o-ree)
an Aboriginal ceremony which includes singing and dancing.
Word use: This word comes from the Dharug language of New South Wales. See the map of Australian Aboriginal languages at the end of this book.

cost
1. the price of something: *What is the **cost** of this mobile phone?*
2. a loss: *They won the war at the **cost** of many lives.*
Word building: If something costs a lot, it is **costly**.

costume (**cos**-tyoom)
the clothes you wear for dressing up or to do something special.

cosy (**co**-zee)
Something is **cosy** if it's friendly and makes you feel comfortable.
Word building: more cosy = **cosier**, most cosy = **cosiest**

cot
a bed with raised sides for babies and small children.

cottage (**cot**-ij)
a small house.

cotton (**cot**-n)
1. a light cloth made from part of a plant.
2. thread you use for sewing.

couch (*cowch*)
a long seat for two or more people.
Word building: For more than one we use **couches**.

cough (*coff*)
the loud, sudden noise you make when something's stuck in your throat.

could (*rhymes with **wood***)
See **can**[2].

council (**coun**-sil)
a group of people who meet often to talk about and to decide things: *The school **council** will meet on Monday to decide how much to spend on new computers.* | *The city **council** needs to do something about the rubbish on the streets.*
Word building: If you're a member of a council, then you're a **councillor**.

count[1]
1. to add up: *Let's **count** how many clouds are in the sky.*
2. to name the numbers: *Can you **count** up to one hundred?*
3. to include: *When you are working out how many will be at the party, don't forget to **count** Tegan.*
4. to matter: *That rule doesn't **count** in this game.*
5. **count on**, to depend on: *Dad **counts on** me to help with the baby.*

count[2]
a man who is part of a noble family.
Word building: The female is a **countess**.

counter *(count-er)*
1. a long shelf in a shop where you can pay for the things you want to buy.
2. something you use to count with in a game. It's often thin, round and made of plastic.

country *(cun-tree)*
1. an area of land that has its own government: *France is a country in Europe.*
2. the land outside a town or a city: *Many people from the city like to go to the country for their holidays.*

Word building: For more than one we use **countries**.

country and western
a type of music that started in the southern part of the United States, consisting mainly of country songs played on a guitar or fiddle with somebody singing.

Word use: Another word for this is **country music**.

couple *(cup-l)*
1. two people who belong together.
2. two things: *We hired a couple of DVDs because it was raining.*

courage *(cu-rij)*
the strength to do something that frightens you.

Word building: If you have courage, then you are **courageous**.

course *(corse)*
1. one part of a meal: *We had roast turkey for the main course.*
2. the ground or stretch of water over which you hold a race.

court *(rhymes with short)*
1. the hard ground where games such as tennis and basketball are played.
2. the palace of a king or queen and the people who live or work there.
3. a place where specially trained people argue about whether someone has broken a law or not.

courteous *(ker-tee-us)*
polite, or with very good manners: *It was courteous of you to hold the door open for me. Thank you.*

Word building: If you are courteous, then you do things with **courtesy** *(ker-te-see)*.

courtyard
an outside area surrounded by walls or buildings.

cousin *(cuz-in)*
a child of your uncle or aunt.

cove
a small bay: *Let's go for a swim in the cove.*

cover *(cuv-er)*
1. to lie over something or be spread over it: *She hoped the mat would be big enough to cover the whole floor.*
2. something you put over a thing to keep it safe: *Here's the cover for the butter dish.*

cow
1. the female of cattle.
2. a female elephant, whale or seal.

Word use: The male is a **bull**.

coward *(cow-ard)*
someone who runs away from the things that make them afraid.

Word building: A coward does **cowardly** things and is full of **cowardice** *(cow-ard-iss)*.

crab
a sea animal with a hard, flat shell, eight legs and two large claws that can pinch things.

crack
1. to break or split with a sharp sound.
2. the line that you can see when something has a split in it: *I was disappointed to discover that my favourite cup had a crack in it.*

cracker (*crack*-er)
1. a roll of paper with twisted ends. It makes a bang when you pull it and you can find a surprise inside.
2. a firework.
3. a thin biscuit with no sugar in it.
Word use: Another name for definition 1 is **bonbon**.

cradle (*cray*-dl)
a small bed for a baby, which you can rock.

craft
a job or hobby which needs you to use your hands in a clever way: *Pottery is a craft.*

crafty
clever at finding ways to trick people.
Word building: more crafty = **craftier**, most crafty = **craftiest**

cramp
a sudden pain in your arms, your legs or your stomach.

crane
1. a machine with a long arm for lifting and moving heavy things around.
2. a large bird with long legs, a long neck and a long bill. It wades in shallow water looking for food.

cranky (*crang*-kee)
You're **cranky** when you're cross or when you have a bad temper.
Word building: more cranky = **crankier**, most cranky = **crankiest**

crash
1. to run into something or hit it with a lot of noise.
2. an accident in which one thing bumps into another thing.
Word building: For more than one we use **crashes**.

crater (*cray*-ter)
1. the opening at the top of a volcano.
2. a round hole in the ground made by a meteor or a bomb.

crawl (*crorl*)
1. to move along on your hands and knees: *The baby is learning to crawl.*
2. to go very slowly: *The traffic had to crawl around the accident which blocked the road.*

crayfish (*cray*-fish)
an animal with a hard shell, which looks like a small lobster. It lives in creeks and rivers because it doesn't like salty water.
Word building: For more than one we use **crayfish**.
Word use: This is sometimes called a **yabby**.

crayon (*cray*-on)
a stick of coloured wax or chalk that you use for drawing or colouring.

crazy (*cray*-zee)
1. mad or likely to do strange things.
2. silly: *What a crazy song!*
Word building: more crazy = **crazier**, most crazy = **craziest**

creak
to make a high squeaking sound: *Her eyes flew open when she heard the stairs begin to creak.*
Word building: Things that creak are **creaky**.
Word use: Don't confuse **creak** with **creek**.

cream
1. the thick part you find at the top of milk.
2. anything which is thick and feels smooth when you touch it: *When I hurt my arm, Mum rubbed a special cream on it to make it better.*

create (cree-*ate*)
to make or invent something: *I'm going to create a beautiful painting.*
Word building: If you are good at creating things, you are **creative**. Something you have created is a **creation**.

creature (*cree*-cher)
any animal that's alive.

a b **c** d e f g h i j k l m n o p q r s t u v w x y z

53

credit card (*cred*-it card)

a plastic card which is used to make a record of what someone owes when they buy something but don't pay cash for it.

creek

a small stream.

Word use: Don't confuse this with **creak**.

creep

1. to go somewhere as slowly and quietly as you can.
2. an everyday word for someone you don't like: *I'm not going to sit next to that* **creep** *again.*

Word building: I **crept**, I am **creeping**

Word use: If something gives you **the creeps** it makes you feel frightened or uncomfortable.

crew (*croo*)

all the people who work on a ship or plane.

cricket[1] (*crik*-et)

an insect which jumps like a grass-hopper. It makes a loud noise by rubbing its wings together.

cricket[2] (*crik*-et)

a game for two teams to play with a ball, bats and wickets.

criminal (*crim*-i-nal)

someone who has done things that are against the law.

Word building: A criminal is guilty of a **crime**.

crisp

Food is **crisp** if it's so hard and fresh that you can break it easily: *I can't wait to bite into this* **crisp** *apple.*

croak

to make a low, rough sound: *Listen to the frogs* **croak** *in the pond.*

Word building: If you have a cold and you can only croak, then your voice is **croaky**.

crocodile (*croc*-o-dile)

a large animal like a lizard, which lives in the rivers of very hot countries. Its nose and jaws are thinner than those of an alligator.

crooked (*crook*-ed)

with curves or not straight: *I drew a* **crooked** *line because I didn't use my ruler.*

crop

the plants a farmer grows for food.

cross

1. anything that has the shape '+' or 'x'.
2. to go from one side of something to the other side: *Hold my hand and we'll* **cross** *the road.* | *The two bridges* **cross** *the river next to each other.*
3. angry.

crossing

a place where a road, river or railway line can be crossed.

crouch (*crowch*)

to bend your knees and lean forward: *If we* **crouch** *behind the bush they won't see us.*

crow[1] (*cro*)

a big, black bird with shiny feathers.

crow[2] (*cro*)

to make the sound a rooster makes.

Word building: it **crew** or it **crowed**, it has **crowed**, it is **crowing**

crowd

a large number of people.

Word building: If a place has a crowd in it, then it's **crowded**.

crown

the circle of gold and jewels a king or queen wears on their head.

cruel (*croo*-el)

You're **cruel** if you like to hurt people.

Word building: The things cruel people do show their **cruelty**.

cruise *(crooze)*
a holiday on a ship.

cruise ship
a large ship on which people take a holiday and sail from place to place.

crumb *(crum)*
a small piece of bread, cake or biscuit.

crumble *(**crum**-bl)*
to break into little pieces: *The building was so old, the stone walls had started to **crumble**.*
Word building: it **crumbled**, it is **crumbling**

crunch *(rhymes with **bunch**)*
to break crisp food into little pieces with your teeth: *I like the noise celery makes when I **crunch** it.*

crush
to break something into little pieces by pressing it or by squeezing it hard.

crust
the hard part on the outside of something.

crutch *(cruch)*
a stick which fits under your arm and helps you to walk if you have a sore leg.

cry
1. to feel so sore or sad that tears fall from your eyes.
2. to shout.
Word building: I **cried**, I am **crying**

cube *(kyoob)*
a shape with six square sides which are all the same size. See the picture at the end of this book.

cuddle *(**cudd**-l)*
to hug someone gently.
Word building: I **cuddled**, I am **cuddling** | If people or things are nice to cuddle, then they're **cuddly**.

culprit *(**cul**-prit)*
someone who does something wrong: *After the robbery, the police hunted for the **culprit** all night.*

cunning *(**cunn**-ing)*
You're **cunning** if you're good at thinking of clever plans or at tricking people.

cup
a small container, with a handle on the side, used for drinking.

cupboard *(**cub**-ed)*
a piece of furniture with shelves and with doors. You use it for keeping things like clothes, cups or plates.

cure *(rhymes with **pure**)*
to make someone better again.
Word building: I **cured**, I am **curing**

curious *(**kyoo**-ree-us)*
You're **curious** if you want to learn new things: *I'm **curious** to know what makes this computer work.*
Word building: If you're curious, then you have feelings of **curiosity**.

curl *(rhymes with **girl**)*
1. a small ring of hair.
2. to make curves, twists or rings: *When I read I always **curl** my legs up under me.* | *This vine has started to **curl** around the tree.*
Word building: If you have curls, then your hair is **curly**.

currant *(**cu**-rent)*
a small grape with no seeds, dried until it's very sweet and hard.
Word use: Don't confuse this with **current**.

current *(**cu**-rent)*
a flow or movement of water, air or electricity in one direction: *My surfboard was swept out to sea by the strong **current**.* | *There's a cool **current** of air from the fan blowing on my face.* | *Don't touch that wire — the **current** through it will give you a shock.*
Word use: Don't confuse this with **currant**.

a b **c** d e f g h i j k l m n o p q r s t u v w x y z

curry *(rhymes with **hurry**)*
food such as meat and vegetables, cooked with spices to make it taste so hot that it can burn your mouth.
Word building: For more than one we use **curries**.

curse *(rhymes with **purse**)*
1. a strong wish that something bad will happen to someone: *The witch put a **curse** on the prince and turned him into a toad.*
2. the sort of words someone uses when they swear at someone.

cursor *(**ker**-ser)*
a small moving arrow or line on a computer screen to show you where you can key in.

curtain *(**kert**-n)*
a piece of material you hang from a rod over a window or across the front of a stage.

curve *(kerv)*
a line that bends or a shape with no pointed corners: *Look out — there's a **curve** in the road!*

cushion *(**coosh**-on)*
a soft pad you use to sit on or to lean your back against, usually on a chair.

custard *(**cus**-ted)*
a soft food you make from milk, eggs and sugar and eat as a dessert.

custom *(**cus**-tom)*
a habit, or something that you usually do.

customer *(**cus**-tom-er)*
someone who buys things in a shop.

cut
1. to make an opening in something with something sharp: *Be careful not to **cut** your finger with that knife.*
2. to separate or make shorter with something sharp: *Use the scissors to **cut** some ribbon.*
3. the result of cutting: *You have a **cut** on your hand.*
Word building: I **cut**, I have **cut**, I am **cutting**

cycle *(**sy**-kl)*
to ride a bicycle.
Word building: I **cycled**, I am **cycling** | Someone who cycles is a **cyclist**.

cyclone *(**sy**-clone)*
a storm with very strong winds.

cylinder *(**sil**-in-der)*
something that has the shape of a tube with round ends. See the picture at the end of this book.

Dd

Dinosaurs dine on delicious desserts.

dad
an everyday word for a father.

daffodil *(daf-o-dil)*
a yellow flower which grows from a bulb.

dagger *(dagg-er)*
a short, pointed sword.

daily *(day-lee)*
Something is **daily** if it happens every day: *I write **daily** emails to my best friend, who is in China for the holidays.*

dainty *(dain-tee)*
small and delicate: *Cinderella wore **dainty** glass dancing shoes to the ball.*
Word building: more dainty = **daintier**, most dainty = **daintiest**

dairy *(dair-ree)*
1. **Dairy** foods, like cheese and yoghurt, come from milk.
2. a place on a farm where you milk cows.
Word building: For more than one we use **dairies**.
Word use: Don't confuse this with **diary**.

daisy *(day-zee)*
a flower which has a yellow centre and lots of white or coloured petals.
Word building: For more than one we use **daisies**.

dam
1. a lot of water held back by a strong wall built across a river.
2. a big hole filled with water on a farm.

damage *(dam-ij)*
1. to hurt or harm something: *Eating too many sweets can **damage** your teeth. | Don't leave your painting on the floor where someone could **damage** it.*
2. the harm that has been done to something: *We were shocked to see the **damage** caused by the storm.*
Word building: I **damaged**, I am **damaging**

damp
a little bit wet, like washing that hasn't quite dried.
Word building: If you make something damp, you **dampen** it, and then it has a feeling of **dampness**.

damper *(dam-per)*
a kind of bread that you cook over a camp fire.

dance *(dance or darnce)*
to move your feet and body in time to music.
Word building: I **danced**, I am **dancing** | Someone whose job is to dance is a **dancer**.

dandelion *(dan-de-lion)*
a weed with bright yellow flowers that turn into soft, fluffy balls of seeds.

danger (*dain*-jer)

something that could hurt you: *The broken glass on the floor is a **danger**.*

Word building: Something that is a danger to you is **dangerous**.

dare (*dair*)

1. to be brave enough or naughty enough to do something: *The teacher was so angry that we didn't **dare** speak.*
2. to challenge somebody to do something silly or something that might harm them or get them into trouble: *I **dare** you to step into that puddle with your best shoes on.*

Word building: I **dared**, I am **daring**

dark

1. without light: *It was very **dark** inside the cave.*
2. more black than white: *A **dark** storm cloud blocked the light of the sun.*
3. night: *We will be home before **dark**.*

Word building: Something that is dark is full of **darkness**.

dash

to move very quickly: *I had to **dash** inside to answer the phone.*

data (*dart*-a or *day*-ta)

facts and information: *I've got lots of **data** for my project on ants.*

date

the day, month and year when something happens, or the numbers that show you this: *The **date** on the old newspaper was 11 November, 1918.*

daughter (*dor*-ter)

someone's girl child.

dawn

the part of the day when the sun comes up.

day

1. the time between sunrise and sunset when the sky is light.
2. the 24 hours between midnight of one day and the following midnight: *A week has seven **days**.*

day care

a place where you can go during the day where people look after you: *My little brother isn't old enough to come to school yet, so he goes to **day care**.*

dazed

You are **dazed** when you can't think properly because something has happened to you: *Uma was **dazed** after the accident and couldn't tell us what had happened.*

dead (*ded*)

not alive: *I think this plant with the brown leaves is **dead**.*

deaf (*def*)

not able to hear properly or not able to hear at all.

Word building: If you are deaf, you suffer from **deafness**.

deal

to hand out: *It's my turn to **deal** the cards.*

Word building: I **dealt** (*delt*), I am **dealing**

dear (*rhymes with **ear***)

1. greatly loved: *She is a **dear** friend.*
2. costing a lot: *This new dress was very **dear**.*

Word use: Don't confuse this with **deer**.

death (*deth*)

the end of life: *I was very upset by the **death** of my old cat.*

debate (*de-**bate***)

a contest in which two teams argue about a subject.

debt *(det)*
something that you owe someone.

decade *(**dec**-aid)*
ten years.

decay *(de-**cay**)*
to rot or go bad: *This bridge is not safe because the wood has begun to **decay**.*

deceive *(de-**seev**)*
to trick someone or to tell them lies.
Word building: I **deceived**, I am **deceiving**

decide *(de-**side**)*
to make up your mind to do something or to think something: *I can't **decide** whether to join the netball team or the soccer team.*
Word building: When you decide to do something, you make a **decision**.

decimal *(**des**-i-mal)*
Decimal numbers and fractions are written in a special way that is based on the number ten. For $\frac{1}{10}$ we write 0.1, for $\frac{1}{2}$ we write 0.5, and for $1\frac{3}{10}$ we write 1.3.

deck
the floor on a ship.

declare *(de-**clair**)*
to say something in a formal way: *'I **declare** this skate park open!', said the mayor.*

decorate *(**dek**-o-rate)*
to make bright and pretty by adding things: *Let's **decorate** the classroom with streamers and balloons for Ahmed's birthday.*
Word building: If you decorate a room, you make it look **decorative** by using **decorations**.

decrease *(de-**creese**)*
to make or get smaller or less: *The sea breeze will **decrease** the temperature.*
Word use: The opposite of this is **increase**.

deed
something done: *I've done my good **deed** for the day.*

deep
Something is **deep** if it goes a long way down: *The hole was so **deep** that we couldn't see the bottom.*
Word building: If you make something deep you **deepen** it and increase its **depth**.

Deepavali *(dee-pa-**vah**-lee)*
a Hindu festival held in October or November, when people eat feasts and light lamps to celebrate the victory of good over evil.

deer *(rhymes with **ear**)*
a big animal that eats grass: *The male **deer** has horns that branch out.*
Word building: For more than one we use **deer**.
Word use: A female deer is a **doe**. A male deer is a **stag**. | Don't confuse this with **dear**.

defeat *(de-**feet**)*
to beat someone in a contest or in a battle.

defence
protection against attack: *Many ancient towns were surrounded by high walls for **defence**.*
Word building: Something that is used for defence is **defensive**.

defend
to protect or keep safe: *I'll **defend** you from the bullies.*

define
to explain the meaning of something: *Can you **define** this word for me?*
Word building: If something has been defined, it has a **definition**.

definite *(**def**-i-nit)*
very sure: *Jack was **definite** about the best way to bowl a cricket ball.*

a
b
c
d
e
f
g
h
i
j
k
l
m
n
o
p
q
r
s
t
u
v
w
x
y
z

defy *(de-fy)*

to do something that you've been told not to do: *Mei tried to **defy** her mum by sneaking out the back door after she had been sent to her room.*

Word building: I **defied**, I am **defying**

degree *(de-gree)*

a unit you use for measuring some things, like an angle or the temperature: *It's two **degrees** hotter than yesterday.*

Word use: We use the mark ° to mean **degrees**, so **30°** means **thirty degrees**.

delay *(de-lay)*

1. to make someone or something late: *The stormy weather may **delay** the plane.*
2. to put something off until later: *We will **delay** our swim until the weather gets warmer.*

delicate *(del-i-ket)*

Something is **delicate** if it can easily be damaged: *The butterfly spread its **delicate** wings.*

delicatessen *(del-i-ca-tess-en)*

a shop which sells foods like cheeses, special meats and sausages.

delicious *(de-lish-us)*

Something is **delicious** if it tastes very good.

delight *(de-lite)*

to please someone very much: *The new toys are sure to **delight** the children.*

Word building: Something that delights you is **delightful**.

deliver *(de-liv-er)*

to take something to someone's place: *Can you **deliver** these books to Mrs Wong on your way to school?*

Word building: When you deliver something, you make a **delivery**.

demand *(de-mand or de-marnd)*

to ask for something as if you think it's your own: *I **demand** my money back — you sold me a printer that doesn't work!*

demolish *(de-mol-ish)*

to knock something down: *We are going to **demolish** the old garage.*

demonstration *(dem-on-stray-shon)*

1. a meeting or a march through the streets by a lot of people to show everyone what they think about something.
2. showing and telling people how to do a particular thing: *The teacher gave us a **demonstration** of how to use the new scanner.*

dense *(rhymes with fence)*

very thick: *It was difficult to push our way through the **dense** bush.*

dent

a small hollow made in something by hitting it: *We got a **dent** in our car when Dad backed it into a post.*

dentist *(den-tist)*

somebody whose job is to help you look after your teeth.

deny *(de-ny)*

to say that something isn't true: *I **deny** I drew on the wall.*

Word building: I **denied**, I am **denying** | When you deny something, you make a **denial**.

depart *(de-part)*

to go away or leave.

Word building: When you depart from somewhere, you make a **departure**.

department

a separate part of a large organisation such as a government, a college or a store: *The children's **department** is on the top floor.*

department store

a very large shop, with many parts to it, where you can buy many different kinds of things.

depend *(de-**pend**)*

to trust someone or something to be there when you need them: *We **depend** on the firefighters to help us when there is a fire.*

Word building: Somebody or something that you can depend on is **dependable**.

deposit *(de-**poz**-it)*

a sum of money that you put into your bank account.

depth

how deep something is: *She dug the hole to a **depth** of ten centimetres.*

deputy *(**dep**-yu-tee)*

the person who is second in charge and who takes control when the boss is away.

Word building: For more than one we use **deputies**.

descend *(de-**send**)*

to go down: *We watched the plane **descend** to the runway.*

Word use: The opposite of this is **ascend**.

describe *(de-**scribe**)*

to say how something looks or how something is: *Can you **describe** what the thief was wearing?*

Word building: I **described**, I am **describing** | When you describe something, you give a **description** of it.

desert[1] *(**dez**-et)*

a dry place where very few plants can grow.

Word use: Don't confuse this with **dessert** or **desert**[2].

desert[2] *(de-**zert**)*

to run away because you don't want to be part of something: *When things start to go wrong it's not good to **desert** your mates.*

Word use: Don't confuse this with **dessert** or **desert**[1].

deserted *(de-**zert**-ed)*

A place is **deserted** if there are no people there: *Nothing moved on the **deserted** railway station.*

deserve *(de-**zerv**)*

to have earned a reward if you've been good or a punishment if you've been bad: *You have trained so hard that you **deserve** to win the race.*

Word building: I **deserved**, I am **deserving**

design *(de-**zine**)*

to draw plans for: *I'm going to **design** a new cage for my bird.*

desire *(de-**zire**)*

to want something very much: *What I **desire** most after a hard day walking in the bush is a long, hot bath.*

Word building: I **desired**, I am **desiring**

desk

a table where you can write and keep your books and pencils.

despair *(de-**spair**)*

a feeling of great sadness because you think there is no hope: *He was filled with **despair** because she had gone.*

dessert *(de-**zert**)*

the fruit or sweets you eat at the end of your meal.

Word use: Don't confuse this with **desert**[1] or **desert**[2].

destroy *(de-**stroy**)*

to break up or ruin something: *If you step on my sandcastle you will **destroy** it.*

detail *(**dee**-tale)*

one of many small parts or happenings that make up a whole thing: *Tell us every **detail** of your visit to the circus.*

a b c d e f g h i j k l m n o p q r s t u v w x y z

detective (de-**tek**-tiv)
someone whose job is to try to find out who did a crime.

determined
If you are **determined**, you are certain you will do something and you won't stop trying until it is done: *She is a **determined** person. | He is **determined** to learn to ski.*

detour (**dee**-toor)
a road or path which you have to use when the way you wanted to go is closed.

develop (de-**vel**-op)
to make something larger or better: *My big brother exercises every day to **develop** his muscles.*
Word building: If you develop something, you make a **development**.

devil (**dev**-il)
somebody who is bad, mean or naughty: *The little **devil** pushed me into the mud and then laughed.*

devoted (de-**vote**-ed)
You are **devoted** to somebody if you love and care about them a lot.

dew (rhymes with **new**)
tiny drops of water that you find on things outside in the early morning.
Word use: Don't confuse this with **due**.

diabolo (dee-**ab**-o-lo)
a game in which you balance a spinning top on a piece of string that is connected to two sticks, one held in each hand.

diagonal (dy-**ag**-on-al)
a sloping line which goes from one corner of a square or rectangle to the opposite corner.

diagram (**dy**-a-gram)
a drawing or plan which shows you how something works: *The model plane kit has a **diagram** of how you put it together.*

dial (**dy**-al)
the part of a clock, radio or measuring instrument that has numbers or letters on it.

diameter (dy-**am**-e-ter)
a straight line which goes across a circle from one side to the other side, passing through the centre.

diamond (**dy**-mond)
1. the hardest of all stones. It sparkles like glass and is used in jewellery.
2. a shape a bit like a squashed square, which is on some playing cards.

diarrhoea (dy-a-**ree**-a)
an illness that gives you pains in the stomach and makes you go to the toilet a lot.

diary (**dy**-ree)
a book in which you can write down what happens each day.
Word building: For more than one we use **diaries**.
Word use: Don't confuse this with **dairy**.

dibbler (**dibb**-ler)
a small mouse with spots that lives in Western Australia. It is almost extinct. See the table at the end of this book.
Word use: This word comes from the Nyungar language of Western Australia. See the map of Australian Aboriginal languages at the end of this book.

dice
small cubes that you use in games. Each side of one of the cubes has a different number of spots, from one to six.
Word use: Dice is the word we use for more than one. For one we use **die**.

dictator (dik-**tay**-tor)
somebody who has all the power in ruling a country.

dictionary *(dik-shon-ree)*
a book which has a list of words in alphabetical order. You can use it to find out what a word means, how to spell it and how to say it.
Word building: For more than one we use **dictionaries**.

didjeridu *(dij-e-ree-**doo**)*
an Aboriginal musical instrument. It is a long, wooden tube that you blow down.
Word use: Some people spell this **didgeridoo**.

die *(rhymes with **my**)*
to stop living: *Those plants will **die** if you don't water them every day.*
Word building: he **died**, he is **dying**
Word use: Don't confuse this with **dye**.

diesel oil *(**dee**-zel oil)*
a type of fuel for vehicles such as trucks.

diet *(**dy**-et)*
the sort of foods that you eat: *It's important to have a healthy **diet**.*

differ *(**diff**-er)*
1. to be not the same: *I **differ** from my sister in the colour of my eyes.*
2. to disagree: *If my brother and I **differ** about which TV show to watch, we have to ask Mum to decide.*
Word building: If something differs from another thing, then it is **different** and you can see the **difference** between them.

difficult *(**diff**-i-cult)*
hard to do or understand.
Word building: If something is difficult, you talk about its **difficulty**.

dig
1. to break up or turn over with a spade: *The gardener will **dig** the soil.*
2. to make by digging: *The dog is starting to **dig** another hole in the garden.*
Word building: I **dug**, I have **dug**, I am **digging**

digger *(**digg**-er)*
an Australian soldier, especially one from World War I.

digital
1. using digits or numbers but no pointers: *My alarm clock is a **digital** clock.*
2. working by storing and using information like a computer does: *I have a **digital** camera, so it doesn't need a film.*

dillybag *(**dill**-ee-bag)*
a small bag made out of string or something like this, that you use to carry food or other things.
Word use: This comes from the Yagara language of Queensland. See the map of Australian Aboriginal languages at the end of this book.

dim
not bright: *It was difficult to see clearly in the **dim** light.*

dimple *(**dim**-pl)*
a small hollow in your cheek, which gets deeper when you smile.

dine *(rhymes with **mine**)*
to have dinner.
Word building: I **dined**, I am **dining**

dinghy *(**ding**-gee)*
a small boat that you row.
Word building: For more than one we use **dinghies**.

dingo *(**din**-go)*
an Australian wild dog. It has brownish-yellow fur and pointed ears.
Word building: For more than one we use **dingoes**.
Word use: This word comes from the Dharug language of New South Wales. See the map of Australian Aboriginal languages at the end of this book.

a b c **d** e f g h i j k l m n o p q r s t u v w x y z

dining room

a room where you eat dinner and other meals: *I will help you carry the food from the kitchen into the dining room.*

dinner *(dinn-er)*

the main meal of the day. Some people eat it in the middle of the day and some people eat it in the evening.

dinosaur *(dy-no-saw)*

an animal like a huge lizard, which lived millions of years ago.

dip

1. to put into a liquid for a short time: *Let's dip our toes in the water.*
2. to slope down: *The path gets slippery when it starts to dip towards the creek.*
3. a soft tasty mixture that you dip biscuits into.
4. a downward slope: *There's a dip in the road ahead.*
5. a short swim: *She went for a quick dip in the ocean.*
Word building: I **dipped**, I am **dipping**

direct *(di-rect)*

to show or tell someone the way: *Can you direct me to the nearest bus stop?*

direction *(di-rec-shon)*

the way you go to get to a particular place: *We ran as fast as we could in the direction of the smoke.*

director

1. the boss of a department in a company or other organisation.
2. the person who gives instructions to actors in a play or a film.

dirt

soil or dust: *Luca fell in the dirt and his clothes got covered in black marks.*
Word building: When something gets dirt on it, then it's **dirty**.

disagree *(dis-a-gree)*

to think differently to someone else: *I sometimes disagree with Mum about what clothes I should wear.*
Word building: When you disagree with someone you have a **disagreement** with them.

disappear *(dis-a-peer)*

to go out of sight or vanish: *They watched the ship disappear slowly over the horizon.*

disappoint *(dis-a-point)*

to become unhappy because something you hope will happen doesn't happen: *It will disappoint the children if it rains and they can't go to the beach.*
Word building: When something disappoints you, you are filled with **disappointment**.

disaster *(diz-ar-ster)*

something terrible that happens suddenly: *The bushfire was a disaster for the people in the small town.*
Word building: Something that causes a disaster is **disastrous**.

disc *(disk)*

any thin, flat object in the shape of a circle.

disco *(dis-co)*

a place or club in which you dance to music.

discover *(dis-cuv-er)*

to find or to find out something: *They set off with a map and a shovel to discover some buried treasure.* | *Did you discover who left the back gate open?*
Word building: When you discover something, you make a **discovery**.

discuss *(dis-kus)*

to talk about something: *Today our class is going to discuss how much pocket money children should get.*

discussion *(dis-**kush**-on)*
1. a talk between people to share opinions.
2. writing which gives more than one opinion on something. See the 'Types of writing and speaking' table at the end of this book.

disease *(di-**zeez**)*
a serious sickness.

disguise *(di-**skies**; the last part rhymes with **eyes**)*
the clothes or make-up that you put on so that you won't look like yourself.

disgust *(dis-**gust**)*
to give someone a strong feeling of dislike: *It will **disgust** you when you hear how cruel some people are to animals.*
Word building: Something that disgusts you is **disgusting**.

dish
1. a shallow bowl that you use to put food in.
2. a serving of a particular kind of food: *Spaghetti with meatballs is my favourite **dish**.*

dishwasher *(**dish**-wash-er)*
a machine that washes dishes automatically.

disintegrate *(dis-**in**-ta-grate)*
to break up into small parts: *The cardboard box will **disintegrate** if you put it in the water.*

disk
a thin, flat object used in computers for storing information.
Word building: This word is a short way of saying **computer disk**.

disk drive
a machine that allows data to be read from or recorded onto a disk.

dislike *(dis-**like**)*
to not like something or someone: *I **dislike** the way Marcus always forgets to say 'thank you'.*
Word building: I **disliked**, I am **disliking**

dismal *(**diz**-mal)*
sad: *The **dismal** news is that we can't go camping on the weekend because Mum has to work.*

dismiss *(dis-**miss**)*
to tell somebody to leave: *The teacher will **dismiss** the class when the bell rings.*

disobedient *(dis-o-**bee**-dee-ant)*
You're **disobedient** if you refuse to do something that you've been told to do: *My puppy is still **disobedient** even after we've been to dog-training classes.*
Word building: If you're disobedient, you **disobey**, and you show **disobedience**.

display *(dis-**play**)*
to show something: *Mia decided to **display** her painting by hanging it on her bedroom door.*

disqualify *(dis-**kwol**-i-fy)*
to put somebody out of a contest because they have broken a rule: *The judges will **disqualify** you if you start running before the whistle blows.*
Word building: I **disqualified**, I am **disqualifying**

distance *(**dis**-tance)*
1. the length of space between two places: *There is a **distance** of one metre between my bed and the window.*
2. a place far away from where you are: *If you listen carefully at night you can hear the trains in the **distance**.*

distant
far away: *He has moved to a **distant** town.*

distress *(dis-tress)*
a lot of sadness, worry or pain: *I could see the look of **distress** on her face when she saw the ferry had left without her.*

district
a particular area or neighbourhood: *We live in the same **district**.*

disturb *(di-sterb)*
to interrupt what someone is doing: *Don't **disturb** Grandpa when he's having a rest.*

ditch *(dich)*
a long, narrow hole dug in the ground.
Word building: For more than one we use **ditches**.

dive
to jump head first into water.
Word building: I **dived**, I am **diving**

divide *(di-vide)*
1. to cut up something into smaller parts: *I will **divide** the cake into six pieces so that we can all have a bit.*
2. to split one number into smaller parts which are the same size: *When you **divide** 10 by 5 you get 2.*
Word building: I **divided**, I am **dividing** │ In maths when you divide one number by another number you are doing **division**.

divorce *(di-vorce)*
If a husband and wife don't want to be together any more, they can end their marriage by getting a **divorce** from a court.

dizzy *(diz-ee)*
You're **dizzy** if you feel as if your head is spinning around.
Word building: more dizzy = **dizzier**, most dizzy = **dizziest**

do
to carry out a task or movement: *What did you **do** on the weekend?*
Word building: I **do**, you **do**, he **does**, I **did**, I have **done**, I am **doing** │ A short way of writing **do not** is **don't**.

dock
the place where the cargo of a ship is loaded or unloaded.

docket *(dock-et)*
a piece of paper that shows that you have bought something.

doctor *(doc-tor)*
someone whose job is to look after sick or hurt people and give them medicine.

dodge *(doj)*
to move quickly out of the way of something: *Every time I got close enough to grab him he would **dodge** past me.*
Word building: I **dodged**, I am **dodging**

doe
a female deer.
Word use: The male is a **stag**.

dog
a four-legged mammal which eats meat and is often kept as a pet.

doll
a child's toy which is made to look like a person.

dollar *(doll-ar)*
an amount of money. There are 100 cents in one dollar.

dolphin *(dol-fin)*
a playful animal with a long, pointed nose, which lives in the sea.

domino *(dom-i-no)*
a flat, oblong piece of wood or plastic with a number of dots on it, that you use to play a game.
Word building: For more than one we use **dominoes**.

donkey *(dong-kee)*
an animal with long ears and a body like a small horse.

door *(rhymes with **for**)*
something that goes across the opening into a house, room, cupboard or car.

dose
the amount of medicine that you take at one time.

dot
a very small spot: *I put a red **dot** on the map to show where my grandmother was born.*

dot painting
a picture made out of many dots of paint. This is an Aboriginal style of art.

double *(dub-l)*
1. twice as big or twice as many.
2. to make something twice as big or twice as many: *This tree will **double** its size in one year.* | *You **double** 2 to get 4.*
Word building: I **doubled**, I am **doubling**

doubt *(dowt)*
to feel unsure about something: *I **doubt** that a clever person like Hiroto would do such a silly thing.*
Word building: If you doubt something, then you're **doubtful** about it.

dough *(doh)*
a mixture of flour and water that you can bake to make bread.

down
1. towards the ground: *The bird flew **down**.* | *Don't look **down**.*
2. from high to low: *Please turn the volume **down**.*
Word use: The opposite of this is **up**.

download *(down-lode)*
to copy data from one computer or the internet to another computer: *I'll **download** the fact sheet from the internet.*

downstairs
down the stairs: *Ben went **downstairs**.* | *My bedroom is **downstairs**.*

Down syndrome *(down sin-drome)*
a condition that some people are born with that makes them look a bit different from other people and means that they sometimes can't do all the same things in school.

downwards *(down-wards)*
down from a high to a low place: *The plane glided **downwards**.*
Word use: The opposite of this is **upwards**.

dozen *(duz-n)*
a group of twelve.

draft
a rough drawing or piece of writing: *This is the first **draft** of my story.*
Word use: Don't confuse this with **draught**.

drag
to pull something along slowly: *Can you **drag** that box of tools over here, please?*
Word building: I **dragged**, I am **dragging**

dragon *(drag-on)*
an imaginary creature that breathes out fire and looks like a giant lizard with wings.

dragonfly *(drag-on-fly)*
a large insect which lives near water. It has a long, thin body and four long, clear wings.
Word building: For more than one we use **dragonflies**.

drain
a pipe or gutter for taking away water.

drake
a male duck.
Word use: The female is a **duck**.

a b c **d** e f g h i j k l m n o p q r s t u v w x y z

drama (*dra-ma*)
1. an exciting, sad or serious play acted on stage, radio or television.
2. any exciting event: *Fatima got caught up in the **drama** of the fire drill.*
3. writing that is meant to be acted out. See the 'Types of writing and speaking' table at the end of this book.

draught (*draft*)
air that blows into a room: *There is a cold **draught** coming through the window.*

Word building: If there is a draught in the room, then the room is **draughty**.

Word use: Don't confuse **draught** with **draft**.

draw
1. to make a picture with a pen or pencil.
2. a game which nobody has won because both sides ended with the same score.

Word building: I **drew**, I have **drawn**, I am **drawing**

Word use: Don't confuse this with **drawer**.

drawer (*draw*)
an open box that slides in and out of a piece of furniture such as a cupboard. You use it to keep things in.

Word use: Don't confuse this with **draw**.

drawing
a picture that you make using a pencil, pen or crayon.

dreadful (*dred-ful*)
very bad: *Did you hear the **dreadful** news about the plane crash?*

dream
the thoughts and pictures that come into your mind when you're asleep.

Dreaming (*dreem-ing*)
an Aboriginal person's special stories about how things began.

Word use: Another word that means nearly the same is **Dreamtime**.

dress
1. a piece of clothing that girls and women wear.
2. to put clothes on: *I'll **dress** the baby now.*

dribble (*dribb-l*)
1. to let a little bit of spit come out of your mouth: *Babies **dribble** a lot when they are growing their teeth.*
2. to move a ball along the ground with little kicks or pushes.

Word building: I **dribbled**, I am **dribbling**

drift
to move gently along in water or in air: *We dropped sticks into the river and watched them **drift** slowly away.*

drill
a tool for making holes.

drink
to swallow liquid: *I like to **drink** hot chocolate on a cold afternoon.*

Word building: I **drank**, I have **drunk**, I am **drinking**

drip
to let liquid fall in small drops: *You'd better take off that wet coat, or you'll **drip** water all through the house.*

Word building: I **dripped**, I am **dripping**

drive
to control something and make it move along: *My big brother is learning to **drive** a car. | The farmer will **drive** the cattle through the gate.*

Word building: I **drove**, I have **driven**, I am **driving** | If you drive something like a car, you are a **driver**.

droop
to bend over or hang down: *The plants **droop** if I don't water them.*

drop
1. a small round bit of liquid: *A **drop** of rain trickled down my back.*
2. to fall or to let something fall: *Be careful not to **drop** that vase.*
Word building: I **dropped**, I am **dropping**

drought *(drowt)*
dry weather which lasts for a long time.

drover *(rhymes with **over**)*
someone who makes cattle or sheep travel a very long way to get to market.
Word building: A drover's job is **droving**.

drown
to die from being under the water for so long that you run out of air to breathe.

drug
1. a medicine the doctor gives you to make you feel better.
2. a substance that some people take to try to make themselves feel good, even though it is against the law.

drum
a hollow musical instrument that makes a deep sound when you hit it.
Word building: If you play the drum, then you're a **drummer**.

drunk
Someone is **drunk** if they have had too much alcohol to drink. They are less able to control their movements or think as clearly as usual.

dry
1. not wet or damp: *My shoes got wet, but my socks are still **dry**.*
2. without much rain: *We've had a very **dry** winter.*
3. **the dry**, the season when it doesn't rain in central and northern Australia, from May to November.
Word building: more dry = **drier**, most dry = **driest**

drycleaner *(dry-**cleen**-er)*
someone who cleans clothes with chemicals, not with water.

duchess *(**duch**-ess)*
a woman who is part of a noble family.

duck[1]
a bird that uses its short legs and webbed feet to swim in the water.
Word building: A young duck is a **duckling**.
Word use: The male of this bird is a **drake**.

duck[2]
to quickly get your head down out of the way of something: *If you don't **duck** now, you'll be hit by the boat's sail.*

due *(rhymes with **new**)*
Something that's **due** is expected to be ready or to arrive: *The train from Melbourne is **due** at 5 o'clock.*
Word use: Don't confuse this with **dew**.

duel *(**dyoo**-el)*
a fight between two people who both use a pistol or a sword.

duet *(dyoo-**et**)*
a piece of music for two people.

duke
a man who is part of a noble family.

dull
1. Something is **dull** if it's boring or not interesting: *What a **dull** talk he's giving — I wish he'd show us some pictures.*
2. not bright or clear: *What a **dull**, rainy day it is — I'll have to turn the light on.*

dumb *(dum)*
1. Someone is **dumb** if they are not able to speak.
2. stupid or silly: *Did you hear the **dumb** answer he gave?*

dummy *(**dum**-ee)*
1. a piece of rubber that you give a baby to suck.
2. a model of a person. You use it to show how clothes look: *She's dressing the **dummy** in the shop window.*
Word building: For more than one we use **dummies**.

a
b
c
d
e
f
g
h
i
j
k
l
m
n
o
p
q
r
s
t
u
v
w
x
y
z

dump

1. to throw something down in a careless way: *Don't just **dump** your clothes in a pile on the floor.*
2. a place where you throw things you don't need: *I'll take our old fridge to the rubbish **dump**.*

dungeon *(dun-jen)*

a small dark prison, usually under the ground.

dunnart *(dunn-art)*

a type of mouse found only in Australia. It is endangered. See the table at the end of this book.

Word use: This word comes from the Nyungar language of Western Australia. See the map of Australian Aboriginal languages at the end of this book.

during *(dyoo-ring)*

for the given length of time of: *They kept talking **during** the film.*

dusk

the time at the end of the day when it's starting to get dark.

dust

earth that's fine and dry like powder.

Word building: If a place is full of dust, then it's **dusty**.

duty *(dyoo-tee)*

something you have to do: *It's my **duty** to tell the police I saw the thief.*

Word building: For more than one we use **duties**.

DVD

a disc for storing information such as film, sound and text, which can be read by a machine such as a computer.

Word use: A machine that you play DVD movies on is called a **DVD player**.

dwarf *(dworf)*

1. a person, animal or plant that is much shorter than usual.
2. a small character in a fairytale.

dye *(dy)*

a liquid like paint. You use it to colour cloth, your hair and other things.

Word use: Don't confuse this with **die**.

dynamite *(dy-na-mite)*

stuff that explodes when you set it off or light it. It can cause a lot of damage.

Ee

Emus explore every exit.

each *(eech)*
1. every: *Put **each** present under the Christmas tree.* | ***Each** of them stayed for dinner.*
2. for every one: *The peaches cost $1 **each**.*

eager *(eeg-er)*
You're eager if you want something very much: *I'm **eager** to have my present right now.*
Word building: If you're eager for something, then you wait for it **eagerly**, with a lot of **eagerness**.

eagle *(eeg-l)*
a large bird with a strong curved beak and claws. It is very good at seeing small animals which it hunts for food.

ear
the part of your body that you hear with.

early *(er-lee)*
Something is **early** if it happens before you think it will or before it usually does: *Ji-min arrived **early** and her friends weren't ready.* | *We had an **early** breakfast so that we wouldn't miss the train.*
Word building: more early = **earlier**, most early = **earliest**
Word use: The opposite of this is **late**.

earn *(ern)*
to get money in return for the work you do: *Anna will **earn** $20 for helping in the takeaway shop.*

earth *(erth)*
1. the planet we live on: *The spaceship was a long way from the **earth**.*
2. dirt or soil: *I put the seed in the hole and covered it with **earth**.*

earthquake *(erth-kwake)*
a violent shaking of the ground, which can cause a lot of damage.

east *(eest)*
the direction you face to watch the sun come up in the morning
Word use: The opposite of this is **west**. The other directions are **north** and **south**.

Easter
the special time each year when Christians remember how Jesus Christ came back to life after he had been killed on the cross.

easy *(eez-ee)*
Something is **easy** if you can do it or understand it without any trouble: *It's **easy** for me to touch my toes.*
Word building: more easy = **easier**, most easy = **easiest** | If something is easy, then you can do it **easily** or with a lot of **ease**.

eat
to chew food and then swallow it.
Word building: I **ate**, I have **eaten**, I am **eating**

ebb
to flow back or away like the sea does: *We watched as the tide began to **ebb** further and further down the beach.*

eccentric *(ek-**sen**-tric)*
Someone is **eccentric** if they do things in a strange or unusual way: *The **eccentric** old man made hats for his cats.*

echidna *(e-**kid**-na)*
a small Australian animal which is covered in long spines and which eats ants. It lays eggs and feeds its babies with its own milk.

echo *(**ek**-o)*
a sound that has bounced back at you after you've made it: *I called into the empty hall, but the only answer I got was the **echo** of my own voice.*
Word building: For more than one we use **echoes**.

eclipse *(e-**clips**)*
1. the darkness that comes when the moon is between the sun and the earth and blocks the sun's light. This is called a **solar eclipse**.
2. the darkness that comes over the moon when the earth is between the moon and the light of the sun. This is called a **lunar eclipse**.

eco-friendly *(ee-co-**frend**-lee)*
If something is **eco-friendly**, it does not damage the natural environment: *We live in an **eco-friendly** house.*

ecology *(e-**col**-o-gee)*
the science or study of the relationship between living things and their environment.

economy *(e-**con**-o-mee)*
looking after your money, your food, and anything else that's yours, in a careful way: *She spent a small amount each day and because of this **economy** her pocket money lasted all week.*
Word building: If you use **economy** and don't waste things, then you're **economical**.

ecosystem *(**ee**-co-sis-tem)*
a group of living things and the environment that they share: *The frogs are a very important part of the **ecosystem** of the pond.*

edge *(ej)*
a line or side where two parts meet: *Cut around the **edge** of the picture.*

educate *(**ej**-u-cate)*
to instruct or give knowledge to: *The teacher **educates** the students at school.*
Word building: I **educated**, I am **educating**

education *(ej-u-**cay**-shon)*
teaching people what they should know: *We get our **education** at school.*

effect *(e-**fect**)*
something that happens because of something else: *One **effect** of rising temperatures is that icebergs melt more quickly.*
Word use: This word is sometimes confused with **affect** which means 'to make something different'.

effort *(**ef**-et)*
You are making an **effort** if you are trying very hard: *We are making a big **effort** at home to use less water.*

EFTPOS *(**eft**-poss)*
a way of paying for things in supermarkets and shops, using a coded plastic card and a PIN.

egg
a roundish object with a thin shell, which a bird lays. A baby bird grows inside it.

either *(**eye**-dher or **ee**-dher)*
one or other of two: *Sit on **either** chair.*

elastic *(e-**las**-tic)*
Something is **elastic** if you can stretch it and then let it go back into shape again: *I'll twist this **elastic** band around my hair.*

elastics *(e-las-tics)*
a game played with a very large circle of elastic which is stretched around people who act as posts that the players must jump around while also jumping over the elastic: *Let's play* **elastics** *at lunchtime!*

elbow *(el-boe)*
the bony part in the middle of your arm where the top half joins the bottom half.

elder *(el-der)*
1. older: *Mario is Angelo's* **elder** *brother.*
2. an older and more important person who knows a lot about the world: *The Aboriginal* **elder** *taught the young people how to make a spear.*

eldest *(eld-est)*
oldest or born first.

elect *(e-lect)*
to choose someone by voting for them: *My Mum hopes they'll* **elect** *her to be our member of parliament.*
Word building: The person you elect to do a job has won an **election**.

electrician *(e-lek-trish-an)*
someone whose job is to work with anything that uses electricity.

electricity *(e-lek-triss-i-tee)*
power that you can use to light and heat a room, or to drive an engine. It moves along a wire in a current and you turn it off or on with a switch.
Word building: If something uses electricity, then it's **electric**.

electronic whiteboard *(e-lek-tron-ic wite-bord)*
a whiteboard that can be connected to a computer or a printer.

elegant *(el-e-gant)*
You're **elegant** if you move in a beautiful or graceful way.
Word building: If you're elegant, then you have **elegance**.

elephant *(el-e-fant)*
a very large animal with a thick skin. It uses its long nose or trunk to get hold of things.

elevator *(el-e-vay-tor)*
a box-like cage for carrying people up and down inside tall buildings.
Word use: Another word for this is **lift**.

elf
a tiny person in fairytales who can do magic and who often plays tricks on people.
Word building: For more than one we use **elves** *(elvz)*.

eliminate *(e-lim-i-nate)*
to get rid of something or someone: *I'll read through my story again and try to* **eliminate** *all the mistakes.*
Word building: I **eliminated**, I am **eliminating** | If you eliminate something, then you make an **elimination**.

else *(els)*
1. instead: *Take someone* **else**.
2. too: *What* **else** *should we play?*
3. otherwise: *Hurry, or* **else** *we'll miss the bus!*

email *(ee-male)*
messages sent by computer from one person to another person.
Word building: This is a short way of saying **electronic mail**.

embarrass *(em-ba-rass)*
to make someone feel silly in front of other people: *You* **embarrass** *me when you show my friends my old baby photos.*
Word building: Things that embarrass you fill you with **embarrassment**.

embassy *(em-ba-see)*
the office or house of an ambassador in a country far from their home.
Word building: For more than one we use **embassies**.

embrace *(em-brace)*
to hug someone.
Word building: I **embraced**, I am **embracing**

emerald *(em-rald)*
a green jewel which costs a lot of money.

emergency *(e-**mer**-jen-see)*
something serious that happens when you don't expect it and that you have to do something about at once.
Word building: For more than one we use **emergencies**.

emergency exit *(e-**mer**-jen-see **eg**-zit)*
an exit in a vehicle or building used as a way out in an emergency like a fire or accident.

emotion *(e-**mo**-shon)*
a feeling you have, such as love, hate, happiness, sadness or anger.
Word building: When you have a strong emotion, you're **emotional**.

emperor *(em-per-ra)*
a man who rules over a group of countries.

empire *(em-pire)*
a group of countries ruled by an emperor or an empress.

employ *(em-**ploy**)*
to keep someone busy or at work: *These factories **employ** 500 people.*
Word building: If you employ people, then you're an **employer**. If someone employs you, then you're an **employee** and you are in their **employment**.

empress *(em-press)*
a woman who rules over a group of countries.

empty *(em-tee)*
Something that's **empty** holds nothing inside: *I've used the water in the kettle and now it's **empty**.*
Word building: more empty = **emptier**, most empty = **emptiest** | If something is empty, you talk about its **emptiness**.

emu *(eem-yoo)*
a large Australian bird which can't fly.

encourage *(en-**cu**-rij)*
to cheer someone on by giving them your support or help: *We'll **encourage** them and tell them to try again next time.*
Word building: I **encouraged**, I am **encouraging** | If you encourage someone, you give them your **encouragement**.

encyclopedia *(en-sy-clo-**peed**-ee-a)*
a book, usually in many volumes, of information which is arranged in alphabetical order.
Word use: This is sometimes spelt **encyclopaedia**.

end
1. the place or time when something stops or finishes: *I've come to the **end** of my talk, so thank you very much for listening.*
2. to stop or finish: *When will the cartoon **end**?*

endanger *(en-**dane**-jer)*
to cause somebody or something to be in danger or at risk: *If you go swimming in those big waves you could **endanger** your life.*
Word building: A group of animals or plants which is in danger of all dying is called an **endangered species**.
Word use: Compare this with definition 2 of **vulnerable**.

endeavour *(en-**dev**-or)*
to try or attempt to do something.

endless
with no end: *As we drove on and on, the road ahead seemed **endless**.*

enemy *(en-e-mee)*
someone who hates you or who wants to hurt you.
Word building: For more than one we use **enemies**.

energy *(en-er-jee)*
1. the power to be strong and active: *I'm so worn out from playing tennis that I haven't got the **energy** for another game.*
2. fuel.
Word building: If you have plenty of energy, then you're **energetic**.

engaged *(en-gaged)*
1. busy or already being used: *Her phone is **engaged** so I'll ring again later.*
2. You're **engaged** if you're going to be married.
Word building: If you're engaged, you tell everyone of your **engagement**.

engine *(en-jin)*
a machine which uses petrol, oil, steam or electricity to move and then to make something else move: *The **engine** in our old car is always hard to start.*

engineer *(en-ji-near)*
someone whose job is to plan and build roads, bridges or machines.

enjoy *(en-joy)*
to like something: *I **enjoy** going surfing with my friends.*
Word building: If you enjoy something, then you find it **enjoyable** and it gives you **enjoyment**.

enormous *(e-norm-us)*
extremely large: *Whales are **enormous** creatures.*

enough *(e-nuff)*
as much as you want or need: *Have you got **enough** money to pay for your ice-cream?*

enter *(en-ter)*
1. to come in or go in: *We'll **enter** the house through the front door.*
2. to start or take part in something: *Will you **enter** the race too?*

entertain *(en-ter-tain)*
to amuse and interest someone: *A clown will **entertain** the children at the party.*
Word building: Someone whose job is to entertain you is an **entertainer**.

enthusiastic *(en-thoo-zee-as-tic)*
full of lively interest in something: *I'm very **enthusiastic** about the new project I'm doing at school.*
Word building: If you're enthusiastic about something, then you have **enthusiasm** for it.

entire *(en-tire)*
Something is **entire** if it's whole or it isn't broken up into parts.

entrance *(en-trance)*
the way in.

entrepreneur *(on-tre-pre-ner)*
someone who takes a risk by owning or working at a particular business.

entry *(en-tree)*
1. coming in or going in: *Everyone turned and looked when the bride made her **entry** into the church.*
2. the way in: *The **entry** to our drive was blocked by a van.*
Word building: For more than one we use **entries**.

envelope *(en-ve-lope or on-ve-lope)*
a paper cover for a letter, with a flap you stick down.

environment *(en-vy-ron-ment)*
1. everything around you in your daily life: *I grew up in a city **environment** with tall buildings, traffic, smog and noise.*
2. everything in nature, such as plants, animals, rivers and the sea.
Word building: Something that has to do with the environment is **environmental**.

a
b
c
d
e
f
g
h
i
j
k
l
m
n
o
p
q
r
s
t
u
v
w
x
y
z

envy *(en-vee)*
the wish to have what belongs to someone else: *He's full of **envy** because I have a new BMX bike.*
Word building: If you're full of envy, then you're **envious**.

equal *(ee-kwal)*
1. Things that are **equal** have the same number, the same value and are the same in every other way: *We'll have an **equal** share of the pie — half each.*
2. to add up to the same number as something else: *I'm sure that 5 plus 5 must **equal** 10.*
Word building: it **equalled**, it is **equalling** | If two things are equal, then they have **equality**.

equator *(e-kway-tor)*
the circle we imagine around the earth, halfway between the North Pole and the South Pole.

equip *(e-kwip)*
to give someone all the things they need to do something: *I can **equip** you with all the safety gear you'll need for rockclimbing.*
Word building: I **equipped**, I am **equipping** | If you equip someone, then you give them **equipment**.

eraser *(e-raze-er)*
a small piece of soft rubber that you can use to clean off pencil marks.
Word use: Another word for this is **rubber**.

erosion *(e-ro-zhon)*
damage to the land caused when soil is worn away, usually by the weather.
Word building: Erosion happens when soil **erodes**.

errand *(e-rand)*
a small job someone gives you to do: *My dad sent me on an **errand** to the shop.*

error *(e-ror)*
a mistake.

escalator *(es-ca-lay-tor)*
moving stairs that take people up or down.

escape *(e-scape)*
to get away from something or someone: *I'm sure the prisoner will try to **escape** from jail.*
Word building: I **escaped**, I am **escaping** | If someone escapes, then they are an **escapee** *(es-ca-pee)*.

especially
more than usually: *It is **especially** cold today.* | *Dress warmly in winter, **especially** at night.*

estimate *(es-ti-mate)*
to try to guess or judge the price, amount or size of something.
Word building: I **estimated**, I am **estimating**

etc. *(et set-ra)*
and many other things: *The lolly shop has chocolate, sweets, toffee, **etc.***
Word building: This is short for the Latin words **et cetera**.

ethnic *(eth-nic)*
Something is **ethnic** if it has to do with a race or group of people: *We watched some **ethnic** dancing — first from Greece, then from Japan.*

eucalypt *(yoo-ca-lipt)*
a gum tree.

euro[1] *(yoo-ro)*
a type of wallaroo with reddish short hair.
Word building: For more than one we use **euros**.
Word use: This word comes from the Adnyamathanha language of South Australia. See the map of Australian Aboriginal languages at the end of this book.

euro²

a type of money that is used in many countries, but not in Australia.

Word building: For more than one we use **euros**.

evaporate *(e-**vap**-o-rate)*

to dry up and disappear: *There are puddles of water now, but they will probably **evaporate** during the day.*

eve

1. the day before: *I like to celebrate New Year's **Eve**.*
2. the time just before something takes place: *The soldiers were ready on the **eve** of war.*

even *(**ee**-ven)*

1. A number is **even** if you can divide it by two: *Four, six, eight and ten are **even** numbers.*
2. equal in size: *Try to cut the cake into eight **even** slices.*

Word use: For definition 1, the opposite is **odd**. | For definition 2, the opposite is **uneven**.

evening *(**eev**-ning)*

the end of the afternoon and the beginning of the night.

event *(e-**vent**)*

something that happens: *Our school fete is a big important **event**.*

ever *(**ev**-er)*

at any time: *Have you **ever** felt like this before?*

every *(**ev**-ree)*

each: *We walk the dog **every** day.* | *She finished **every** level in the game!*

everyday *(**ev**-ree-day)*

Something is **everyday** if it has to do with the ordinary things that usually happen: *An **everyday** word is one that you'd use in talking to your friends at school.*

everyone

every person: ***Everyone** in my family has black hair.*

everything

all things: ***Everything** outside got soaked in the rain.* | *I'll teach you **everything** I know about cooking.*

everywhere

in all places: *I've looked **everywhere** in my room for that missing sock.*

evil *(**eev**-il)*

Someone is **evil** if they do wicked things that harm people.

evolution *(e-vol-**oo**-shun)*

a gradual change, over many years, that makes an animal or plant suit its environment better: ***Evolution** has made humans taller over thousands of years.*

evolve *(e-**volv**)*

to change in a gradual way over time: *Many living things will continue to **evolve** as their environments change over the years.*

ewe *(yoo)*

a female sheep.

Word use: The male is a **ram**.

exact *(eg-**zact**)*

Something is **exact** if every part is just right: *These shoes are an **exact** fit.*

Word building: If something is done in an exact way, it is done **exactly**.

exaggerate *(eg-**zaj**-e-rate)*

to say more about something than is true: *We'll have to **exaggerate** the story — instead of saying you were a bit sick, we'll say you nearly died.*

Word building: I **exaggerated**, I am **exaggerating** | If you exaggerate, then you make an **exaggeration**.

examination (eg-zam-i-**nay**-shon)
a test that shows how much you know or how well you can do something.

Word building: This word is often shortened to **exam**.

examine (eg-**zam**-in)
to look at or test something in a very careful way: *The dentist will **examine** your teeth.*

Word building: I **examined**, I am **examining**

example (eg-**zam**-pl or eg-**zarm**-pl)
1. a part or piece of something which shows you what the rest is like and makes it easy to understand: *Can you give us an **example** of the kind of poem you want us to write?*
2. a model you should copy: *Set an **example** to the younger children and don't run near the pool.*

excellent (**ex**-e-lent)
very good.

Word building: Something that's excellent is an example of **excellence**.

except
leaving out: *We're all in the same class **except** Omar.*

Word use: Don't confuse this with **accept**.

exchange (ex-**change**)
to give one thing and get another thing in return: *I'd like to **exchange** this red top for that blue one.*

Word building: I **exchanged**, I am **exchanging**

excite (ex-**site**)
to make someone feel very eager about something: *Your visit will **excite** them because they haven't seen you for a year.*

Word building: I **excited**, I am **exciting** | Things that excite you are **exciting** and fill you with **excitement**.

exclaim (ex-**claim**)
to cry out suddenly because you're pleased or frightened.

Word building: When you exclaim, you make an **exclamation**.

excursion (ex-**sker**-shen)
a short trip you take for a special reason: *Our class went on an **excursion** to the museum to see the dinosaurs.*

excuse (ex-**cuce**)
1. a reason you give to explain why someone should forgive you or let you off something: *What's your **excuse** for being late today?*
2. (ex-**cuze**) to forgive someone: *I'll **excuse** you this time, but don't be late again.*

Word building: I **excused**, I am **excusing**

execute (**ex**-e-cute)
to kill someone because they have done something wrong: *In some countries they **execute** people who smuggle drugs.*

Word building: he **executed**, he is **executing** | When they execute someone, they have an **execution**.

exercise (**ex**-er-size)
things you do to make your body fit and healthy, like sport.

exhausted (eg-**zorst**-ed)
very tired or worn out.

Word building: When you're exhausted, you feel **exhaustion**.

exhibition (ex-i-**bish**-on)
a show or display that everyone can come and see: *There's an art **exhibition** at our school.*

exist (eg-**zist**)
to be real: *Do Tasmanian tigers still **exist**?*

Word building: Things that exist have **existence**.

exit (*eg*-zit or **ex**-it)
1. the way out: *We slowly made our way to the **exit**.*
2. to leave: *Please **exit** through the side door.* | *Before you turn off the computer, you should **exit** from that program.*

exotic (ex-**o**-tic)
1. from another country, or not native to an area: ***Exotic** plants and animals have been brought into Australia.*
2. strange, or unusually colourful or beautiful: *When we were on holiday we saw many **exotic** places and ate **exotic** food.*

expand (ex-**pand**)
to get bigger or make something bigger: *A balloon will **expand** when you blow it up.*

expect (ex-**pect**)
to think that something is likely to happen or that someone is likely to come: *I **expect** we'll go home soon.* | *I'll **expect** you at the party at 5 o'clock.*

expedition (ex-pe-**dish**-on)
a journey you make for a special reason: *Emily and Ivan began to plan their next **expedition** to the market.*

expensive (ex-**pen**-sive)
Something is **expensive** if it costs a lot of money: *That phone is perfect, but it's too **expensive**.*

experience (ex-**peer**-ree-ence)
1. something that happens to you: *I had a strange **experience** on my way to school.*
2. the things you learn from doing or seeing things: *My friend has a lot of **experience** in looking after small children.*

experiment (ex-**pe**-ri-ment)
a test you do to find something out.

expert (**ex**-pert)
someone who knows a lot about a special thing: *She's an **expert** in computers.*

explain (ex-**plain**)
to make something easy for people to understand: *Can you **explain** how to do that sum?*

explanation (ex-pla-**nay**-shon)
1. If someone gives an **explanation**, they tell how or why something happens.
2. writing which tells how or why something happens. See the 'Types of writing and speaking' table at the end of this book.

explode (ex-**plode**)
to blow up or burst into pieces with a loud noise.
Word building: it **exploded**, it is **exploding** | When something explodes, there's an **explosion**.

explore (ex-**plore**)
to look around a place you've never been to before and find out what's there: *Are you coming with us to **explore** the island?*
Word building: I **explored**, I am **exploring** | If you go to faraway places to explore, you're an **explorer** and your job is **exploration**.

exposition (ex-po-**zish**-on)
1. a show or display that everyone can come and see.
2. writing which gives only one opinion on something. See the 'Types of writing and speaking' table at the end of this book.
Word building: Definition 1 is sometimes shortened to **expo**.

express (ex-**press**)
1. to put your thoughts or feelings into words.
2. a very fast train or bus that doesn't make all the usual stops.

a
b
c
d
e
f
g
h
i
j
k
l
m
n
o
p
q
r
s
t
u
v
w
x
y
z

expression *(ex-presh-on)*

the look on someone's face: *You can tell Adam's cross — just look at his angry* **expression**.

expressway

a large road people use if they want to drive fast, without having to stop.

Word use: Another name we use for this is **freeway**.

extend *(ex-tend)*

to pull out or to stretch out: *We will* **extend** *the ladder until it can reach the roof.* | *These roads* **extend** *for hundreds of kilometres across the desert.*

Word building: If you **extend** something, then you stretch it out to its full **extent**.

exterior *(ex-teer-ree-or)*

Something is **exterior** if it's on the outside of a place or building.

Word use: The opposite of this is **interior**.

external *(ex-ter-nal)*

on the outside: *My only* **external** *injury was a black eye.*

Word use: The opposite of this is **internal**.

extinct *(ex-tinct)*

1. no longer existing: *A dinosaur is an* **extinct** *type of reptile.*
2. no longer active: *We live in a small town beside an* **extinct** *volcano.*

Word building: When something is extinct, it is in a state of **extinction**.

extinguish *(ex-ting-gwish)*

to put out a light or a fire.

Word building: You can extinguish a fire with an **extinguisher**.

extra *(ex-tra)*

more than usual: *We need to buy an* **extra** *bottle of milk today.*

extraordinary *(ex-traw-den-ree)*

so unusual that you can't help noticing it: *Did you see that* **extraordinary** *hat in the shape of a banana?*

extreme *(ex-treem)*

very great: *She felt ready to burst with* **extreme** *happiness.*

Word building: If you feel extreme happiness, then you're **extremely** happy.

eye *(rhymes with my)*

the part of your body that you see with.

Four frogs float on fuzzy flowers.

fable *(fay-bl)*
a short story that teaches people about how they should behave: *My favourite **fable** is the one about the tortoise and the hare.*

face
1. the front part of your head.
2. the outside part of anything: *I can see the **face** of my watch in the dark.*
3. to look towards something: ***Face** the light so I can see you.*
Word building: I **faced**, I am **facing**

fact
something that is true.

factory *(fac-tree)*
a building where people use machines to make things you can buy.
Word building: For more than one we use **factories**.

fade
to lose its colour or strength: *The paint on this side of the house is beginning to **fade** in the sun.*
Word building: I **faded**, I am **fading**

fail
to have no success in something you try to do: *I'm sure I'll **fail** my maths test as I just can't do those sums.*
Word building: If you fail something then you have had a **failure**.

faint
1. to feel so weak and dizzy that you fall over and everything goes black.
2. weak or distant: *We heard a **faint** rumble of thunder in the distance.*

fair[1]
1. If something is **fair**, it's done honestly, according to the rules: *It's not **fair**! You've had three rides and I've only had one.*
2. light in colour: *I have **fair** hair, but my sister has dark hair.*

fair[2]
a travelling group of people performing shows, offering special rides and games, and selling food and drink.

fairly
1. in a fair way: *We divided the lollies between us **fairly**.*
2. rather, quite: *I'm **fairly** good at soccer, but my sister is better.*

fairy *(fair-ree)*
a tiny person in stories, who can do magic things.

fairytale
an old story about magic or fairies.

faith
1. trust in someone or something.
2. the beliefs of a religion: *He believes in the Jewish **faith**.*

a
b
c
d
e
f
g
h
i
j
k
l
m
n
o
p
q
r
s
t
u
v
w
x
y
z

faithful *(faith-ful)*
You are **faithful** if you can be trusted and always do what you have promised.

fake
something which is not real that you use to trick people: *Let me check to see if this fifty dollar note is a fake.*

fall *(rhymes with tall)*
to drop suddenly from a higher to a lower place.
Word building: I **fell**, I have **fallen**, I am **falling**

false
1. not true: *The story he told the police was false.*
2. not real: *Grandpa has false teeth.*

familiar *(fa-mil-yar)*
Something is **familiar** if you are used to seeing, doing or hearing it.

family *(fam-lee)*
your brothers and sisters, parents and grandparents and other relatives.
Word building: For more than one we use **families**.

famine *(fam-in)*
a time when there's hardly any food.

famous *(fame-us)*
very well known: *Everyone knows that famous singer.*

fan¹
something which makes the air move so that you feel cooler.

fan²
someone who's a strong supporter of a sport or a team or a person.

fancy *(fan-see)*
decorative: *We used gold paper and red ribbon to make a fancy cover for the book.*
Word use: When you dress up in special clothes and pretend to be someone else, you are in **fancy dress**.

fang
a long, pointed tooth. Dogs, wolves and some snakes have them.

fantastic
an everyday word you use to describe something very good or wonderful: *The new cafe has fantastic food.*
Word building: If you do something in a fantastic way, you do it **fantastically**.

far
Something is **far** if it is a long way off.
Word building: This word is part of the set **far, further, furthest**.

fare *(rhymes with care)*
money that you pay to travel on a bus, train, boat or plane.

farm
a piece of land where you grow crops or keep animals for food.
Word building: Someone whose job is to work on a farm is a **farmer**.

fashion *(fash-on)*
a particular way of dressing that a lot of people like and try to copy: *I always choose clothes in the latest fashion.*

fast¹ *(rhymes with last)*
quick: *She is a fast swimmer and should win this race.*

fast² *(rhymes with last)*
to go without food, usually for a special reason.

fasten *(far-sen)*
to close or do up something: *You must fasten your seatbelt whenever you get in a car.*

fat
1. You are **fat** if you weigh a lot more than you should.
2. the white, greasy part of meat.

fatal *(fay-tl)*
Something is **fatal** if it makes someone die.

fate
something you can't control that seems to control the things that happen to you: *It was **fate** that I should see you again.*

Word building: If something seems to have been caused by fate, it is **fateful**, and it happened **fatefully**.

Word use: Don't confuse **fate** with **fete**.

father *(far-dher)*
a male parent.

fault *(fawlt or folt)*
1. a mistake that makes something bad happen or makes something go wrong: *It is my **fault** that the dog is lost because I left the back gate open.*
2. something wrong: *There must be a **fault** with this torch — it won't work.*

Word building: When something has a fault, then it is **faulty**.

favour *(fay-vor)*
a kind thing that you do for someone: *Will you do me a **favour** and post this letter while you're out?*

favourite *(fave-ret)*
the one that you like the most.

fawn[1] *(rhymes with **horn**)*
1. a young deer.
2. yellowish-brown in colour.

fawn[2]
to try to get special treatment from someone by saying nice things about them and showing them lots of attention: *You don't have to **fawn** to get a good mark from your teacher.*

fax
written messages or pictures that are sent along a telephone line.

Word building: To send a fax you use a **fax machine**.

Word use: This comes from a longer word, **facsimile**, which means 'an exact copy' and is pronounced *(fax-**sim**-i-lee)*. The first part of the word was chosen and the spelling was changed to match how you say it.

fear *(rhymes with **ear**)*
the feeling you have when you think that something bad might happen to you: *He had a **fear** of the beach, because he thought he might drown.*

feast *(feest)*
a large meal for a lot of people.

feather *(fedh-er)*
one of the light, soft parts that cover a bird's body.

feeble *(fee-bl)*
weak: *The thin legs of the newly-born foal are too **feeble** for it to walk.*

feed
to give food to.

Word building: I **fed**, I am **feeding**

feel
1. to know something by touching: ***Feel** how smooth this table is.*
2. to know how you are inside yourself: *I **feel** sick. | I **feel** sad.*

Word building: I **felt**, I am **feeling** | If you feel something then you have a **feeling**.

felt
a thick, smooth cloth made of wool.

felt pen *(felt pen)*
a thick, brightly coloured pen that is used to fill in the blank parts of a picture.

Word use: This is sometimes called a **texta**.

female *(fee-male)*
a person or animal that can have babies.

Word use: The opposite of this is **male**.

feminism
the belief that women and men should be treated the same.

Word building: A person who believes in feminism is called a **feminist**.

fence
a wall or barrier around or across something.

fern
a green, leafy plant that grows in damp places and does not have flowers.

ferry *(rhymes with **berry**)*
a boat that carries people and sometimes cars.
Word building: For more than one we use **ferries**.

fertile *(**fer**-tile)*
Ground is **fertile** if it can grow healthy plants.

festival *(**fes**-ti-val)*
a special time with parades, music and dancing.

fetch
to go and get something: *Could you **fetch** me a glass of water, please?*

fete *(rhymes with **hate**)*
a small fair which people hold to make money for a school or a charity.
Word use: Don't confuse this with **fate**.

fever *(**fee**-ver)*
the hot and dizzy feeling you sometimes have when you are sick.

few
not many: ***Few** people swim in winter.*

fiction *(**fic**-shon)*
a story or book about people and happenings that are not real: *Fairytales are my favourite type of **fiction**.*

fiddle *(**fidd**-l)*
1. to play about with something: *If you **fiddle** with Mum's camera you might damage it.*
2. a violin.
Word building: I **fiddled**, I am **fiddling**

fidget *(**fij**-et)*
to keep moving about in an annoying way: *Don't **fidget** while I'm trying to cut your hair.*

field *(feeld)*
a piece of open ground where people grow crops or keep animals or where you can play sport.

fierce *(feerce)*
strong, wild and angry: *Beware! **Fierce** dogs guard this factory at night.*

fig
a small soft fruit shaped like a pear, with a lot of small seeds inside.

fight *(fite)*
to take part in an argument or struggle.
Word building: I **fought**, I am **fighting**

figure *(**fig**-er)*
a sign that we use for a number: *Now make a **figure** 8.*

file[1]
a line of people: *The children entered the hall in single **file**.*

file[2]
a collection of information stored in a computer.

file[3]
a flat tool with a rough surface that you rub against things to make them smooth.

fill
to put as much into something as it will hold.

film
1. a moving picture shown on a screen: *I cried at the end of the sad **film**.*
2. a roll of thin plastic that you put in older types of cameras to take photographs: *Dad still uses **film** in his old camera, but I have a digital camera.*
Word use: Another word for definition 1 is **movie**.

filthy *(**fil**-thee)*
very dirty.
Word building: more filthy = **filthier**, most filthy = **filthiest** | If something is filthy, then it's covered with or full of **filth**.

fin
one of the thin, flat parts that stick out of a fish's body and help it to swim.

final *(fine-l)*
last: *The next race will be the **final** event.*

finalist *(fine-a-list)*
a person who is in the last round of a competition.

find *(rhymes with **dined**)*
to come across something, either by accident or because you were looking for it: *I can't **find** my keys anywhere.*
Word building: I **found**, I am **finding**

fine[1]
1. very good: *She is a **fine** writer.*
2. very thin: *This cloth is so **fine** that you can almost see through it.*
3. sunny and dry: *I hope it is **fine** tomorrow for our picnic.*
4. healthy: *I felt sick this morning, but I'm **fine** now.*

fine[2]
money that you have to pay because you have done something wrong.

finger *(fing-ger)*
one of the five long parts at the end of your hand.

finish *(fin-ish)*
1. the end.
2. to come to an end: *Will the party **finish** before five o'clock?*

fir *(fer)*
a tree with woody cones and long, thin leaves like needles.

fire
1. the heat and flames that come from things that are burning.
2. to shoot: *Hold the gun very still and then **fire** at the target.*
Word building: I **fired**, I am **firing**

fireworks *(fire-works)*
containers filled with a powder that burns with brightly coloured sparks and sometimes makes a bang.

firm[1] *(ferm)*
hard or solid: *I like my boiled eggs to be **firm** in the centre.*

firm[2] *(ferm)*
a group of people joined together in a company to do business: *Emma is going to work in the same **firm** of lawyers as Rania.*

first *(ferst)*
before any other: *My baby brother took his **first** step yesterday.*

first aid *(ferst **aid**)*
help that you give quickly before a doctor arrives to someone who is hurt.

fish
an animal with fins and scales, that lives and breathes under water.
Word building: For more than one we use **fish** or **fishes**.

fist
your hand with all the fingers tightly closed.

fit
1. healthy: *My Mum does exercises every morning to keep **fit**.*
2. to be the right shape and size: *Do those jeans **fit** or are they too tight?*
Word building: more fit = **fitter**, most fit = **fittest** | I **fitted**, I am **fitting** | If someone is fit, they have a certain level of **fitness**.

fix
to mend something or make it right.

fizzy *(fiz-ee)*
full of tiny bubbles: *Lemonade is my favourite **fizzy** drink.*
Word building: more fizzy = **fizzier**, most fizzy = **fizziest**

flag
a piece of cloth with a pattern on it which shows that it belongs to one country or group, or that it has a special meaning.

flake
a small, flat, thin piece of something: *Flakes of paint are coming off the house.*

flame
the yellow, dancing part of a fire.

flammable
easily set on fire: *Make sure you don't take anything flammable near the camp fire.*

flap
1. to move up and down: *I saw the bird flap its wings and fly away.*
2. something flat and thin that is joined to something else along one edge: *When you've folded the paper, tuck in the flap.*
Word building: I **flapped**, I am **flapping**

flash
a sudden burst of bright light: *A flash of lightning lit up the sky.*
Word use: A flood that happens quickly and unexpectedly is a **flash flood**.

flask *(rhymes with ask)*
a bottle that you put drink into.

flat¹
smooth or without any bumps: *The sea is flat today because there is no wind.*

flat²
a home that is a group of rooms in a larger building.

flavour *(flay-vor)*
taste: *Do you like the flavour of lemon?*

flea *(flee)*
a small insect without wings, which sucks blood from animals like cats and dogs, and moves by jumping.
Word use: Don't confuse this with **flee**.

flee
to run away from something or someone.
Word building: I **fled**, I am **fleeing**
Word use: Don't confuse this with **flea**.

fleece *(rhymes with geese)*
the wool that covers a sheep.

fleet
a group of ships sailing together.

flesh
the soft part of an animal's body, between the skin and the bone.

flicker *(flick-er)*
to burn brightly and then dimly, so that the light keeps on changing: *Please close the window because the wind is making the candle flicker.*

flight *(flite)*
1. a movement or journey through the air: *'I hope you enjoyed your flight', said the captain when the plane landed.*
2. a set of stairs.

flight attendant *(flite a-tend-ant)*
a person who works on a plane and looks after the passengers.

fling
to throw something away from you: *She screwed the paper into a ball to fling at her brother.*
Word building: I **flung**, I am **flinging**

flipper
1. the broad flat body part of an animal such as a seal or whale that is used for swimming.
2. a piece of rubber shaped like a flipper that you wear on your foot to help you swim.

float *(rhymes with boat)*
to rest gently on the top of water or something like that: *I gave the baby a plastic duck to float in the bath.*

flock
a group of birds, sheep or goats.

flood *(rhymes with **mud**)*
a lot of water that covers land which is usually dry.

floor *(rhymes with **door**)*
1. the lowest flat part of a room or any other place: *The ship sank to the **floor** of the ocean.*
2. a storey of a building.

flour *(rhymes with **power**)*
the powder you get when you crush up wheat or some other grain. You use it in cooking.
Word use: Don't confuse this with **flower**.

flow *(flo)*
to move along smoothly.

flower *(rhymes with **power**)*
1. the part of a plant that makes the seed. It usually has coloured petals and some flowers have a sweet smell.
2. to grow flowers: *Most plants **flower** in the spring.*
Word use: Don't confuse this with **flour**.

flu *(floo)*
an illness that makes you ache all over, sneeze and feel very hot and tired.
Word building: This word has been shortened from **influenza**.

fluff
soft light bits that come from wool or cotton.
Word building: Something that is soft and light like a piece of fluff is **fluffy**.

fluoro *(floo-ro)*
an extremely bright colour: *My favourite coloured pen is my green **fluoro** one.*
Word building: This is a short way of saying **fluorescent** *(flu-**ress**-ent)*.

flute
a musical instrument that you play by blowing across a hole near the top.
Word building: Someone who plays the flute is a **flautist** *(**floor**-tist)*.

flutter *(**flutt**-er)*
to move up and down with quick jerks: *Watch the butterfly **flutter** by.*

fly[1] *(rhymes with **my**)*
to move through the air: *I am going to **fly** to Sydney on the afternoon plane.*
Word building: I **fly**, he **flies**, I **flew**, I have **flown**, I am **flying**

fly[2] *(rhymes with **my**)*
an insect with two wings.
Word building: For more than one we use **flies**.

foal *(rhymes with **hole**)*
a young horse.

foam *(rhymes with **home**)*
a lot of bubbles on top of water or some other liquid.

fog
a layer of wet air near the ground. It looks like a cloud and is difficult to see through.
Word building: When there is a lot of fog, then it is **foggy**.

fold *(rhymes with **cold**)*
to bend one part of something over onto another part of the same thing: ***Fold** your letter and put it into this envelope.*

folder *(**fold**-er)*
a cardboard cover for keeping your papers in.

foliage *(**foe**-lee-ij)*
the leaves of a plant.

follow *(**foll**-oe)*
to come along after someone or something: *You go ahead and I'll **follow**.*

fond

You're **fond** of something or someone if you like them very much.

font

a style of printing type: *Let's use a different **font** for the heading.*

food

anything that you eat to keep you alive and to help you grow.

food chain

a series of living things that eat each other to survive. Something lower on the food chain is eaten by something higher on the food chain: *Grass is lower than cows on the **food chain** and cows are lower than people.*

fool

someone who is very silly.

Word building: A fool often does **foolish** things.

foot *(rhymes with **put**)*

1. the part of your body at the end of your leg.
2. a measure of length equal to about 30 centimetres. We used it in Australia before we used centimetres and metres.

Word building: For more than one we use **feet**.

football *(**foot**-ball)*

a game in which two teams kick or throw a ball and try to score goals.

for

to be used by or given to: *The bottle is **for** the baby.* | *I bought a present **for** you.*

forbid *(for-**bid**)*

to tell someone that they are not allowed to do something.

Word building: I **forbade**, I have **forbidden**, I am **forbidding**

force

1. power or strength: *The **force** of the wind was so great that we were nearly blown over.*
2. to make someone do something by frightening them or by hurting them: *The bully tried to **force** me to hand over my money, but my classmates stood up for me.*
3. to use your strength to do something: *Can you **force** this door open? It's stuck.*

Word building: I **forced**, I am **forcing**

forecast *(for-cast)*

to tell what might happen in the future: *Did they **forecast** that there will be rain tomorrow?*

Word building: I **forecast**, I have **forecast**, I am **forecasting**

forehead *(forrid)*

the part of your face between your eyebrows and where your hair starts.

foreign *(forrin)*

from another country: *The only **foreign** language I've learned is Indonesian.*

Word building: Someone who is foreign is a **foreigner**.

forest *(fo-rest)*

a lot of trees growing together.

forever

without ever ending: *I wish this holiday could go **forever**.*

forge *(forj)*

to make a copy of something and use it to trick someone: *The naughty girl tried to **forge** her mother's signature.*

Word building: I **forged**, I am **forging** | Something that someone forges is a **forgery**.

forget *(for-**get**)*

1. to have no memory of something: *I always **forget** people's names.*
2. to leave behind: *Don't **forget** your umbrella — it looks like it will rain.*

Word building: I **forgot**, I have **forgotten**, I am **forgetting** | If you forget things, you are **forgetful**.

forgive *(for-give)*
to stop having bad feelings about what someone has done or said: *I think you should forgive your little sister — she didn't mean to tear your book.*
Word building: I **forgave**, I have **forgiven**, I am **forgiving**

fork
1. a tool with several long, thin, pointed parts which you use for lifting food when you are eating.
2. the place where a tree, a river or a road divides into two or more parts.

form
1. the shape that something has: *My cake was in the form of a '6'.*
2. a printed paper with spaces where you have to write.

formal
1. not relaxed or casual: *It was an important occasion, so we had to get dressed up in formal clothes.*
2. following the official procedure: *You need to make a formal complaint in writing.*
Word building: If you say or do something in a formal way, then you say or do it **formally**.

format *(for-mat)*
shape, plan or style: *You can now get the book in a new format with a softer cover, coloured pictures and bigger print.*

fort
a strong building like a castle, which is difficult for an enemy to get into.

fortnight *(fort-nite)*
two weeks.

fortunate *(for-tune-at)*
lucky: *You are fortunate to live so close to the beach.*
Word building: If something happens in a fortunate way, it happens **fortunately**.

fortune *(for-tune)*
1. a huge amount of money: *The queen's jewels are worth a fortune.*
2. luck: *It was my bad fortune to miss the bus.*

forwards *(for-wards)*
facing or moving ahead: *I didn't see the boy behind me because I was facing forwards.* | *The car moved forwards when the light turned green.*
Word use: The opposite of this is **backwards**.

fossil *(foss-l)*
an animal or plant that lived long ago and which has become as hard as rock.

fossil fuel *(foss-l fewl)*
a fuel such as coal or petrol, which has formed underground from fossils.

foul *(rhymes with growl)*
1. very dirty: *Fish can't live in the foul water of a polluted river.*
2. something in a game that breaks the rules or isn't fair.
Word use: Don't confuse this with **fowl**.

foundations *(fown-day-shons)*
the base on which a building stands.

fountain *(fown-ten)*
a jet of water that shoots into the air from a pipe.

fowl
a bird that is kept for its meat or eggs, such as a hen, duck, goose or turkey.
Word use: Don't confuse this with **foul**.

fox
an animal that looks like a small dog. It has reddish fur and a long bushy tail.
Word building: For more than one we use **foxes**.

fraction *(frac-shen)*
a part of a whole number, such as $\frac{1}{2}$, $\frac{3}{4}$ and $\frac{5}{8}$.

a b c d e f g h i j k l m n o p q r s t u v w x y z

fragile *(fra-jile)*

easily damaged or broken: *Eggs are fragile.*

Word use: Another word that means nearly the same is **delicate**.

fragment *(frag-ment)*

a piece that has come off something: *The museum has a fragment from an ancient Egyptian vase.*

frame

the part which fits around something or holds it up and which gives it its shape: *This picture needs a frame so I can hang it up.* | *Our house has a wooden frame.*

fraud *(frawd)*

someone who tries to trick you by pretending to be someone else.

freak *(freek)*

someone or something that is very strange or different from usual.

freckle *(freck-l)*

a small brown spot on your skin from being in the sun.

free

1. Something is **free** if it doesn't cost you anything: *We won some free movie tickets.*
2. able to choose where to go and what to do: *The bird is free now that it has flown out of its cage.*

Word building: If you are free, then you have **freedom** and you can do things **freely**.

free-range *(free-raynj)*

If an animal is **free-range**, it is not kept in a cage and can walk around freely: *We get our eggs from free-range chickens.*

freeway *(free-way)*

a large road people use if they want to drive fast, without having to stop.

Word use: Another name we use for this is **expressway**.

freeze

1. to turn to ice: *The pond will freeze in this cold weather.*
2. to be or to feel very cold: *You'll freeze if you don't wear a jumper.*

Word building: I **froze**, I have **frozen**, I am **freezing** | If you freeze something, it's **frozen**.

frequent *(free-kwent)*

Something is **frequent** if it happens often.

Word building: If something happens in a frequent way, it happens **frequently**.

fresh

1. not frozen or put in a can: *We're having fresh prawns for lunch today.*
2. new: *Go and get a fresh piece of paper and start again.*

fridge *(frij)*

an everyday word which is short for **refrigerator**.

fried rice *(fride rice)*

rice that is fried with egg, pork, onion and soy sauce. This dish is Chinese.

friend *(frend)*

someone you like and who likes you too.

Word building: If you have a friend, then you feel **friendly** towards them and you have a **friendship** with them.

fright *(frite)*

a sudden scare or shock: *Sam jumped out of the bushes and gave me a fright.*

Word building: When someone gives you a fright, they **frighten** you and you feel **frightened**.

frill

a strip of lace or material put on a curtain or on a dress to make it look pretty.

fringe *(frinj)*

1. loose threads hanging from the ends of something like a scarf or a rug.
2. hair which has been cut straight across your forehead.

frog
a small animal that uses its webbed feet and its long back legs for swimming in the water or for jumping about on land.

from
From is a very common word that is used in many ways. It usually has to do with where someone was before, or where something was made. You also use it if you want to talk about direction or time, or the difference between things: *Ricardo is from Peru.* | *This olive oil is from Spain.* | *The track goes from our house to the beach.* | *She ran from the room.* | *She works from early in the morning until late at night.* | *Can you tell this colour from that one?*

front *(frunt)*
the part which faces forward or that you see most of the time.

frost
the tiny bits of ice that cover the ground on a very cold morning.

froth
all the small bubbles that come to the top of water when you shake it.
Word building: If a liquid has froth on top, then it's **frothy**.

frown
to make lines come on your forehead when you're cross or worried: *I made Mum frown when I told her I'd lost my jumper again.*

fruit *(rhymes with boot)*
the part of a plant which grows from its flowers and which you can often eat.

fry *(rhymes with my)*
to cook something in a pan using fat or oil: *I'll fry the bacon, if you make the toast.*
Word building: I **fried**, I am **frying** | Food you fry is **fried**.

fuel *(fewl)*
anything that burns and gives heat or makes an engine work: *This wood will make good fuel for the fire.*

full *(rhymes with pull)*
filled up so that no more will fit.
Word use: The opposite of this is **empty**.

fun
1. enjoyment: *Let's have some fun!*
2. a word to describe something you enjoy: *Basketball is fun.*
3. If you make **fun** of someone, you tease them.

funeral *(few-ne-ral)*
a ceremony held before the body of a dead person is burnt or buried.

fungus *(fung-gus)*
a type of plant which grows in dark or damp places. It does not have a green stem or green leaves.
Word building: For more than one we use **fungi**.

funnel *(funn-l)*
1. the chimney of a ship or a steam engine.
2. a cone with both ends open, which you use for pouring things into bottles.

funny *(funn-ee)*
1. Something is **funny** if it can make you laugh: *What a funny joke!*
2. strange: *There's something funny about this cake — I think you've added salt instead of sugar.*
Word building: more funny = **funnier**, most funny = **funniest**

fun run *(fun run)*
a long running race, often used to raise money.

fur *(fer)*
the hair that covers some animals.
Word building: An animal with fur is **furry**.

a b c d e f g h i j k l m n o p q r s t u v w x y z

furious *(few-ree-us)*

very angry: *She was **furious** when I turned off the computer because she hadn't saved her work.*

Word building: If you're furious, you are full of **fury**.

furniture *(fer-ni-cher)*

the chairs, beds, tables and other things like this that belong in a room or in a house.

further *(fer-dher)*

at or to a greater distance: *He's waiting for you **further** down the road. | I can run **further** than you can.*

Word building: This word is part of the set **far, further, furthest**.

Word use: You can use **farther** instead if you want to.

fuse *(fuze)*

the twisted threads you light to set off anything that explodes.

fuss

too much bother about things that aren't important.

Word building: Someone who makes a fuss about little things is **fussy**.

future *(few-cher)*

the time ahead which hasn't come yet: *We went to see a film about how people might live in the **future**.*

fuzzy *(fuzz-ee)*

1. covered with a fluffy coat or with lots of fluff: *This is a very **fuzzy** mat.*
2. Something is **fuzzy** if you can't see it clearly: *I can't tell who that is because the photo is too **fuzzy**.*

Word building: more fuzzy = **fuzzier**, most fuzzy = **fuzziest** | If something is fuzzy, then it has a lot of **fuzziness**.

Gg

Guinea pigs gobble green grapes.

gadget *(gaj-et)*
a small machine that someone invents to do a special job: *This new gadget for peeling and slicing apples is great.*

gag
to cover someone's mouth to stop them from speaking or from making any noise.
Word building: I **gagged**, I am **gagging**

gain
to get or win something: *You will gain everyone's respect if you run in the marathon.*

galah *(ga-lah)*
an Australian parrot with pink and grey feathers.
Word use: This word comes from the Yuwaalaraay language of New South Wales. See the map of Australian Aboriginal languages at the end of this book.

gale
a very strong wind.

gallery *(gal-e-ree)*
a room or a building where you can go to see paintings and other sorts of art.
Word building: For more than one we use **galleries**.

gallop *(gal-op)*
to ride a horse as fast as it can go.

gamble *(gam-bl)*
to play a game in which you have a chance of winning some money.
Word building: I **gambled**, I am **gambling** | A person who gambles is a **gambler** and does a lot of **gambling**.

game
something you can play, often with rules you have to follow: *Let's have a game of soccer.*

gander *(gan-der)*
a male goose.
Word use: The female is a **goose**.

gang
a group of people who do things together: *Tell the rest of the gang that we're riding our bikes in the park.*

gaol *(jale)*
another spelling of **jail**.
Word use: Don't confuse this with **goal**.

garage *(ga-rahzh or ga-rahzh)*
1. a building to keep your car in.
2. a place where someone will mend your car or sell you petrol.

garbage *(gar-bij)*
the rubbish someone throws away.

garden (*gar*-den)
a place with trees, grass and flowers, where you can play or sit.

Word building: Someone who works in a garden is a **gardener**.

garlic (*gar*-lic)
a plant with a white bulb you use in cooking to give food a strong flavour.

garment (*gar*-ment)
any of the clothes you wear, such as a dress or a shirt.

gas
1. any stuff like air that fills up all the space it's in.
2. the fuel which is like air, that we get from burning coal or that we find trapped under the ground: *Turn on the **gas** and I'll heat the water.*

Word building: For more than one we use **gases**.

Word use: Think about how gas is different from **liquid** and **solid**.

gate
a kind of door made of wood, iron or wire in an outside wall or fence.

gather (*gadh*-er)
1. to collect or pick something: *I'm going to **gather** some strawberries.*
2. to come together: *A crowd began to **gather** as people saw the fire.*

gaze
to look at someone or something for a long time without stopping.

Word building: I **gazed**, I am **gazing**

gear
1. part of a machine such as a car or a bicycle. You use the gears to make it easier to keep the wheels going at the speed you want.
2. all the special things you need for something: *Have you got your bats, the balls and all the rest of the **gear** you need for the game?*

gelato (*je-lar*-to)
an Italian kind of ice-cream.

gem (*jem*)
a beautiful stone you use to make jewellery.

gene (*jeen*)
one of the units in your body which is responsible for passing on things like eye colour or hair colour from parents to their children.

Word building: If something is passed on by genes, it is **genetic**.

general (*jen*-rel)
1. If something is **general**, most people have it: *The **general** feeling at our school is that we hate the new green uniforms.*
2. one of the most important soldiers who leads an army.

Word building: If something is done in a general way, it is **generally** done.

generation
all of the people born about the same time: *He is part of the older **generation**.*

generous (*jen-e-rus*)
ready to give what you have to other people: *Ella's such a **generous** person that she was happy to share her lunch with me.*

Word building: A generous person is full of **generosity**.

genius (*jee-nee-us*)
a very clever person.

Word building: For more than one we use **geniuses**.

gentle (*jen*-tl)
kind or calm: *He's a **gentle** man who likes helping people.* | *A **gentle** breeze blew through my hair.*

gentleman (*jen*-tl-man)
a polite name for any man.

Word building: For more than one we use **gentlemen**.

genuine *(jen-yoo-en)*
true or real: *I can tell the difference between a fake diamond and a **genuine** one.*

geography *(jee-og-ra-fee)*
the study of the earth and the different parts of it.

geometry *(jee-om-e-tree)*
the part of maths that has to do with shapes such as squares and triangles.

germ *(jerm)*
a living thing that is so tiny you need a microscope to see it. Some germs can make you sick.

get
1. to obtain or be given: *What DVD did you **get**?*
2. to bring or fetch: *Can you **get** me the scissors from the kitchen? | I'll go and **get** you some lunch.*
3. to arrive: *What time will they **get** here?*
4. to become: *I will **get** very fit if I keep playing sport.*
Word building: I **got**, I have **got**, I am **getting**

ghost *(rhymes with toast)*
the spirit of someone who is dead.

giant *(jy-ant)*
1. someone in stories who looks like a man but who is much bigger and much stronger.
2. very, very large: *Nadia has a **giant** peach.*
Word building: If you're a giant, you're **gigantic** *(jy-gan-tic)* in size.

gift
something you give as a present.

giggle *(gig-l)*
to laugh in a silly way: *I made faces at my friend and he started to **giggle**.*
Word building: I **giggled**, I am **giggling** | If you giggle a lot, you're **giggly**.

gill
the part of the body that fish and other sea animals use for breathing.

ginger *(jin-jer)*
1. the root of a plant, which you use in cooking to make food hot and spicy.
2. reddish-brown in colour.

gipsy *(jip-see)*
another spelling of **gypsy**.

giraffe *(ji-rarf)*
an African animal with spots on its skin, long legs and a very long neck.

girl *(gerl)*
a female child.

give *(giv)*
to hand something over to someone: *I'd like to **give** you this present.*
Word building: I **gave**, I have **given**, I am **giving** | You give someone a **gift**.

glacier *(glay-see-a)*
a large river of ice which moves slowly.

glad
happy or pleased: *I'm so **glad** to see you!*
Word building: If you are glad, then you're full of **gladness** and you do things **gladly**.

glance *(rhymes with dance)*
to look at someone or something quickly: *I only had time to **glance** at my notes before we went into the exam.*
Word building: I **glanced**, I am **glancing**

glass *(rhymes with class)*
1. hard stuff you can see through. It is used for things such as windows and bottles.
2. a cup for cold drinks, with no handle.

glasses *(glass-ez)*
two pieces of curved glass in a frame which you wear over your eyes to help you see better.
Word use: Another name for these is **spectacles**.

a
b
c
d
e
f
g
h
i
j
k
l
m
n
o
p
q
r
s
t
u
v
w
x
y
z

gleam *(gleem)*
to shine with a dim light: *I polished the table until it began to* **gleam**.

glide
to move along smoothly: *I sat beside the lake and watched the swans* **glide** *through the water.*
Word building: I **glided**, I am **gliding**

glider *(glide-er)*
1. an aeroplane without an engine that flies by using wind and currents of air.
2. a possum with thick skin stretched between its front and back legs to help it fly smoothly through the air. It is endangered. See the table at the end of this book.

glisten *(gliss-en)*
to shine with a light that sparkles: *The waves* **glisten** *in the sun.*

glitter *(glitt-er)*
to shine with bright flashes of light: *We looked down and saw the lights of the city* **glitter** *in the dark below.*

global warming *(glo-bl warm-ing)*
an increase in temperature in the earth's atmosphere which harms our natural environment. It is thought by many people to be caused by things that humans do, such as driving cars and chopping down forests.

globe
1. a round ball-shaped map of the earth.
2. anything shaped like a round ball.
3. an electric light bulb.
4. the earth: *One day we'll travel all over the* **globe** *together.*
Word building: If something happens all over the earth, it is **global** and it happens **globally**.
Word use: Another word for definition 2 is **sphere**.

glory *(glor-ree)*
the good thoughts or admiration of other people: *Winning the dance competition will bring lots of* **glory** *to our school.*
Word building: If something is full of glory, it's **glorious**.

glove *(gluv)*
a covering for your hand with a separate part for each finger and for your thumb.

glow *(glo)*
to give out light and heat without any flame: *I blew the ashes in the fireplace and they began to* **glow**.

glue
a thick paste you use to stick things together.

gnome *(nome)*
a little old person in fairytales.

go
1. to move: *Where will you* **go**?
2. to work properly: *The car won't* **go**.
3. to become: *The children* **go** *quiet when I read them a story.*
4. to make a particular sound or movement: *The fireworks will* **go** *bang!*
Word building: I **went**, I have **gone**, I am **going**

goal *(gole)*
the posts, or other sort of marker that you kick or throw the ball through to score in a game such as football.
Word use: Don't confuse this with **gaol**.

goanna *(go-an-a)*
a large Australian lizard.

goat
an animal with horns which can live in rocky places.
Word building: A male goat is a **billy goat**. A female goat is a **nanny goat**.

gobble *(gobb-l)*
to eat food quickly in large bits: *Cut your meat up and don't **gobble** it.*
Word building: I **gobbled**, I am **gobbling**

goblin *(gob-lin)*
a small, ugly man in fairytales who makes bad things happen to people.

god
a person or thing that is worshipped.

goddess *(godd-ess)*
a female person or thing that is worshipped.

goggles *(gogg-lz)*
special glasses with pieces at the side. You use them to keep wind, dust, water or bright light out of your eyes.

gold *(rhymes with **cold**)*
1. a yellow metal which is hard to find and which costs a lot of money.
2. yellow in colour.
Word building: Something that is made of gold or that is a gold colour is **golden**.

good
1. right, fair or well-behaved: *Be **good** for the new teacher.*
2. useful or of fine quality: *Have you seen the **good** scissors? | I will wear my **good** suit to the party.*
3. clever or skilful: *She's a **good** soccer player.*
Word building: more good = **better**, most good = **best** | If something is good, you talk about its **goodness**.

goodbye
a word you use when you leave someone.
Word building: This word is often shortened to **bye**.

goods
products that you can buy: *The **goods** are stacked on the shelves.*

goose
a large bird with a long neck and feet that are good for swimming.
Word building: For more than one we use **geese**.
Word use: The male of this bird is a **gander**. A young one is a **gosling** *(goz-ling)*.

gorilla *(go-ril-a)*
the largest kind of monkey, with no tail.

gossip *(goss-ip)*
silly or unkind talk about other people: *You shouldn't spread that **gossip** about my brother because it isn't true.*

government *(guv-en-ment)*
the group of people who are in charge of your country or your State.
Word building: A government has the power to **govern**.

governor *(guv-er-nor)*
someone who acts for the Queen in one of the States of Australia.

gown
a flowing dress or anything like this that you wear to a special place or at an important time: *The princess wore a lovely white **gown** to the ball. | The judge wore a **gown** and wig at the trial.*

grab
to take something suddenly: *I'll just **grab** my coat and then we can go.*
Word building: I **grabbed**, I am **grabbing**

grade
a class in some schools: *I've finished kindergarten so I'll be in first **grade** next year.*

gradual *(grad-ju-al)*
Something is **gradual** if it happens a little bit at a time: *There has been a **gradual** change in your work and now it's always very good.*
Word building: If something happens in a gradual way, it happens **gradually**.

a b c d e f **g** h i j k l m n o p q r s t u v w x y z

graduate *(graj-oo-uht)*
1. someone who has finished studying at a university or college: *My big sister is a graduate.*
2. *(graj-oo-ayt)* to receive a certificate after finishing studying at a university or college: *My brother will graduate this year.*
Word building: If you graduate from university, you will attend a **graduation**.

grain
1. a small, hard seed of a plant like rice or wheat, which we use for making food.
2. any small, hard bit of something: *There's a grain of sand in my eye.*

gram
a small measure you use to find out how much something weighs. There are 1000 grams in a kilogram.

grammar *(gram-ar)*
the way the words of a language are combined into phrases and sentences.

grand
Something is **grand** if it looks very important or if it's very large.

grandchild *(grand-child)*
the child of someone's son or daughter.
Word building: For more than one we use **grandchildren**.

granddaughter *(grand-dor-ter)*
a daughter of someone's son or daughter.

grandfather
the father of your father or mother.

grandmother
the mother of your father or mother.

grandparent *(grand-pair-rent)*
the mother or father of your mother or father.

grandson
a son of someone's son or daughter.

grape
a small, round, green or purple fruit which grows in bunches on a vine.

graph *(graf or grarf)*
a picture which shows different measurements: *We made a graph showing each day's rainfall for a week.*

grass *(rhymes with glass)*
a plant with thin, green leaves that you can cut very short to make a lawn.

grasshopper *(grass-hopp-er)*
an insect with large back legs for jumping, that eats plants.

grassland *(grass-land)*
an area in nature covered with grass and with not many trees.

grateful *(grate-ful)*
You are **grateful** if you feel like thanking someone for something they've done.

grave[1]
a hole in the earth for burying a dead person.

grave[2]
1. You look **grave** when you're thinking serious thoughts and you don't feel like joking.
2. very serious or full of danger: *Patrick's condition is grave and he may die.*

gravel *(grav-l)*
small stones, sometimes mixed with sand.

gravity *(grav-i-tee)*
the strong force that pulls things or that makes them fall towards the earth.

gravy *(gray-vee)*
a hot, brown sauce you make to pour over meat before you eat it.

graze[1]

to eat grass that's growing: *We'll put the cows out to **graze** in that paddock now.*

Word building: it **grazed**, it is **grazing**

graze[2]

to rub or scratch the skin from part of your body: *Wear knee pads when you skate so you don't **graze** your knees if you fall.*

grazier *(gray-zee-er)*

a farmer with lots of land for keeping cattle or sheep.

grease

thick sticky oil.

great *(grate)*

1. large: *A **great** elephant stood in front of the small mouse.*
2. important: *Can you name a **great** explorer?*
3. an everyday word you use to describe something very good: *The movie was great.*

greed

a very strong wish for food or for money.

Word building: People who feel greed are **greedy**.

green

Something is **green** if it is the colour of growing leaves.

greenhouse *(green-house)*

a glass house where plants are grown, which gets very warm inside.

greenhouse effect *(green-house e-fect)*

a condition when the weather gets hotter because the air all around the earth traps the heat from the sun, in the same way that the glass of a greenhouse does.

greeting *(gree-ting)*

the friendly words you use when you meet or when you welcome someone.

Word building: If you give someone a greeting, you **greet** them.

grey *(gray)*

between black and white in colour.

grid

a square or rectangle shape made up of lots of little squares: *I used my ruler to draw a **grid** in my maths book. | We can use the **grid** on the map to help us find the treasure!*

grief *(greef)*

the sad feeling you have when something bad happens or when someone you love dies.

Word building: If you feel grief, then you **grieve** *(greev)*.

grill

to cook food on metal bars you slide under heat or put over a flame.

grin

to give a big smile.

Word building: I **grinned**, I am **grinning**

grind *(rhymes with find)*

to crush something into a powder: *They **grind** the wheat to make flour.*

Word building: I **ground**, I am **grinding**

grip

to hold something tightly: ***Grip** my hand — I won't let you fall.*

Word building: I **gripped**, I am **gripping**

groan *(grone)*

the low, sad sound you make if you are in pain or if you feel very sad.

grocer *(groce-er)*

a person who sells food, drinks and other things for the house.

Word building: A grocer works in a **grocery**. Things that you buy from a grocer are called **groceries**.

grommet *(gromm-et)*

a small tube put into the ear by a doctor to prevent ear infections: *I can't swim today because I have a **grommet** in my ear.*

groom (groom)
1. someone who looks after horses.
2. another word for **bridegroom**.

groove (groov)
a long, narrow cut you make with a tool: *I made a **groove** in the wood.*

ground (rhymes with **round**)
the dry land we walk about on.

group (groop)
a number of people or things that do things together or that belong together: *I'm in your **group** for reading.*

grow (gro)
1. to get bigger: *The puppies are starting to **grow**.*
2. to plant something and look after it so that it gets bigger: *I'm going to **grow** some vegetables.*
Word building: I **grew**, I have **grown**, I am **growing** | Something that grows has **growth**.

growl
to make a deep, angry sound: *When the dog saw me it started to **growl**.*

grub
the young of some insects.

grumble (grum-bl)
to keep on saying in a cranky way that you are not happy about something: *I hope you're not going to **grumble** all day about missing out on the trip.*
Word building: I **grumbled**, I am **grumbling**

grunt
to make a sound like a pig: *Don't just **grunt** when I try to talk to you.*

guard (gard)
to keep something safe: *I'll **guard** your bag until you come back.*

guess (gess)
to try to give an answer when you don't really know: *Can you **guess** what we did while you were at school?*

guest (gest)
someone you invite to visit you.

guide (rhymes with **ride**)
1. to show someone the way.
2. someone who helps you find your way around.
3. a member of a worldwide club for girls that organises fun and interesting activities.
Word building: I **guided**, I am **guiding** | If you guide someone, you give them **guidance**.

guilty (**gil**-tee)
You feel **guilty** if you've done something that you know is wrong: *Joshua began to feel **guilty** about stealing the bag, so he gave it back.*
Word building: more guilty = **guiltier**, most guilty = **guiltiest** | If you're guilty, then you feel **guilt**.

guinea pig (**gin**-ee pig)
a small animal with short fur, short ears, short legs and no tail.

guitar (gi-**tar**)
a musical instrument that you play by moving your fingers across the strings.

gully (**gull**-ee)
a small valley dug out by water running through it.

gulp
to swallow something quickly: *If you **gulp** your food like that you might get a stomach ache.*

gum[1]
glue.

gum[2]
the part of your mouth that your teeth grow from.

gum tree *(gum tree)*

an Australian tree that makes a thick, sticky liquid which oozes from its trunk.

Word use: Another name for this tree is **eucalypt**.

gun

a weapon which fires bullets.

guru *(goo-roo)*

1. a teacher in the religion of Hinduism.
2. any wise teacher.

gutter *(gutt-er)*

1. a ditch along the side of a road, that carries away water.
2. a long, open pipe along the edge of your roof that carries away rainwater.

gym *(jim)*

1. a gymnasium.
2. a place with special exercise equipment you use to keep fit.

gymnasium *(jim-nay-zee-um)*

a building or room in which you do gymnastics and sport.

gymnastics *(jim-nas-tics)*

a sport that involves difficult exercises that require your body to be strong and to move and bend easily.

Word building: Someone who does gymnastics is called a **gymnast**.

gypsy *(jip-see)*

one of a group of people who travel about from place to place and who often live in caravans.

Word building: For more than one we use **gypsies**.

Word use: Some people spell this **gipsy**.

a
b
c
d
e
f
g
h
i
j
k
l
m
n
o
p
q
r
s
t
u
v
w
x
y
z

Hh

Hippopotamuses on holiday hide in hammocks.

habit *(hab-it)*
something that you do without thinking and in your own special way: *You have a **habit** of rubbing your eyes when you're tired.*

habitat *(hab-i-tat)*
the place in nature where a plant or animal normally lives or grows: *We must protect the koala's **habitat**.*

hail *(hale)*
balls of ice that fall from the clouds like frozen rain.

hair
the fur-like covering that grows on the skin of people and some animals.
Word building: Someone or something that is covered with hair is **hairy**.
Word use: Don't confuse **hair** with **hare**.

haircut
1. a cutting of the hair.
2. the style in which your hair is cut and arranged.

hairdresser *(hair-dress-er)*
someone whose job it is to wash hair, cut it, and sometimes arrange it in a special way.

half *(harf)*
one of the two equal parts that you can divide something into.
Word building: For more than one we use **halves**. | To get one half of something you **halve** it.

hall *(rhymes with **all**)*
1. a building or a very large room where a lot of people can meet.
2. the small room just inside the front door of a house.
Word use: Don't confuse this with **haul**.

Halloween *(hal-o-**ween**)*
the night of 31 October, when children dress up in costumes and ask people for treats. If they don't get a treat, then they play a trick.

halo *(**hay**-lo)*
a circle of light which glows around something: *In paintings there is often a **halo** around the head of an angel.*
Word building: For more than one we use **haloes**.

halt *(holt)*
to stop.

ham
the meat from the top part of a pig's leg.

hamburger *(**ham**-berg-er)*
a bread roll containing a flat, round piece of cooked, minced meat, and often other things like lettuce and tomato.

hammer *(**hamm**-er)*
a tool with a wooden handle and a heavy end, that you use to hit in things like nails.

hammock *(ham-ock)*
a hanging bed made from strong cloth or net.

hand
1. the end part of your arm, below your wrist.
2. to pass something to someone: *Hand me the remote control, please.*

handbag
a small bag, usually used by women, for carrying money and personal items. It is held in the hand, or has a strap so it can be worn over the shoulder.

handkerchief *(hang-ker-cheef)*
a small piece of cloth that you use when you blow your nose.

handle *(hand-l)*
a part put onto something to hold it with or to open it with: *I turned the handle and the door opened.*

handlebars *(hand-l-bars)*
the metal bar with rubber-covered ends which you hold to steer a bike.

handsome *(han-sum)*
Men are **handsome** if they are good to look at.

hang
to attach something at the top but not at the bottom: *Hang those wet clothes on the line to dry, please.*
Word building: I **hung**, I am **hanging**

Hanukkah *(han-oo-kah)*
a Jewish festival known as the Feast of the Dedication, which usually happens in November or December and lasts for eight days.

happen *(happ-en)*
to take place: *Where did the accident happen?*

happy *(happ-ee)*
very pleased or full of joy.
Word building: more happy = **happier**, most happy = **happiest** | When you are happy, you are full of **happiness**.

harbour *(har-bor)*
a part of the sea near the coast where the water is deep and calm and ships are safe from the wind and from big waves.

hard
1. solid and firm when you touch it: *A stone floor is hard.*
2. difficult or not easy: *This puzzle is too hard for me.*
Word building: If you make something hard, then you **harden** it. If it gets hard, it **hardens**.

hard disk *(hard disk)*
a computer disk that is built into the computer and is not easily removed.

hard drive *(hard drive)*
a computer disk drive for a hard disk.

hardly *(hard-lee)*
almost not at all: *The room was so crowded that I could hardly move.*

hardware *(hard-wair)*
1. the materials used in building something.
2. the mechanical parts of a computer.

hare *(hair)*
an animal like a large rabbit. It has long back legs and can move very quickly.
Word use: Don't confuse this with **hair**.

harm
to hurt or damage someone or something: *That gentle old dog would never harm anyone.*

harness *(har-ness)*
straps that you put around the head and shoulders of a horse to help you control it or attach a cart to it.

harp
a musical instrument made from a large frame shaped like a triangle, with strings stretched across that you pluck.

harvest *(har-vest)*
crops like wheat or grapes that have been picked because they are ripe.

hat
a covering for your head, usually with a brim, worn outdoors.

hatch
to break out of an egg: *Perhaps some baby chickens will hatch today.*

hate
to have a very strong feeling of not liking someone or something: *I hate people who are cruel to dogs.*
Word building: I **hated**, I am **hating** | If you hate someone, you feel **hatred** for them.

haul *(rhymes with all)*
to pull hard: *It was not easy to haul the heavy canoe out of the river.*
Word use: Don't confuse this with **hall**.

haunt *(hornt)*
to visit a place often as a ghost.

have *(hav)*
1. to own: *Do you have a red hat?*
2. to contain: *Each bag should have six apples.*
3. to experience, enjoy or suffer: *I have a sore foot.*
Word building: I **have**, he **has**, I **had**, I am **having**

hawk
a bird that looks like an eagle and hunts for small animals to eat.

hay
dry grass that is used to feed animals.

hazard *(haz-ard)*
something that might be a danger to you: *That hole in the road is a hazard.*

he *(hee)*
a word you use when you are talking about a man or boy: *He will come with us.*

head *(hed)*
1. the part of your body above your neck. It contains your brain, eyes, nose, ears and mouth.
2. the top or front of anything: *Go to the head of the queue.*

headache
a pain in your head.

head lice *(hed lice)*
very small insects that can live in your hair and make your head itchy. They lay eggs called nits.
Word building: This word is often shortened to **lice**.

heal *(heel)*
1. to make someone well again: *A doctor's job is to heal sick people.*
2. to get better: *That cut will take a few days to heal.*
Word use: Don't confuse this with **heel**.

health *(helth)*
the way your body feels. Your **health** is good if you are not sick.
Word building: If your health is good, you are **healthy**.

heap *(heep)*
a lot of things lying one on top of the other: *There's a heap of dirty dishes in the sink.*

hear
to take in sounds through your ears: *I can hear the birds singing.*
Word building: I **heard**, I am **hearing**
Word use: Don't confuse this with **here**.

heart *(hart)*
1. the part of your body that pumps the blood around.
2. the curved shape that is printed on some playing cards and is sometimes used as a sign for love.

heat *(heet)*
1. great warmth.
2. a contest where the winners go into a final contest: *There are ten swimmers in the first* **heat**.
3. to make something hot: *I'll* **heat** *the soup for lunch.*

heaven *(hev-en)*
the place where Christians believe God and the angels live.

heavy *(hev-ee)*
difficult to lift or carry because it weighs so much.
Word building: more heavy = **heavier**, most heavy = **heaviest**

hedge *(hej)*
a row of bushes planted close together to make a fence.

heel
1. the back part of your foot.
2. the back part of a shoe or of a sock.
Word use: Don't confuse this with **heal**.

height *(hite)*
how high something is.

heir *(air)*
someone who will get what belongs to someone else when the owner dies: *The young prince is the* **heir** *to the kingdom.*

helicopter *(hel-i-cop-ter)*
a machine like a small plane without wings, which can fly straight up because it has a large propeller on the top.

hello
a word you use when you meet someone.

help
1. to save someone from danger or to look after someone who is hurt or in trouble.
2. to do something that makes things easier for someone else: *Will you* **help** *me set the table?*
Word building: Someone who helps is a **helper** and does **helpful** things.

hen
a female bird, especially a chicken.

her
1. a word you use when you are talking about a woman or girl: *Sadie would like us to visit* **her**.
2. a word you use when you are talking about something that belongs to a woman or girl: *Did Lisa tell you about* **her** *new skateboard?*

herb
one of different sorts of plants that you can use for medicines or add to food to make it taste better.

herd
a large group of animals.

here *(heer)*
in this place: *Leave your coat* **here**.
Word use: Don't confuse this with **hear**.

hermit *(her-mit)*
someone who chooses to live alone and who keeps away from other people.

hero *(hear-ro)*
a person who has done a very brave thing.
Word building: For more than one we use **heroes**. | A hero does **heroic** things.

a b c d e f g h i j k l m n o p q r s t u v w x y z

hers

a word you use when you are talking about something that belongs to a woman or girl: *Mia said the last ice-cream was **hers**.*

herself *(her-**self**)*

a word you use when you are talking about a woman or girl doing something to their own body or doing something without help: *She washed **herself**. | She designed the house **herself**.*

he's *(heez)*

a short way of saying **he is** or **he has**.

hiccup *(**hic**-up)*

a sudden movement in your chest that you can't stop and which makes you give a short, sharp sound like a cough.

hide

1. to go into a place where people can't see you.
2. to put something in a secret place: *Where did Lachlan **hide** Maria's present?*

Word building: I **hid**, I have **hidden**, I am **hiding**

high *(hi)*

1. tall or far above the ground.
2. from the bottom to the top: *The fence is one metre **high**.*

Word building: If you make something high you **heighten** it and increase its **height**.

highlighter *(**hy**-light-er)*

a fluoro coloured pen used to colour over special words or pictures that you want to be noticed.

highway *(**hy**-way)*

a main road.

hike

a long walk in the country for enjoyment.

Word building: Someone who is on a hike is a **hiker**.

hill

a slope of the earth's surface, smaller than a mountain.

him

a word you use when you are talking about a man or boy: *Let's go with **him**.*

himself *(him-**self**)*

a word you use when you are talking about a man or boy doing something to their own body or doing something without help: *He cut **himself**. | He made the cake **himself**.*

hind *(rhymes with **dined**)*

back: *The dog stood up on its **hind** legs.*

Hinduism *(**hin**-doo-izm)*

the main religion of India. The followers of this religion worship many gods and goddesses.

Word building: Someone who follows Hinduism is called a **Hindu**.

hint

a helpful idea: *I'll give you a **hint** — the password starts with 'G'.*

hip

the bony part on each side of your body, just below your waist.

hippopotamus *(hip-o-**pot**-a-muss)*

a large, heavy animal with short legs, that lives near lakes and rivers in Africa.

Word building: For more than one we use **hippopotamuses**.

hire *(rhymes with **fire**)*

to pay money to borrow something: *You can **hire** the boat for two hours.*

Word building: I **hired**, I am **hiring**

his

a word you use when you are talking about something that belongs to a man or boy: *Do you know where David left **his** hat? | David said this jacket is **his**.*

hiss
to make the sound 'ssss', like a snake.

history *(hiss-tree)*
things that happened in the past.

hit
to strike something: *She **hit** the ball with the bat.*
Word building: I **hit**, I am **hitting**

hive
a place that bees live in.

hoarse *(horse)*
low and croaky, like a loud whisper: *Our voices were **hoarse** from cheering for our team all afternoon.*
Word use: Don't confuse this with **horse**.

hoax *(hokes)*
something that is done to trick people.

hobby *(hobb-ee)*
something interesting that you enjoy doing in your spare time: *My **hobby** is collecting stickers.*
Word building: For more than one we use **hobbies**.

hockey *(hock-ee)*
a game played on a field or on ice in which two teams try to hit a ball into a goal using a stick with a curved end.

hold
1. to have someone or something in your hands or arms: *My aunt let me **hold** the new baby for a few minutes.*
2. to have the right amount of room for something: *This box should **hold** all your magazines.*
Word building: I **held**, I am **holding**

hole
1. an opening or gap in something.
2. a small tunnel in the ground that an animal like a rabbit or wombat makes.

holiday *(hol-i-day)*
a special time off from school or work.

hollow *(holl-oe)*
1. with an empty space inside: *When I hit the **hollow** log it sounded like a drum.*
2. a dip on the surface of something: *You can make a **hollow** in clay by pressing it in with your finger.*

holy *(hole-ee)*
special because it has to do with God or with religion: *Good Friday is a **holy** day.*
Word building: more holy = **holier**, most holy = **holiest**

home
1. the place where you live or where you were born.
2. the base on a softball or baseball field where the batter stands to hit the ball and tries to run back to in order to score a point.

home page *(home page)*
a **home page** on the internet has information about what a website contains.

homework *(home-work)*
school work that is done at home.

honest *(on-est)*
You are **honest** if you tell the truth, and you don't steal or cheat.
Word building: An honest person shows **honesty**.

honey *(hun-ee)*
a sweet, sticky food that is made by bees.

honour *(on-a)*
1. fame and glory: *I wanted to bring **honour** to my family by doing well in the contest.*
2. great respect: *The princess was treated with **honour**.*
Word use: Other words that mean nearly the same are **glory** and **praise**.

hood *(rhymes with good)*
a part of a jacket which covers your head and neck.

hoof
the hard part that covers the feet of animals like horses and cows.

Word building: For more than one we use **hoofs**.

hook
a piece of curved metal for hanging things on or for catching hold of things.

hop
to jump up and down, usually on one leg only.

Word building: I **hopped**, I am **hopping**

hope
to wish that something will happen: *I hope you can come with us to the party.*

Word building: I **hoped**, I am **hoping** | If you hope for something and you expect it to happen, then you're **hopeful**. If there is no hope of something happening, the situation is **hopeless**.

hopscotch *(hop-skoch)*
a game where you throw a stone onto one of a pattern of squares drawn on the ground, and then hop on the other squares.

horizon *(ho-rise-n)*
the line where the land or the sea seems to meet the sky.

horizontal *(ho-ri-zon-tal)*
level or in line with the ground: *A ladder has horizontal rungs.*

Word use: Think about how this is different from **vertical**.

horn
1. a pointed bone that grows on the head of animals like cattle and sheep.
2. a musical instrument that you blow.
3. something that makes a sound to warn you or attract your attention: *The driver blew the horn when I started to walk in front of the car.*

horrible *(ho-ri-bl)*
nasty or not pleasant: *The rotten egg had a horrible smell.*

horror *(ho-ra)*
a feeling of very great fear: *My little brother has a horror of spiders.*

horse
a large animal with four legs and hoofs. You can ride on it.

Word use: Don't confuse this with **hoarse**.

hose
a long tube that you can bend, for water to go through.

hospital *(hos-pi-tal)*
a place where people who are sick or hurt are looked after by nurses and doctors.

hot
1. high in temperature: *The fire is hot.*
2. feeling lots of heat in your body: *I am too hot sitting next to the heater.*

Word building: more hot = **hotter**, most hot = **hottest**

hot dog *(hot dog)*
a long, red sausage served hot in a bread roll, usually with tomato sauce or mustard.

hotel *(ho-tel)*
1. a place where you pay for a room to stay for a night and for meals.
2. a place that has special rooms where adults can go to drink beer and other drinks like that.

hour *(our; rhymes with flower)*
a length of time equal to sixty minutes.

house
a building where people live.

housework
work that you do in your house, such as cleaning and cooking.

hovercraft *(hov-er-craft)*
a vehicle without wheels that can travel quickly on land and water.

how *(rhymes with **cow**)*
in what way or condition: ***How** did you do that?*

however
no matter how much, or in what way: *I'll never be able to swim as fast as Leah, **however** hard I try.*

howl
a long, loud cry, like a dog in pain.

huddle *(hudd-l)*
to gather close together: *We all had to **huddle** under the same umbrella.*

huge
very big.
Word use: Other words that mean nearly the same are **giant** and **gigantic**.

hum
1. a buzzing sound, like the one a bee makes.
2. to sing with your lips closed: *Can you **hum** that tune?*
Word building: I **hummed**, I am **humming**

human *(hew-man)*
a woman, man or child.

humankind
all humans.

humble *(hum-bel)*
1. You are **humble** if you don't boast about yourself.
2. Something is **humble** if it is ordinary, and not big, new or different: *The **humble** meat pie is very popular.*

hummus *(hoom-us or hom-us)*
a Middle Eastern dish made from chickpeas, oil, lemon and garlic.
Word use: Another spelling is **hommos**.

humorous *(hew-mo-rus)*
funny: *Sasha's **humorous** description of the surprise birthday party made us all laugh.*
Word building: Something that is humorous is full of **humour**.

hump
a big lump on the back of an animal, like the camel, or on a person.

humpy *(hum-pee)*
a bush hut traditionally used by Aboriginal people.
Word use: This word comes from the Yagara language of Queensland. See the map of Australian Aboriginal languages at the end of this book.

hundred
ten times ten (100).

hungry *(hung-gree)*
You are **hungry** if you feel you want to eat some food: *Tamara got **hungry** and wandered off to find a snack.*
Word building: more hungry = **hungrier**, most hungry = **hungriest** | When you're hungry, you feel **hunger**.

hunt
1. to chase an animal because you want to kill it for food or sport: *Owls **hunt** mice at night.*
2. to look for something or someone: *Could you **hunt** for some string in the bottom drawer?*

hurry *(hu-ree)*
to go fast: ***Hurry**, or we will be late!*
Word building: I **hurried**, I am **hurrying**

hurt *(hert)*
to make a person or an animal feel pain: *I **hurt** my arm when I tripped over.*

husband *(huz-band)*
the man a woman marries.

hush
> to stop making a noise: **Hush**, *or you won't be able to hear the baby birds.*

hydrofoil *(hy-dro-foil)*
> a boat with special parts on it like large skis that help the boat travel very fast along the surface of the water.

hymn *(him)*
> a song that praises God.

Ii

Insects use the internet for information on igloos.

I
a word you use when you are talking about yourself: *I like ice-cream.*

ice
water that has frozen solid.

iceberg *(ice-berg)*
a very large piece of ice that breaks off from a glacier and floats in the sea.

ice-cream
a sweet frozen food made with cream or milk.

ice skate *(ice skate)*
a special boot with a blade running from the front of the sole to the back of the sole.
Word building: This word is often shortened to **skate**. | If you wear ice skates to move around on ice, you **ice-skate**. A person who ice-skates is called an **ice-skater**.

icicle *(ice-i-kel)*
a piece of ice that hangs down in a point. It is made when dripping water freezes.

icing *(ice-ing)*
sugar, water and the other things you mix together and use for covering cakes.

icon *(eye-con)*
a small picture on a computer screen that stands for something else and can be clicked on to do something, like open files.

idea *(eye-deer)*
a thought or picture that comes into your mind.

identical *(eye-den-tik-l)*
People or things are **identical** if they are the same as each other in every way: *I can't tell those identical twins apart.*

idiot *(id-ee-ot)*
a very stupid person.
Word building: An idiot is likely to do **idiotic** things.

igloo *(ig-loo)*
a hut that Inuit people build out of blocks of hard snow.

ignorant *(ig-no-rant)*
You are **ignorant** if you don't know very much.
Word building: If you are ignorant, then you have a lot of **ignorance**.

ignore *(ig-nore)*
to take no notice of what someone says: *Please don't ignore me when I ask you to set the table.*
Word building: I **ignored**, I am **ignoring**

a
b
c
d
e
f
g
h
i
j
k
l
m
n
o
p
q
r
s
t
u
v
w
x
y
z

ill
sick or not very well.

Word building: When you're ill, you have an **illness**.

illustration *(il-us-tray-shon)*
a picture in a book.

Word building: If you draw illustrations, then you're an **illustrator** and you **illustrate**.

I'm *(ime)*
a short way of saying **I am**.

imagination *(im-aj-i-nay-shon)*
the power you have to make pictures in your mind or to think of interesting stories.

Word building: If you can use your imagination, then you're **imaginative**.

Word use: Don't confuse **imaginative** with **imaginary**, which means not real.

imagine *(i-maj-n)*
to make a picture in your mind: *Imagine the beach in summer and all the people swimming in the sea.*

Word building: I **imagined**, I am **imagining** | Things people imagine that aren't real or true are **imaginary**.

Word use: Don't confuse **imaginary** with **imaginative**, which describes someone with imagination.

imam *(i-mahm)*
a leader of the religion of Islam.

immediate *(i-mee-dee-it)*
Something is **immediate** if it happens straight away.

Word building: If something happens in an immediate way, it happens **immediately**.

impatient *(im-pay-shent)*
You are **impatient** if you want to do something right now and if you don't want to wait.

Word building: If you are impatient, then you're filled with **impatience**.

important *(im-por-tant)*
1. Something is **important** if it means a lot to you: *Your birthday is an important day for you.*
2. You are **important** if you're in charge of other people or if you have a lot of power.

Word building: If something or someone is important, then they have **importance**.

impossible *(im-poss-i-bel)*
Something is **impossible** if it can't be done: *It's impossible for him to be there if he's at home in bed.*

Word building: An impossible thing is an **impossibility**.

improve *(im-proov)*
to make something better or to get better: *I need to improve the way I hit the ball.*

Word building: I **improved**, I am **improving** | If you improve something or if it improves, then there's an **improvement**.

in
inside: *The milk is in the fridge.* | *Stay in the house.*

inch
a measure we once used in Australia to find out how long things are. One inch is about 2.5 centimetres.

include *(in-clude)*
to have something as a part: *Your reading group will include George, Ji-hun and Sophie.*

Word building: I **included**, I am **including**

income *(in-cum)*
the money that comes to you because you go to work or for other reasons like that.

increase *(in-creese)*
to make something bigger or higher, or to get bigger or higher: *I need to increase the speed of my computer.*

Word building: I **increased**, I am **increasing**

Word use: The opposite of this is **decrease**.

incredible (in-**cred**-i-bl)
very hard to believe: *What an **incredible** story — are you sure it's true?*

indeed
truly or in fact: ***Indeed** she did it.*

index (**in**-dex)
a list of all the things that are in a book and where you can find them.

indicate (**in**-di-cate)
to point to something: *Can you **indicate** your house when we go past it?*
Word building: I **indicated**, I am **indicating**

indigenous (in-**dij**-en-us)
1. Someone who is **indigenous** to a place belongs to that place, and their ancestors were the first people there. Australia's **Indigenous** people are the Aboriginal and Torres Strait Islander people.
2. An **indigenous** plant or animal belongs to a place: *The kangaroo is an **indigenous** Australian animal.*
Word use: When you are writing about Australia's Indigenous people, or things to do with them, you use a capital letter, as in *Indigenous art, Indigenous languages*.

indoors (in-**doors**)
inside a house: *Let's go **indoors** — it's raining.*
Word use: The opposite of this is **outdoors**.

industry (**in**-duss-tree)
a type of business for making lots of things in a factory and selling them to people.
Word building: For more than one we use **industries**. | Anything that has to do with an industry is **industrial**.

infant (**in**-fant)
a baby or a very young child.

infect (in-**fect**)
to give your germs or your illness to other people: *Cover your mouth when you cough or you'll **infect** the whole family with your cold.*
Word building: You can infect people if you're **infectious** or if you have an **infection**.

inferior (in-**fear**-ree-or)
not as good as something else: *This is an **inferior** brand of chocolate.*
Word use: The opposite of this is **superior**.

inferno (in-**fer**-no)
a place where there is a lot of fire and heat.

inflammable (in-**flam**-i-bel)
easy to set on fire.
Word use: Another word that means the same is **flammable**.

inflate (in-**flate**)
to fill up with gas or air: *My job is to **inflate** the balloons for the party.*
Word building: I **inflated**, I am **inflating**

informal
1. casual or relaxed: *It will be an **informal** meeting.*
2. not following the usual procedure: *It was an **informal** agreement.*
Word building: If something is informal, it is an **informality**. If something is done in an informal way, it is done **informally**.

information (in-for-**may**-shon)
facts about someone or something: *I need some **information** about sugar for my project.*
Word building: If you give someone information, then you **inform** them of something.

information report (in-for-**may**-shon re-**port**)
writing which gives facts on something. See the 'Types of writing and speaking' table at the end of this book.

a b c d e f g h **i** j k l m n o p q r s t u v w x y z

ingredient *(in-**gree**-dee-ent)*
one of the parts of a whole thing: *Flour is one **ingredient** you need to make a cake.*

inhabit *(in-**hab**-it)*
to live in a place: *Some Aboriginal people still **inhabit** the Australian desert.*
Word building: Someone who inhabits a place is an **inhabitant**.

inherit *(in-**he**-rit)*
to get something as a gift from someone who has died: *Nadia will **inherit** a gold ring from her grandmother.*
Word building: Something you inherit is your **inheritance**.

initial *(i-**nish**-al)*
the first letter of a word or of your name.

injection *(in-**jec**-shon)*
You have an **injection** when a doctor or nurse uses a special hollow needle to put medicine into your body.
Word building: When you have an injection, the doctor or nurse **injects** you.

injure *(in-jer)*
to hurt someone: *You'll **injure** yourself if you fall on those sharp rocks.*
Word building: I **injured**, I am **injuring** | When something injures you, you get an **injury**.

ink
a dark liquid used for writing or printing.

inland *(in-land)*
A place is **inland** if it is in the middle of a country or if it's a long way from the sea.

inn
a small hotel where travellers can stay the night.

inner
1. further in: *Go through the **inner** door.*
2. private or personal: *I write my **inner** feelings in my diary.*

innocent *(in-o-sent)*
You are **innocent** if you haven't done anything wrong.
Word building: If someone is innocent, then you talk about their **innocence**.

insect *(in-sect)*
a small animal with three parts to its body, six legs and often wings. Bees, ants and flies are insects.

inside
1. the inner part or side: *Check the label on the **inside** of your jumper.*
2. **insides**, an everyday word for your stomach and other inner parts of your body.
3. indoors, or into the inner part: *Dad's gone **inside**.*
Word use: The opposite of this is **outside**.

insist *(in-**sist**)*
to say that someone must do something: *I **insist** that you come inside.*

inspect *(in-**spect**)*
to look over something in a very careful way: *Can I **inspect** your ticket please?*
Word building: If your job is to inspect, then you are an **inspector** and you make an **inspection**.

instant *(in-stant)*
1. a very short time: *The thief was gone in an **instant**.*
2. in a form that makes preparation quick and easy: *Can you make me an **instant** coffee?*

instead *(in-**sted**)*
in place of someone or something else: *Send me **instead** of him.*

instinct *(in-stinct)*
the strong wish or need to do some things that people and animals are born with: *A bird's **instinct** is to fly to a warm place in the winter.*

instruct (in-**struct**)

to tell someone what to do: *I want to learn to ride and she'll* **instruct** *me.* | **Instruct** *them to march in a straight line.*

Word building: If you instruct someone in something like swimming, then you are an **instructor** and you give them **instruction**.

instrument (**in**-stru-ment)

1. any tool or machine that helps you to do a job: *The doctor put a special* **instrument** *to my chest to listen to my heartbeat.*
2. something you use to make a musical sound: *A violin is a string* **instrument**.

insult (in-**sult**)

1. to behave or to speak to someone rudely: *Sam tried to* **insult** *me by calling me a baby.*
2. (**in**-sult) a rude action or remark: *Calling me a baby was an* **insult**.

intend (in-**tend**)

to have it in your mind to do something: *I* **intend** *to check my email after I've finished my breakfast.*

Word building: If you intend to do something, then it's your **intention** to do it.

interactive whiteboard (in-ter-**ac**-tiv **wite**-bord)

a whiteboard that can be connected to a computer, a printer or the internet.

interest (**in**-trest)

to make you want to know more: *The stories you tell me about your childhood really* **interest** *me.*

Word building: People or things that interest you are **interesting**, and they make you **interested**.

interfere (in-ter-**fear**)

to get in somebody's way when they don't want you: *Don't* **interfere** *with my work — I can do it by myself.*

Word building: I **interfered**, I am **interfering** | Anything that interferes is an **interference**.

interior (in-**teer**-ree-or)

the inside of something.

interjection

a remark made to interrupt a conversation or a speech: *Please do not interrupt me with your* **interjections**.

Word building: If you make an interjection, you **interject**, and you are an **interjector**.

internal (in-**ter**-nal)

on the inside: *Your heart and your liver are two of the* **internal** *parts of your body.*

international (in-ter-**nash**-nal)

between two or more countries: *India, England and Australia are some of the countries that play in* **international** *cricket matches.*

internet (**in**-ter-net)

the, the linking of computers all around the world so that you can share information.

Word building: This is often shortened to **the net** or **the Net**.

interrupt (in-ter-**rupt**)

to stop someone in the middle of what they are doing.

Word building: Anything that interrupts is an **interruption**.

intersection (in-ter-**sec**-shon)

a place where streets cross each other.

interval (**in**-ter-val)

a short break in the middle when you're at the movies, a play or a concert.

into

If something or someone goes **into** something else, they go inside it, and if something turns **into** something, they become it: *He walked* **into** *the room.* | *She dived* **into** *the pool.* | *The tadpole turned* **into** *a frog.*

a b c d e f g h i j k l m n o p q r s t u v w x y z

introduce (in-tro-**duce**)

to make someone known to people who don't already know them: *I'll **introduce** you to my brother Aziz — I don't think you've met him before.*

Word building: I **introduced**, I am **introducing** | When you introduce someone, you make an **introduction**.

invade (in-**vade**)

to attack another country and go into it with your army: *Hundreds of years ago the Romans decided to **invade** Britain.*

Word building: they **invaded**, they are **invading** | If you invade a country, you're the **invader** and you carry out an **invasion**.

invalid (**in**-va-lid)

someone who is sick, or someone who needs to be cared for after an illness.

invaluable (in-**val**-ya-bl)

worth more than you can tell: *You have given me **invaluable** help with my homework.*

invent (in-**vent**)

to make or think up something new: *I'm going to **invent** a time machine when I grow up!*

Word building: If you invent something, you have an **invention**.

investigate (in-**ves**-ti-gate)

to look into something with a lot of care: *What a loud crash — I'd better **investigate**.*

Word building: I **investigated**, I am **investigating** | When you investigate, you make an **investigation**.

invisible (in-**viz**-i-bel)

Something is **invisible** if it can't be seen.

invite (in-**vite**)

to ask someone to visit you or to take part in something: *We'd like to **invite** you to come for dinner.*

Word building: I **invited**, I am **inviting** | When you invite someone to something you give them an **invitation** (in-vi-**tay**-shon).

iron (**eye**-n)

1. a heavy metal used to make tools and machines.
2. a tool with a handle, which you heat up and smooth clothes with.

irrigate (**i**-ri-gate)

to water the ground by sending the water along canals or pipes: *If we could **irrigate** parts of the desert, we could grow crops.*

Word building: I **irrigated**, I am **irrigating**

irritate (**i**-ri-tate)

to make someone cross or angry.

Word building: I **irritated**, I am **irritating** | Things that irritate you cause **irritation**.

Islam (**iz**-lam)

a religion started by a special teacher called Mohammed who lived a long time ago. This religion teaches that we should do whatever Allah (God) wants us to do. The followers of Islam worship in a mosque.

Word use: Someone whose religion is Islam is called a **Muslim**.

island (**eye**-land)

a piece of land which has water all around it.

isolate (**eye**-so-late)

to keep people or things all alone or all by themselves: *We'll have to **isolate** that prisoner until he stops hurting the others.*

Word building: I **isolated**, I am **isolating** | If you isolate people or things, you keep them in **isolation**.

it

a word you use when you are talking about an animal or a thing: *The duck swam across the pond and **it** quacked at me! | **It** is my favourite toy. | **It** was a very good movie.*

itch

to have a feeling on your skin which makes you want to scratch: *My legs itch*.

Word building: When your skin starts to itch it's **itchy**.

item *(eye-tem)*

one thing from a list: *The first item on my shopping list is cheese.*

its

a word you use when you are talking about something that belongs to an animal or a thing: *The duck shook its feathers.* | *The torch won't work without its batteries.*

Word use: Don't confuse this with **it's**, which is short for 'it is', as in *It's a hot day.*

itself

a word that you use when you are talking about an animal or thing doing something to its own body or form: *The dog scratched itself.* | *The computer turned itself off.*

ivory *(eye-vo-ree)*

the hard white tusk of elephants. It is worth a lot of money and was used for things like the white keys of pianos.

ivy *(eye-vee)*

a plant with shiny, green leaves. As it grows it climbs higher by holding onto walls or by twisting around branches.

Jj

Judges wearing jeans juggle juicy jellies.

jabiru *(jab-i-**roo**)*
a white bird with a greenish-black head, neck and tail and with long legs and a long beak. It catches fish and you can find it in Australia.

jackaroo *(jack-a-**roo**)*
a young man who is learning to work on a cattle or a sheep station.
Word use: Another spelling is **jackeroo**.

jacket *(**jack**-et)*
a short coat.

jackpot *(**jack**-pot)*
the biggest prize that you can win in some competitions or games.

jagged *(**jagg**-ed)*
with very sharp edges: *We cut our feet on the **jagged** rocks.*

jail *(jale)*
the place where prisoners are kept.
Word use: Another spelling is **gaol**.

jam[1]
1. to get stuck: *This door always seems to **jam** when it's wet.*
2. a lot of people or things all pushed or squeezed together: *We sat in the traffic jam for hours.*
Word building: it **jammed**, it is **jamming**

jam[2]
a sweet food made of fruit and sugar. You can spread it on bread or scones.

jar
a glass container with a lid. You use it for keeping things like honey and jam in.

jarrah *(**ja**-ra)*
a tall gum tree with red wood.
Word use: This word comes from the Nyungar language of Western Australia. See the map of Australian Aboriginal languages at the end of this book.

jaw
one of the two bones between your chin and your nose that your teeth grow in.

jazz
a type of music with strong rhythms, first played by African Americans.

jealous *(**jel**-us)*
You're **jealous** of someone if you want something they have: *Ben is **jealous** of Rachel because she has a new mobile phone.*
Word building: When you are jealous, you feel **jealousy**.

jeans *(jeens)*
strong trousers made of thick cotton. They are usually blue.
Word use: Don't confuse **jeans** with **genes**.

jeer
to make fun of someone or to say nasty things about them: *The mean boys stopped to jeer at him because he came from a different country.*

jelly *(jell-ee)*
a soft food that wobbles when you move it.
Word building: For more than one we use **jellies**.

jerk
a sudden, quick movement.
Word building: If you move with jerks, then your movements are **jerky** and have a lot of **jerkiness**.

jet
1. a stream of water or gas that shoots out of a small opening.
2. a very fast plane with engines that work when hot gas is pushed out an opening at the back.

jetty *(jett-ee)*
a long, stone wall or something like this, that sticks out into a river or into the sea. You can tie boats or ships to it.
Word building: For more than one we use **jetties**.

Jew *(rhymes with new)*
someone whose religion is Judaism.

jewel *(joo-el)*
a stone that is worth a lot of money, such as a diamond or a ruby.
Word building: Jewels made into necklaces, bracelets or rings are **jewellery**. Someone who makes or sells **jewellery** is called a **jeweller**.

jigsaw *(jig-saw)*
a puzzle made up of many different pieces which fit together to make a picture.

jillaroo *(jill-a-roo)*
a young woman who is learning to work on a cattle or a sheep station.

jingle *(jing-gl)*
to make a sound like small bells ringing: *Your keys jingle when you run.* | *She began to jingle the coins in her pocket while she waited.*
Word building: it **jingled**, it is **jingling**

job
1. a piece of work you do for someone.
2. the work you do to earn money: *My cousin has a job working in a factory.*

jockey *(jock-ee)*
someone who rides horses in races.

joey *(jo-ee)*
a baby kangaroo that lives in its mother's pouch.

jog
to run along slowly: *I'm going to jog in the park.*
Word building: I **jogged**, I am **jogging** | If you often jog to get exercise, then you're a **jogger**.

join *(joyn)*
to put things together or to come together: *I'll join these pieces of wood with glue.* | *This is where the two bones join.*
Word building: The place where two things or parts join is a **joint**.

joke
something that someone says or does to make people laugh.

journey *(jer-nee)*
a trip from one place to another: *Our train journey took us from the sea up into the mountains.*

joy
great happiness.
Word building: If you're full of joy, then you are **joyful**.

Judaism *(jew-day-izm)*
a religion that began a very long time ago and which teaches that there is only one God. The followers of Judaism worship in a synagogue.

Word building: Someone whose religion is Judaism is called a **Jew**.

judge *(juj)*
1. someone whose job is to decide between right and wrong or between good and bad.
2. to say what you think or what you've decided about someone or something: *I judge you to be a very good student. | We judge the distance to be about two kilometres.*

Word building: I **judged**, I am **judging** | When you judge something, you make a **judgement**.

judo *(jew-doe)*
a sport based on the Japanese way of defending yourself without using weapons.

Word use: This word comes from the Japanese language and means 'soft way'.

juggle *(jugg-l)*
to throw some things into the air and keep them moving without dropping any.

Word building: I **juggled**, I am **juggling** | Someone who juggles is a **juggler**.

juice *(rhymes with goose)*
the part of fruit and vegetables that you can drink.

Word building: If something has a lot of juice, then it's **juicy**.

jumble *(jum-bl)*
to mix something up in a big mess: *Try not to jumble your clothes in the drawer — I've put them in neat piles.*

Word building: I **jumbled**, I am **jumbling**

jumbo *(jum-bo)*
an everyday word for a very large jet plane or for anything else that's bigger than usual.

jumbuck *(jum-buk)*
a very old-fashioned word for a sheep.

Word use: You've probably only heard this in the song 'Waltzing Matilda'.

jump
to spring suddenly into the air with both your feet off the ground: *How high can you jump?*

jumper *(jum-per)*
a piece of warm clothing that you wear on the top half of your body. It is often made of wool.

jungle *(jung-gl)*
the thick trees and vines which grow in warm, damp parts of the world.

junior *(june-yer)*
younger or smaller than the others: *The junior members of the family aren't old enough to go to that film.*

junk
old things that no-one wants any more.

junk food *(junk food)*
food that is not healthy: *Chips are my favourite junk food.*

jury *(jew-ree)*
the group of people who have to try and decide if someone is innocent or guilty in a law court.

Word building: A member of a jury is a **juror**.

just
1. fair or right: *The referee made just decisions during the football match.*
2. by a very little: *The ball just missed the goal.*
3. exactly: *That's just what he said.*
4. only: *There is just a little bit of pizza left.*

Kookaburras in kurrajongs sing karaoke.

kanga cricket *(kang-ga crick-et)*
a type of cricket for children that uses a softer ball and a plastic bat.

kangaroo *(kang-ga-roo)*
an Australian animal that uses its large tail and strong back legs for jumping. The female carries her babies in a pouch.
Word use: This word comes from the Guugu Yimidhirr language of Queensland. See the map of Australian Aboriginal languages at the end of this book.

karaoke *(karri-o-kee)*
singing along to a video of a song. The singer reads the words to the song displayed on a video screen.

karate *(ka-ra-tee)*
a sport based on the Japanese way of defending yourself by using only your hands, elbows, feet and knees.
Word use: This word comes from the Japanese language and means 'empty hand'.

kebab *(ke-bab)*
cubes of meat and sometimes vegetables, grilled on a thin stick.

keel
a long piece of wood or metal put along the bottom of a ship to hold it together. On a yacht, it goes very deep and is very heavy, to help stop the yacht tipping over.

keen
You are **keen** if you want to do something very much: *Are you keen to try your new computer game?*
Word use: Another word that means nearly the same is **eager**.

keep
1. to make something go on in the same way: *They keep their room very tidy.*
2. to have something as your own: *I'll keep this toy and put the others back on the shelf.*
3. to look after something: *I keep mice.*
Word building: I **kept**, I am **keeping**

kelpie *(kel-pee)*
an Australian dog trained to work with sheep.

kennel *(kenn-l)*
a small house or hut for keeping a dog warm and dry.

kerb
the line of stones or concrete at the edge of a street.

kettle *(kett-l)*
a pot with a handle and a spout, that you boil water in.

key *(kee)*
1. a piece of metal you use to open and close a lock.
2. one of the parts of a piano, a typewriter or a computer that you press down to make it work.

key in *(kee in)*
to type information into a computer: *To log in you must **key in** your name.*
Word building: I **keyed in**, I am **keying in** | When you key in you use a **keyboard**.

kick
to hit or move something with your foot.

kid[1]
1. a baby goat.
2. an everyday word for a child.

kid[2]
to tease someone or try to trick them: *Don't be upset — he always tries to **kid** people like that.*
Word building: I **kidded**, I am **kidding**

kill
to make someone or something die: *Some diseases can **kill** people.*

kilogram *(kil-o-gram)*
a measure you use when you weigh something. There are 1000 grams in a kilogram.

kilometre *(kil-o-mee-ter or ki-lom-o-ter)*
a large measure you use to work out how far it is between two places. There are 1000 metres in a kilometre.

kind[1] *(rhymes with **dined**)*
You are **kind** if you're friendly and if you care about people and try to help them.
Word building: If you are kind, then you show **kindness** and you treat people **kindly**.

kind[2] *(rhymes with **dined**)*
the same sort of things or people: *We drink that **kind** of coffee.*

kindergarten *(kin-der-gar-ten)*
1. a place where some young children go for a year or so before they start primary school.
2. In some Australian States the first class you are in when you go to school is called **kindergarten**.

king
a man who is born to be the ruler of his country.
Word use: Compare this with **queen**.

kingdom *(king-dom)*
the land that a king or a queen rules.

kiosk *(kee-osk)*
a small shop which sells things like newspapers, postcards, drinks and ice-creams.

kiss
to touch someone with your lips to show them that you like them or that you're glad to see them: *Don't forget to **kiss** me goodbye.*

kitchen *(kich-en)*
a room where you cook food.

kite
a toy made of paper or plastic stretched over a light frame. You tie it to a long string and the wind blows it into the air.

kitten *(kitt-n)*
a young cat.

kiwi *(kee-wee)*
a New Zealand bird that can't fly. It has thick legs and a long, thin bill.

knee *(nee)*
the middle of your leg, where it bends.

kneel *(neel)*
to go down on your knees: *Some people **kneel** to pray.*
Word building: I **knelt**, I am **kneeling**

knife *(nife)*
a tool with a sharp edge for cutting things.
Word building: For more than one we use **knives**.

knight *(nite)*
1. a man who has the special name 'Sir' given to him by a queen or king.
2. a brave and good man who fought for the king in times long ago.

knit *(nit)*

to make clothes by weaving long strings of wool together with two long needles: *I am going to **knit** a scarf for winter.*

Word building: I **knitted**, I am **knitting**

knob *(nob)*

a round handle on a door or a drawer.

knock *(nock)*

1. to hit or tap with your hand: *Please **knock** on the door before you go into the room.*
2. to bump something or someone: *Sorry, I didn't mean to **knock** your arm.*

knot *(not)*

the part where something long and thin, like a piece of rope or string, has been tied or has got tangled.

know *(no)*

1. to have learned and understood something: *I **know** how to say some words in Japanese.*
2. to have met someone before: *Do you **know** James?*

Word building: I **knew**, I have **known**, I am **knowing** | What you know now or you can get to know is **knowledge** *(nol-ij)*.

knuckle *(nuk-l)*

the place where your finger bends or where it meets the rest of your hand.

koala *(ko-**wa**-la)*

an Australian animal with grey fur, fluffy ears and no tail. The female carries her babies in a pouch.

Word use: This word comes from the Dharug language of New South Wales. See the map of Australian Aboriginal languages at the end of this book.

kookaburra *(**kook**-a-burra)*

an Australian bird with a call that sounds like someone laughing.

Word use: This word comes from the Wiradjuri language of New South Wales. See the map of Australian Aboriginal languages at the end of this book.

kowari *(ko-**wa**-ree)*

a small, yellow-brown animal with a black, bushy tail that lives in the Australian desert. It is endangered. See the table at the end of this book.

Word use: This word comes from the Diyari language of South Australia. See the map of Australian Aboriginal languages at the end of this book.

kurrajong *(**kurra**-jong)*

an Australian tree whose bark was traditionally used by Aboriginal people to make fishing line and fishing nets.

Word use: This word comes from the Dharug language of New South Wales. See the map of Australian Aboriginal languages at the end of this book.

a
b
c
d
e
f
g
h
i
j
k
l
m
n
o
p
q
r
s
t
u
v
w
x
y
z

L l

Lifesavers on ladders lecture lizards.

label *(lay-bl)*
a piece of paper or cloth put on something to tell you what it is, who it belongs to or where it is going.

laboratory *(la-borra-tree)*
a place where scientists do experiments.
Word building: For more than one we use **laboratories**.

labour *(lay-ber)*
1. hard or tiring work: *There is a lot of labour involved in building a house.*
2. the pain and effort of giving birth to a baby.

lace
1. a material made of fine threads with holes in between. It is like a net but it has patterns in it.
2. a piece of strong, thin cord that you use to tighten up your shoe.

lack
If you **lack** something, you do not have it: *I lack the energy to swim another lap.*

ladder *(ladd-er)*
something that has two long sides with short bars or steps between them, for climbing up or down on.

lady *(lay dcc)*
a name for a woman: *Will you find this lady and gentleman good seats in the front row?*
Word building: For more than one we use **ladies**.

ladybird *(lay-dee-berd)*
a small beetle which has an orange or red back with black spots on it.
Word use: Other names for this are **ladybug** and **lady beetle**.

lagoon *(la-goon)*
a large shallow pond of water near the sea.

lake
a large area of water with land all around it.

lama *(rhymes with farmer)*
a Buddhist priest or monk.
Word use: Don't confuse this with **llama**.

lamb *(lam)*
1. a young sheep.
2. the meat from a young sheep.

lame
having something wrong with your foot or your leg that stops you walking properly.

lamington *(lam-ing-ton)*
a cube-shaped piece of sponge cake covered in chocolate and coconut.

lamp
a light that you can carry around.

land
1. the part of the earth that is not covered by water.
2. a country or a nation.
3. to end a sea or air journey: *The plane will land at Perth airport at two o'clock.*

landing *(land-ing)*
When an aeroplane ends its journey it makes a **landing** on the ground.

lane
1. a narrow road, wide enough for only one car at a time.
2. a part of a running track or of a swimming pool that has been marked out as the space for one person in a race.

language *(lang-gwij)*
the words you use when you speak or write.

lap¹
the front part of your body from your waist to your knees, when you are sitting down: *The kitten went to sleep curled up on my lap.*

lap²
one time around a racing track or down a swimming pool.

laptop *(lap-top)*
a small computer that can be carried around easily and used anywhere. When you use it, it can sit on your lap.

large *(larj)*
big.

larvae *(lar-vee)*
the young of any insect which changes the form of its body before becoming an adult: *Caterpillars are the larvae of butterflies.*
Word use: Larvae is the word we use for more than one. For one we use **larva**.

lasagne *(la-za-nya)*
an Italian dish made from flat sheets of pasta, minced meat, tomato and cheese.

lash
one of the short, curved hairs that grow around the edges of your eye.
Word building: For more than one we use **lashes**. | This word has been shortened from **eyelash**.

last¹ *(larst)*
after everything or everyone else.

last²
to go on or continue: *This movie will last two hours.*
Word building: If something lasts for a long time, it is **lasting**.

late
Something is **late** if it happens after you think it will or after it usually does: *If you miss the bus you will be late for school. | We'll have a late dinner tonight.*
Word building: more late = **later**, most late = **latest**
Word use: The opposite of this is **early**.

lately
recently: *There hasn't been much rain lately.*

laugh *(larf)*
to make a sound that shows that you are happy or amused.
Word building: When you laugh, people can hear your **laughter**.

a b c d e f g h i j k l m n o p q r s t u v w x y z

laundry *(lorn-dree)*
the room in your house for washing dirty clothes.

lava *(lar-va)*
the very hot, melted rock that flows out of a volcano.

law *(lor)*
a rule or a set of rules, especially those that everyone in a country must obey.

lawn *(lorn)*
the part of a garden with grass that has been cut very short.

lawyer *(loy-yer)*
somebody whose job is to advise people about the laws of a country or to argue in court for other people.

lay
1. to put something down flat: *Lay your towel on the sand.*
2. to produce an egg, as birds do.
Word building: I **laid**, I am **laying**

layer
a single thickness of something: *Add another **layer** of paint to your picture.*

lazy *(lay-zee)*
You are **lazy** if you do not like to work hard.
Word building: more lazy = **lazier**, most lazy = **laziest**

lead¹ *(leed)*
1. to be in front or in charge of something.
2. a strap that you attach to the collar of an animal.
Word building: I **led**, I am **leading** | Someone who leads is a **leader**.

lead² *(led)*
a heavy, dark-grey metal that you can bend easily.

leaded petrol *(led-ed pet-rol)*
petrol that contains tiny bits of lead which can harm you and the environment.

leaf *(leef)*
the flat, green part of a plant.
Word building: For more than one we use **leaves**.

league *(leeg)*
a group of people, countries or organisations who have made an agreement between themselves.

leak *(leek)*
a small hole or crack in something that lets liquid or a gas out when you don't want it to get out.

lean *(leen)*
to bend or curve your body towards or against something: ***Lean** over here and I'll whisper in your ear.* | *Can I **lean** my head on your shoulder?*
Word building: I **leaned** or I **leant** *(lent)*, I am **leaning**

leap *(leep)*
to jump or move quickly.
Word building: I **leapt** *(lept)* or I **leaped**, I am **leaping**

learn *(lern)*
1. to discover how to do something: *I am going to **learn** French.*
2. to find out something.
Word building: I **learned** or I **learnt**, I am **learning**

least *(leest)*
smallest in size or amount.
Word use: You can find this word at **little** as well. | The opposite of this is **most**.

leather *(ledh-er)*
the skin of an animal that has been made soft so that it can be used for making things like shoes or bags.

leave *(leev)*
1. to go away from somewhere or something: *When will you **leave** the house?* | *She is going to **leave** her job.*
2. to let something remain as it is: ***Leave** the door open.*
3. to not interfere with somebody: ***Leave** him alone.*
Word building: I **left**, I am **leaving**

lecture *(lec-cher)*
1. a speech that you give before an audience in order to teach or inform them: *I am giving a **lecture** on Australian history.*
2. a long talk that someone usually gives you when you're in trouble: *Mum gave me a **lecture** about not doing my homework.*
Word building: If you give a lecture, you are a **lecturer**.

left
The **left** side of your body is where your heart is.

leg
1. the part of your body from your hip to your foot.
2. one of the parts of a piece of furniture that touches the floor: *Don't swing back on the **legs** of the chair.*

legend *(lej-end)*
a story from long ago which is thought by many people to be at least partly true: *Have you heard of the **legend** of Robin Hood?*
Word building: Something that is a legend is **legendary**.

lemon
a yellow fruit with a sour taste.

lemonade *(lem-o-nade)*
a sweet, fizzy drink.

lend
to let someone use something of yours for a short time.
Word building: I **lent**, I am **lending**
Word use: When you lend someone something, you give them a **loan**. | Compare this with **borrow**.

length
how long something is.

leopard *(lep-ard)*
a large, fierce cat that has yellow fur with black spots and lives in Africa and Asia.

less
smaller in size or amount: *You have **less** money than us because you've already spent some.*
Word use: You can find this word at **little** as well. | The opposite of this is **more**.

lesson *(less-on)*
the time when someone teaches you something.

let
to allow or permit: *Will your parents **let** you go camping?*
Word building: I **let**, I have **let**, I am **letting**

letter *(lett-er)*
1. a written message that you post to someone.
2. one of the signs you use in writing and printing: *'A' is the first **letter** of the alphabet.*

letterbox
a box with a slot for posting or receiving mail.

lettuce *(lett-us)*
a plant with big, green leaves that you eat in salads.

level *(lev-l)*
1. flat or not sloping: *We must set up the tent on **level** ground.*
2. equal: *The scores are **level**.*

a b c d e f g h i j k l m n o p q r s t u v w x y z

lever *(lee-ver)*

a bar which rests across something and when you press down on one end the other end will lift something heavy.

liar *(rhymes with fire)*

someone who doesn't tell the truth.

liberate

to set free: *The president decided to liberate the prisoner.*

Word building: Someone who is liberated receives **liberation**, and someone who liberates is a **liberator**.

library *(libe-ree)*

a place where books are kept for people to read or borrow.

Word building: For more than one we use **libraries**. | Someone who looks after the books in a library is a **librarian**.

lice

a short way of saying **head lice**.

Word use: For one of these we use **louse**.

licence *(ly-sense)*

a printed form that says you can do, use or own something: *You have to have a driving licence before you're allowed to drive a car.*

lick

to move your tongue over something: *Lick the back of the stamp and stick it on the letter.*

licorice *(lik-rish or lik-uh-rish)*

a sweet substance made from the root of a plant and used to make sweets and some medicines.

Word use: Some people spell this **liquorice**.

lid

a top for covering a container: *I've lost the lid of this jar.*

lie[1]

1. something you say that you know is not true.
2. to say something that you know is not true: *If you lie, people won't trust you.*

Word building: I **lied**, I am **lying**

lie[2]

to have your body flat on the ground or on a bed: *Lie on the couch for a while.*

Word building: I **lay**, I have **lain**

lifesaver *(life-say-ver)*

someone who watches people swimming at the beach or at a public swimming pool and rescues them if they are having trouble in the water.

lifetime

the time that your life continues: *There are so many things I want to do in my lifetime.*

lift

1. to move something upwards.
2. a kind of cage or a platform for carrying people and things up and down inside tall buildings.

Word use: Another word for definition 2 is **elevator**.

light[1] *(lite)*

1. something that glows brightly so that you can see when it is dark.
2. to make something start to burn.
3. pale in colour: *My hair is light brown.*

Word building: I **lit**, I am **lighting**

light[2] *(lite)*

Something is **light** if it is easy to lift or carry because it does not weigh very much.

Word use: The opposite of this is **heavy**.

lightning *(lite-ning)*

a bright flash of light in the sky that comes during a storm and is followed by thunder.

like[1]

nearly the same: *I love playing hockey, tennis and other games like that.*

Word building: Things that are like each other are **alike** and you can see the **likeness** between them.

like[2]

to find something or someone very enjoyable or pleasant: *I **like** flying kites.* | *I **like** the new girl at school.*

Word building: I **liked**, I am **liking** | When you like something or someone, then you have a **liking** for them.

likely

probable: *With all those dark clouds in the sky, rain seems **likely**.*

Word building: If you are talking about whether something is likely, then you're talking about its **likelihood**.

limb (*lim*)

1. an arm or leg.
2. the branch of a tree.

limerick (*lim*-e-rick)

a funny poem with five lines.

limit (*lim*-it)

an amount, a speed or a line that you should not go beyond.

line

1. a thin mark or stroke made on paper, wood or some other surface.
2. something arranged like a line: *The **line** of ducklings hurried after their mother.*

link

1. one of the rings in a chain.
2. to join together, like the rings in a chain: *Let's all **link** arms and form a circle.*
3. to join one thing to another so that they work together: *If we **link** our two computers, we can play the game against each other.*

lion (*ly*-on)

a large, fierce cat with fur the colour of honey, found in Africa and India. The male has a mane.

Word use: The female is a **lioness**.

lip

1. Your mouth consists of a top **lip** and a bottom **lip**.
2. the edge or rim of an object.

liquid (*lik*-wid)

anything that can flow like water.

Word use: Think about how this is different from **gas** and **solid**.

liquid paper (*lik*-wid *pay*-per)

a thin, white paint that is used to cover written mistakes on paper.

Word use: Another word for this is **white-out**.

list

a group of things or names written down one under the other.

listen (*liss*-en)

to pay attention so that you can hear something.

litre (*lee*-ter)

a measure you use to work out how much liquid a container holds.

litter

1. scattered rubbish, especially in a public place.
2. baby animals that are born at the same time: *Our cat had a **litter** of six kittens.*

little (*litt*-l)

1. not big: *The baby has **little** feet.*
2. not much: *We spend **little** time inside on sunny days.*

Word building: When it means 'not much', this word belongs to the set **little**, **less**, **least**.

live[1] (*liv*)

1. to exist and breathe or grow: *The old parrot could easily **live** for another five years.*
2. to have your home somewhere: *Fish **live** in the sea.*

Word building: I **lived**, I am **living** | Things that live are **alive** and they have **life**.

live[2] *(rhymes with dive)*

1. something is **live** if it is shown on radio, television or the internet at the same time as it is happening: *This show is coming **live** from the Town Hall.*
2. supplied with electricity: *Don't touch that wire — it's **live**.*

lively *(live-lee; the first part rhymes with dive)*

full of energy.

living

1. A person, animal or plant that has life is **living**.
2. in existence or use: *French is a **living** language.*

living room

a room in a home, used both for entertaining guests and for relaxing: *Come and watch TV with me in the **living room**.*

Word use: Other words for this are **lounge**, **lounge room** and **sitting room**.

lizard *(liz-ard)*

an animal with a long, thin body, four legs, a long tail and skin like a snake.

llama *(rhymes with farmer)*

an animal used to carry heavy loads. It is a bit like a camel, but without humps.

Word use: Don't confuse this with **lama**.

load *(lode)*

1. something that is carried.
2. to put things in or on something that will carry them.

loaf[1] *(lofe)*

bread in one piece as it was baked.

Word building: For more than one we use **loaves**.

loaf[2] *(lofe)*

to be lazy or do nothing.

loan *(lone)*

anything that someone lends you and expects you to return.

lobster *(lob-ster)*

an animal with a hard shell like a crab, that lives in the sea. The first two of its ten legs are like big claws.

local *(loe-cal)*

Something is **local** if it belongs to a place, like your town or suburb: *I swim in the **local** pool.*

lock[1]

something used to keep a door or a box shut. It needs a key to open it.

lock[2]

a short piece of hair.

locust *(loe-cust)*

one of the grasshoppers that fly about in a large group and which can cause great damage by eating all the grass and crops in a place.

log

1. a large branch or the trunk of a tree which has fallen or been cut down.
2. the daily record of a voyage or flight kept by the captain of a ship or plane.

Word building: I **logged**, I am **logging**

log in *(log in)*

to enter your name and password into a computer so that you can begin using it: *You must **log in** before you can access the network.*

Word building: I **logged in**, I am **logging in**

Word use: Another word for this is **log on**.

log off *(log off)*

to exit from a computer network.

Word building: I **logged off**, I am **logging off**

Word use: Another word for this is **log out**.

lolly *(loll-ee)*

a sweet that you suck or chew.

lonely *(lone-lee)*
1. sad because you are not with your friends or family.
2. far away from where people are.
Word building: If you're lonely, then you have a feeling of **loneliness**.

long[1]
1. Something is **long** if it measures a lot from one end to the other: *He wrapped the **long** scarf several times around his neck.*
2. for a great amount of time: *I hope you didn't have to wait **long** in the rain.*
Word building: If you make something long, you **lengthen** it and increase its **length**.

long[2]
to want something very much.

look *(rhymes with book)*
1. to use your eyes to see: ***Look**! There's the picture I painted today.*
2. to search for something: *I can't find my library book — can you help me **look** for it?*
3. to seem: *You **look** very happy today.*
4. look after, to mind or take care of: *My cousins will **look after** our pets when we go away on holiday.*

loom[1]
a machine for weaving threads into cloth.

loom[2]
to appear suddenly, usually in a way that frightens you: *We were terrified to see a big truck **loom** out of the mist.*

loop
a circle shape that you twist in a piece of string, a lace or a ribbon.

loose *(rhymes with goose)*
1. not fastened or tied: *Chloe's **loose** hair blew in the wind.*
2. not tight: *The clown wore big, **loose** trousers that kept falling down.*
Word use: Don't confuse this with **lose**.

lord
a man who is the head of one of the important ruling families in Britain.

lorikeet *(lo-ri-keet)*
a small, brightly coloured parrot.

lose *(looze)*
1. to be without something because you don't know where it is: *You won't **lose** your toys if you keep them in the right place.*
2. to not win: *If our teams **lose** their games this week we will be out of the competition.*
Word building: I **lost**, I am **losing** | Something that you lose is **lost** and you might be unhappy about its **loss**.
Word use: Don't confuse **lose** with **loose**.

lot
a large number or amount: *We found a **lot** of Easter eggs hidden around the garden.*

loud
Something is **loud** if it makes a lot of sound so that you can hear it easily: *The **loud** bang woke us all.*

lounge *(lownj)*
another word for **living room**.

louse *(rhymes with house)*
a very small insect that can live in your hair and make your head itchy. It lays eggs called nits.
Word building: For more than one we use **lice**.

love *(luv)*
to like someone or something very much.
Word building: I **loved**, I am **loving**

lovely *(luv-lee)*
1. beautiful to look at.
2. pleasant: *We had a lovely time in the park.*

Word building: more lovely = **lovelier**, most lovely = **loveliest**

low *(lo)*
near to the ground or the floor.

lower *(lo-er)*
to make something go down.

Word use: The opposite of this is **raise**.

loyal *(loy-al)*
You are **loyal** if you are faithful and true to your friends.

Word building: Someone who is loyal is full of **loyalty**.

luck
something, usually good, that happens to you in a way that has not been planned: *What good luck that I was on the same plane as the famous basketballer.*

Word building: If you have good luck, then you are **lucky**.

luggage *(lugg-ij)*
the bags and cases you use to carry your things when you're travelling.

lump
1. a piece of something solid with no special shape: *The art teacher took a lump of clay and made it into a dainty bowl.*
2. a swelling: *I have a lump on my head where I was hit by a ball.*

lunar *(loo-nar)*
Something is **lunar** if it has something to do with the moon: *A lunar month is the time from one new moon to the next. | The lunar module landed on the surface of the moon.*

lunch
a meal in the middle of the day.

Word building: For more than one we use **lunches**.

lung
one of the two parts inside your chest that you use for breathing.

lunge *(lunj)*
to jump or push forward suddenly towards something: *The cat kept very still and waited for the best time to lunge at the mouse.*

Word building: I **lunged**, I am **lunging**

luxury *(luck-sha-ree)*
something that you enjoy a lot, but that you don't really need.

Word building: For more than one we use **luxuries**.

lyrebird *(ly-a-bird)*
an Australian bird that builds its nest on the ground and can copy the sounds of other birds and animals. The male has a long beautiful tail which he spreads open when he is dancing for the female.

Mm

Mice munch mushrooms at the movies.

machine *(ma-**sheen**)*
something that is made up of parts that work together to do a job: *Put the clothes in the washing* **machine**.
Word building: If you are talking about many machines, then you're talking about **machinery**.

mad
1. crazy or likely to do strange things.
2. angry: *I am **mad** because you took my game without asking.*
Word building: If something is done in a mad way, it is done **madly** and you talk about its **madness**.

madam *(**mad**-am)*
a polite word you use when you're speaking to a woman: *May I carry your parcels, **madam**?*

magazine *(mag-a-**zeen**)*
a kind of thin, soft book with stories, pictures and advertisements in it. It usually comes out every week or every month.

magic *(**maj**-ic)*
the power to do things that no-one can explain or to do tricks which seem impossible.

magician *(ma-**jish**-in)*
someone who can do things using magic.

magnet *(**mag**-net)*
a piece of iron or steel that can pull other metal things towards it.

magnify *(**mag**-ni-fy)*
to make something look larger.
Word building: I **magnified**, I am **magnifying**

magpie *(**mag**-pie)*
a black and white bird, very common in Australia.

maid
a woman who is paid to help look after a house or a hotel.

mail
letters and packages sent by post.
Word use: Don't confuse this with **male**.

main
most important or biggest: *The **main** reason I came was to see you.* | *Will you take the **main** road or the back streets?*
Word use: Don't confuse this with **mane**.

mainly
for the most part: *Koalas have fur that is **mainly** coloured grey.*

major *(**may**-jer)*
1. important: *Vegetables make up one of the **major** food groups.*
2. a soldier in the army.

majority (muh-**jo**-ri-tee)

the greater number or more than half: *The **majority** of my friends play sport on Saturdays.*

Word building: For more than one we use **majorities**.

Word use: The opposite of this is **minority**.

make

1. to bring something into being or to invent something: *I will **make** a paper plane for you.*

2. to cause something to happen or someone to do something: *This rain will **make** the court too wet for playing tennis. | You can't **make** me eat this carrot if I don't want to.*

Word building: I **made**, I am **making**

male

a person or an animal of the sex that doesn't have babies.

Word use: The opposite of this is **female**. | Don't confuse this with **mail**.

mall (*mawl* or *mal*)

an open area surrounded by shops.

mammal (***mamm**-al*)

an animal which feeds its babies with its own milk.

man

a grown-up male human being.

manage (***man**-ij*)

1. to be able to: *Can you **manage** to carry that by yourself?*

2. to control: *The new teacher cannot **manage** the class very well.*

Word building: I **managed**, I am **managing** | A person who manages a business or a sports team is called a **manager**.

mane

the long hair on the head of a lion or along the neck of a horse.

Word use: Don't confuse this with **main**.

mango (***mang**-go*)

a sweet, yellow fruit that grows in hot, rainy areas.

Word building: For more than one we use **mangoes**.

mankind

all humans.

mansion (***man**-shon*)

a very big or grand house.

manual (***man**-yoo-al*)

a car which has gears that you change by hand.

manufacture (*man-yu-**fac**-cher*)

to make a lot of something with machines or by hand: *They **manufacture** cars at this factory.*

Word building: I **manufacture**, I am **manufacturing**

many (***men**-ee*)

of or with a large number of people or things: ***Many** children were sick and only a few came to school.*

Word use: This word is part of the set **many**, **more**, **most**. | Don't confuse this with **much**. | The opposite of this is **few**.

map

a drawing or diagram of an area showing where certain things are, such as towns, roads, mountains and borders: *I think we're lost, so we'd better check the **map**.*

marble (***mar**-bl*)

1. a sort of smooth, hard stone that you use in buildings or to make statues.

2. a small, glass ball you use to play a game.

march

to walk like a soldier, with all your steps exactly the same and with your arms swinging.

mare *(mair)*
a female horse that has grown up.
Word use: The male is a **stallion**.

margarine *(mar-ja-**reen**)*
a food like butter, that you can spread on bread or use for cooking. It is made from vegetable oil.

margin *(**mar**-jin)*
the blank space between the edge of a page and where the writing starts.

marine *(ma-**reen**)*
having to do with or living in the sea: *The dolphin is a **marine** animal.*

mark
1. a spot, a line, a scratch or a stain on anything.
2. to put a number or a tick on someone's work to show how good or bad it is: *Our teacher has a pile of our projects to **mark** tonight.*

market *(**mar**-ket)*
a place with a lot of stalls where you can buy things.

marmalade *(**mar**-ma-lade)*
a jam made with oranges, lemons or other fruit like this.

marry *(rhymes with **carry**)*
to take someone as your husband or as your wife: *My sister is going to **marry** the boy who lives next door.*
Word building: I **married**, I am **marrying** | When you marry someone, you begin your **marriage**.

marsh
low, wet land.
Word building: Land that's a marsh is **marshy**.
Word use: Another word that means nearly the same is **swamp**.

marsupial *(mah-**soop**-ee-al)*
an animal which keeps and feeds its babies in a pouch for a few months after they are born. Kangaroos are marsupials and so are wallabies, koalas and possums.

mask *(rhymes with **ask**)*
something you wear over your face to protect it or to change the way you look.

mass
a large number of things or a big amount of something: *Did you see the **mass** of papers on my desk? | A **mass** of water stretched in front of us.*

massive *(**mass**-iv)*
very big or huge.

mast *(rhymes with **last**)*
a tall pole that goes upwards from the deck of a ship to hold its sails up.

master
1. someone who has control or a special skill: *She is a **master** of several languages.*
2. the owner of a dog or other animal.
3. to get control of: *I will **master** this new computer if it takes all day!*

mat
a piece of plaited or woven material, used to cover a floor.

match[1] *(mach)*
a short, thin piece of wood that makes a flame when you rub it on something rough.
Word building: For more than one we use **matches**.

match[2] *(mach)*
1. a game or a contest.
2. to go together exactly: *The colours you're wearing don't **match**.*
Word building: For more than one we use **matches**.

material (ma-*teer*-ree-al)

1. anything you use to make something with: *Here is some of the building* **material** *for your new house.*
2. cotton, wool, silk or anything that someone weaves and uses to make clothes, curtains and other things like this.

maths

learning how to use numbers and how to find out how big things are.

Word building: This word is short for **mathematics**.

matter

1. the substance of which things are made.
2. a subject: *That is a* **matter** *for my parents to discuss.*
3. trouble or difficulty: *Is there something the* **matter** *with that cat?*
4. If something **matters** it is important: *Everyone's opinion* **matters**.

mattress (*matt*-ress)

the soft, thick part of a bed, that you lie on.

maximum (*max*-i-mum)

the most you can have: *This taxi holds a* **maximum** *of four passengers.*

Word use: The opposite of this is **minimum**.

may

1. to be allowed to do something: *You* **may** *go and play outside now.*
2. could possibly: *We* **may** *see a falling star tonight, if we're lucky.*

Word use: This word is a helping word. It is always used with another one in the form I **may** or I **might** do something.

maybe

perhaps or possibly: ***Maybe** you can come next time.*

mayor (rhymes with *care*)

the person in charge of a city or town council.

me (mee)

a word you use when you are talking about yourself: *Please give* **me** *some ice-cream.*

meal (meel)

the food you eat at about the same time each day.

mean[1] (meen)

1. to have it in your mind to do something: *I do* **mean** *to ask her but she's always too busy.*
2. to stand for or to show something: *The word 'colossal' can* **mean** *'very good' in everyday language.* | *Does the way Youssef is limping* **mean** *that there's something wrong with his leg?*

Word building: I **meant** (ment), I am **meaning**

mean[2] (meen)

You are **mean** if you don't want to give anything of yours away to anyone else.

meaning

what something means or stands for: *Look up the* **meaning** *of this word in your dictionary.*

meanwhile

at the same time: *Molly found the secret cave.* **Meanwhile**, *the other children made their escape from the castle.*

measles (*meez*-lz)

a disease that gives you a fever and red spots on your skin. It is easily caught from someone else.

measure (*mezh*-er)

1. an amount that everyone agrees to use when they want to know how big something is or how much of something there is: *A metre is a* **measure** *of length.*
2. to use something like a ruler or scales to find out how big a thing is or how much of it there is.

Word building: I **measured**, I am **measuring** | When you measure something, you find out its **measurement**.

meat *(meet)*
the soft part of an animal's body used for food.
Word use: Don't confuse this with **meet**.

mechanical *(me-**can**-i-cal)*
Something is **mechanical** if it works by machinery: *You wind the key of this **mechanical** toy to make it move.*
Word building: Anything mechanical, like a car, is cared for by a **mechanic**.

medal *(**medd**-l)*
a metal badge which people are given for being brave or doing something very well.
Word use: Don't confuse this with **meddle**.

medallion *(me-**dal**-yon)*
a large medal, especially one given as a prize.

meddle *(**medd**-l)*
to take part in someone else's business when it has nothing to do with you.
Word building: I **meddled**, I am **meddling**
Word use: Another word that means nearly the same is **interfere**. | Don't confuse this with **medal**.

medical
having to do with medicine: *Mum is a doctor at the **medical** centre.*

medicine *(**med**-i-sin or **med**-sin)*
1. something the doctor gives you to make you better.
2. the science of treating sickness and disease.

meditate *(**med**-i-tate)*
to think long and deeply: *He **meditated** on the problem for many hours before coming up with an answer.*
Word building: I **meditated**, I am **meditating** | If you meditate, you are doing **meditation**. Some people do a special kind of meditation as part of their religion or to relax.

medium *(**mee**-dee-um)*
middle or ordinary in anything: *Thomas is of **medium** height but his older sister is very tall.*

meet
to come together: *The paths **meet** at the big tree in the middle of the park.* | *Let's **meet** tomorrow.*
Word building: I **met**, I am **meeting** | When people arrange to meet for a reason, they have a **meeting**.
Word use: Don't confuse **meet** with **meat**.

melody *(**mel**-o-dee)*
musical sounds that you hear one after another, making a pleasant pattern.
Word building: For more than one we use **melodies**.
Word use: Another word that means nearly the same is **tune**.

melon *(**mel**-on)*
a large fruit with a lot of juice and with a thick skin.

melt
to make something soft and flowing by heating it: *We need to **melt** some chocolate to make the icing for the cake.*

member *(**mem**-ber)*
someone who belongs to a group or a club.
Word building: If you are a member of something, you have **membership**.

memorial *(me-**mor**-ree-al)*
something that helps people remember a person or a special event: *This statue is a **memorial** to the soldiers who died fighting for their country.*

memorise
to put into your memory or learn by heart: *I will **memorise** every word of your song.*
Word building: If you memorise something, you are using the skill of **memorisation**.

memory (mem-o-ree)

1. the ability to keep things in your mind until you need to use them again.
2. something you remember: *I have a clear memory of my friends waving goodbye to me.*

Word building: For more than one we use **memories**.

memory stick (mem-o-ree stick)

a very small computer part that you can store files on, carry around with you, and plug into different computers to access the files.

mend

to make something work properly again: *I have to get someone to mend my broken bike.*

mental (ment-l)

Something is **mental** if it has to do with your mind: *I'm very good at mental arithmetic.*

mention

to speak or write briefly about something: *Did Lena mention her new puppy when you spoke to her?*

menu (men-yoo)

a list of the food that you can order at a restaurant.

mercy (mer-see)

the kindness someone shows when they decide not to punish a person or not to be cruel.

Word building: If someone shows mercy, they are **merciful**.

meringue (ma-rang)

a sweet, white food you make with sugar and the white part of eggs.

merino (ma-ree-no)

a kind of sheep that has very fine wool.

mermaid (mer-made)

a sea creature in stories who looks like a woman from the waist up but looks like a fish from the waist down.

merry (rhymes with berry)

happy or full of fun.

Word building: more merry = **merrier**, most merry = **merriest** | When you are merry, you're full of **merriment**.

mess

something that's dirty or untidy.

message (mess-ij)

important news that one person sends to another.

Word building: Someone who carries a message is a **messenger**.

metal (met-l)

anything like iron, gold or silver that you can polish and that you can bend when it's hot.

meteor (mee-tee-or)

a small rock from outer space which makes a streak of fire across the sky as it falls towards the earth.

meter (mee-ter)

a machine that measures something, especially one that measures the amount of gas, electricity or water passing through it.

Word use: Don't confuse this with **metre**.

method (meth-od)

a way of doing something: *Show me your method for making scones.*

metre (mee-ter)

a measure you use to work out how long something is. There are 1000 metres in a kilometre.

Word use: Don't confuse this with **meter**.

mice
small, furry animals with sharp teeth and long tails, usually brown, white or grey coloured.
Word use: For one of these we use **mouse**.

microphone *(my-cro-fone)*
a thing that turns sound into electricity, which you use when you want to make sounds louder or to record them.

microscope *(my-cro-skope)*
an instrument you look into that makes very tiny things big enough for you to see.

microwave *(my-cro-wave)*
a type of oven that heats and cooks food very quickly.

midday *(mid-day)*
twelve o'clock in the middle of the day.
Word use: Another word that means the same is **noon**.

middle *(midd-l)*
the point that's halfway between two sides or halfway through something: *Don't stop in the **middle** of the road. | Her phone rang in the **middle** of the play.*

midnight *(mid-nite)*
twelve o'clock in the middle of the night.

might[1] *(mite)*
power or strength: *I pushed with all my **might** but the rock wouldn't move.*

might[2] *(mite)*
See **may**.

mighty *(my-tee)*
very powerful.
Word building: more mighty = **mightier**, most mighty = **mightiest**

migrant *(my-grant)*
someone who leaves their own country to go and live in another country.

mild *(rhymes with **wild**)*
gentle: *A **mild** breeze blew through my hair.*

mile
a large measure we once used in Australia to work out how far it is between two places. One mile is about 1.6 kilometres.

milk
the white drink that mothers produce to feed their babies. We often drink cow's milk.

mill
a building with machines for grinding grain into flour.
Word building: Someone in charge of a flour mill is a **miller**.

millimetre *(mil-i-mee-ter)*
a very small measure you use to work out how long something is. There are 1000 millimetres in a metre.

million *(mill-yon)*
a thousand times a thousand (1 000 000).

mime
to act something without using any words.
Word building: I **mimed**, I am **miming**

mimic *(mim-ic)*
to copy the way other people move and speak.
Word building: I **mimicked**, I am **mimicking**

mind *(rhymes with **dined**)*
1. the part of you that thinks, decides or remembers things.
2. to look after someone or something: *I'll **mind** your baby while you go to the shops.*
3. to feel bad about, or not like something: *I try not to **mind** when she teases me but I always end up crying.*

mine[1]

a word you use when you are talking about something that belongs to you: *That jacket is mine.*

mine[2]

1. a large hole people dig in the earth for taking out things like coal, gold or diamonds.
2. a bomb put under the ground or in the sea.

Word building: Someone who works in a mine is a **miner**.

Word use: Don't confuse **miner** with **minor**.

mineral *(min-er-al)*

a substance like stone or coal which is dug out of the ground at a mine.

minimum *(min-i-mum)*

the least you can have: *You have to get a minimum of seven points before you have a chance of winning.*

Word use: The opposite of this is **maximum**.

minister *(min-i-ster)*

1. a person who has been trained to take the services in a church.
2. a very important member of a government. They are in charge of something like education or health.

minor

lesser in size or importance: *Don't worry, that's a minor mistake.*

Word use: Don't confuse this with **miner**.

minority *(my-no-ri-tee)*

1. the smaller part or number, or less than half.
2. a group of people who, for some reason, are different from most other people: *The government should not forget the views of the minority.*

Word building: For more than one we use **minorities**.

Word use: The opposite of this is **majority**.

mint[1]

1. a plant with leaves you can use for cooking.
2. a sort of lolly.

mint[2]

a place where the government makes our money.

minus *(mine-us)*

take away: *5 minus 3 leaves 2.*

Word use: The opposite of this is **plus**.

minute[1] *(min-it)*

1. a small measure of time, 60 seconds long. There are 60 minutes in an hour.
2. any short amount of time: *Wait a minute — I'm not ready yet.*

minute[2] *(my-newt)*

very, very small.

miracle *(mi-ra-kel)*

something that happens which no-one can explain: *It's a miracle she wasn't badly hurt when she fell from the window.*

mirage *(mi-rarzh)*

something you see in the distance that seems much closer than it really is, or that isn't really there at all. People sometimes see one in the desert.

mirror *(mi-ror)*

a piece of special glass that you can see yourself in.

mischief *(miss-chef)*

a way of behaving that is meant to tease or to annoy people.

Word building: Someone who is always up to mischief is **mischievous (mis-chi-vus)**.

miserable *(miz-ra-bl)*

very unhappy or not very comfortable: *Don't be so miserable — I'll share my lunch with you.*

Word building: When you are miserable, you're full of **misery**.

miss[1]

1. to not hit or catch something: *He'll* ***miss*** *that ball because he's not good at catching.*
2. to not see, hear or meet someone or something: *They said they'd wait for us but we will* ***miss*** *them if we don't hurry.*
3. to feel sad that someone isn't there or that something is lost: *I* ***miss*** *my sister when she goes away.*

miss[2]

1. a young unmarried woman.
2. Miss, a title you can put before an unmarried woman's name: *My teacher is* ***Miss*** *Dacey.*

Word use: Some women prefer **Ms** because it doesn't refer to whether they are married or not.

missile *(miss-ile)*

a weapon or anything like this that people can throw or shoot.

mist

a cloud of tiny drops of water which is hard to see through.

mistake *(mi-stake)*

something you have done the wrong way, or something you thought that wasn't right.

Word use: Another word that means nearly the same is **error**.

mitten *(mitt-n)*

a kind of glove with one part to cover your thumb and one part to cover your four fingers together.

mix

to put things together: *You can* ***mix*** *flour and water to make damper.*

Word building: When you mix things together, you make a **mixture**.

moan *(mone)*

a long, low sound you make when you feel sad or when you're in pain.

moat *(mote)*

a deep, wide ditch built around a town or a castle to keep out enemies. It is usually filled with water.

mobile *(mo-bile)*

1. able to be moved: *The* ***mobile*** *library visits our school every week.*
2. a hanging decoration made up of movable parts.
3. a mobile phone.

mobile phone *(mo-bile **fone**)*

a telephone without a cord that you can use anywhere.

mock

to make fun of someone: *I felt angry when I heard the bully* ***mock*** *my friend.*

model *(**mod**-l)*

1. a small copy of something that's much larger: *I'd like that* ***model*** *of a sailing ship for Christmas.*
2. something that you can copy: *Her picture was used as a* ***model*** *by the other children in the class.*
3. someone whose job is to wear new clothes and to show them to the people who want to buy them.

modem *(mo-dem)*

a machine that changes information from one computer into a form that can be sent by telephone to another computer.

modern *(mod-n)*

Something is **modern** if it is new or recent.

moist *(moyst)*

damp or a bit wet: *It was so hot that my skin was* ***moist*** *with sweat.*

Word building: Something that's moist has some **moisture** in it.

moment *(moe-ment)*

a very short length of time.

monarch *(mon-ark)*
a king or a queen.

money *(mun-ee)*
the coins and paper notes you use to pay for the things you buy.

monitor *(mon-i-tor)*
the part of the computer that you look at to read the words and pictures. It looks like a television screen.

monk *(munk)*
one of a group of men who choose to live away from the rest of the world and think about God or religion.

monkey *(mung-kee)*
an animal with a long tail, that lives in the trees of some hot countries.
Word building: For more than one we use **monkeys**.

monorail *(mon-o-rail)*
a train that runs on one rail.

monotreme *(mon-o-treme)*
a special kind of mammal found only in Australia. A platypus is a monotreme, and so is an echidna.

monster *(mon-ster)*
someone or something that frightens you because it is so big, ugly or cruel.

month *(munth)*
one of the twelve parts of the year.
Word building: If something comes or happens each month, then it is **monthly**.

monument *(mon-yu-ment)*
a statue or anything like this that people make to remember a person or something important that's happened.

mood
the way you feel: *I'm in a good mood because we're going to a nice restaurant for dinner tonight.*

moon
the round object that you can see as a light in the sky at night. It moves in a circle around the earth every month.
Word use: Something to do with the moon is **lunar**.

mop
1. a loose bundle of cloth or strings attached to the end of a stick, and used for washing floors.
2. a thick mass: *I can't see your face under that mop of hair.*
3. to clean or wipe up with a mop or something similar.
Word building: I **mopped**, I am **mopping**

more
bigger in size or amount: *That dog is even more enormous than I remember it. | More people came to my party than I thought would come.*
Word use: This word is part of the set **many**, **more**, **most**. | The opposite of this is **less**.

morning *(mor-ning)*
the part of the day between breakfast and lunchtime.

mosque *(mosk)*
a special place where Muslims worship.

mosquito *(mo-skee-to)*
a small insect that flies around trying to find people and animals to suck blood from.
Word building: For more than one we use **mosquitoes**.

moss
a plant with very small leaves. It grows in damp places.

most
biggest or highest in size or amount: *That is the most enormous building I've ever seen. | They've eaten most of the ice-cream in the tub!*
Word use: This word is part of the set **many**, **more**, **most**. | The opposite of this is **least**.

moth
an insect that flies around at night. It is rather like a butterfly.

mother *(mudh-er)*
a female parent.

motor *(mo-tor)*
an engine, usually for a car or a boat.

motorbike *(mo-tor-bike)*
a large heavy bicycle with an engine.

motorway
a large main road which you often have to pay a special fee, called a toll, to use.

mountain *(mount-n)*
a part of the land that's higher than a hill.

Word building: Someone who climbs mountains is a **mountaineer** *(mount-n-eer)*.

mouse *(rhymes with **house**)*
1. a small, furry animal with sharp teeth and a long tail, usually brown, white or grey coloured.

Word building: For more than one we use **mice**.
2. a small object that you move on the desk in the direction that you want the cursor to move on your computer screen.

moustache *(mo-**starsh**)*
the hair that grows on a man's top lip.

mouth *(mowth)*
the opening in your face for eating, drinking and talking.

move *(moov)*
to go from one place to another, or to change position: *Move your chair next to mine.* | *Can you **move** away from the window?*

Word building: I **moved**, I am **moving** | When you move, you make a **movement**.

movie
another word for **film**: *Did you watch that funny **movie** on TV last night?*

Mr
a title put before a man's name: *My history teacher is **Mr** Naidoo.*

Mrs
a title you can put before a married woman's name: *My mum's best friend is **Mrs** Lee.*

Word use: Some women prefer **Ms** because it doesn't refer to whether they are married or not.

Ms *(mz or miz)*
a title put before a woman's name: *The boss of the company is **Ms** Andreas.*

much
a lot of something: *Is there **much** sugar left?*

Word use: Don't confuse this with **many**.

mud
wet, soft, sticky earth.

Word building: When something is covered with mud, it's **muddy**.

mug
a large cup.

mule
an animal whose mother is a horse and whose father is a donkey.

mulga *(**mul**-ga)*
a wattle tree that grows in dry parts of Australia. Cattle like to eat its leaves.

Word use: This word comes from the Yuwaalaraay and Kamilaroi languages of New South Wales. See the map of Australian Aboriginal languages at the end of this book.

mulgara *(mul-**gar**-a)*
a small marsupial that looks like a mouse with a black, hairy tail. It lives in the Australian desert and is endangered. See the table at the end of this book.

Word use: This word comes from the Wangganguru language of South Australia. See the map of Australian Aboriginal languages at the end of this book.

multiply *(mul-ti-ply)*
to add a number to itself a number of times to get an answer: ***Multiply** 4 by 2 to get 8.*
Word building: I **multiplied**, I am **multiplying** | If you have to multiply in a sum, then you're doing a **multiplication**.

mum
an everyday word for a mother.

mumps
an illness which makes your neck and face swell up and feel very sore.

munch
to chew something in a noisy way.

murder *(mer-der)*
the crime of killing someone on purpose.

muscle *(muss-l)*
one of the parts of your body that helps to make it move.

museum *(myoo-zee-um)*
a place where interesting and unusual things are kept for people to go and see.

mushroom *(mush-room)*
a plant that looks like a fat umbrella. They grow in damp places and you can eat them.
Word use: See how this is different from a **toadstool**.

music *(muze-ic)*
the pleasant sounds that people make when they sing or when they play an instrument.
Word building: Someone who is good at music is **musical**, and if their job is to play music, they are a **musician**.

Muslim *(mooz-lim)*
someone whose religion is Islam.

must
have to: *You **must** taste this — it is really delicious!*
Word use: This word is a helping word. It is always used with another one in the form I **must** or I **mustn't** do something.

mustard *(must-ed)*
a brown or yellow food which has a hot taste.

mute *(rhymes with **cute**)*
You're **mute** if you're unable to speak.

mutiny *(mute-i-nee)*
the refusal of soldiers or sailors to obey orders of the officers who are in charge.
Word building: For more than one we use **mutinies**.

mutter
to speak or grumble in a quiet voice that is hard to hear.

my
a word you use when you are talking about something that belongs to you: ***My** book is on the shelf.*

myself *(my-self)*
a word you use when you are talking about doing something to yourself or doing something by yourself without help: *I cut **myself**. | I made lunch **myself**.*

mystery *(miss-tree)*
a strange and puzzling thing that no-one can explain.
Word building: Something that is a mystery is **mysterious** *(mi-stear-ree-us)*.

myth *(mith)*
one of the very old stories about gods, heroes and unusual happenings. They were told to explain natural things like what makes it rain or why the sun goes down every night: *In Aboriginal **myths** the song of kookaburras is said to make the sun rise every morning.*

Nn

Numbats nibble noodles at noon.

nachos *(nar-choss)*
a snack made from corn chips with tomato, chilli, and melted cheese on top.

nag
to keep on complaining about something.
Word building: I **nagged**, I am **nagging**

nail *(nale)*
1. a small, thin piece of metal that is sharp at one end and which you hammer into pieces of wood to join them together.
2. the thin, hard, flat part that covers the end of your finger or toe.

naked *(nay-ked)*
without any clothes on.
Word use: Another word that means nearly the same is **nude**.

name
what you call someone or something.

nanny goat
a female goat.

narrate *(na-rate)*
to tell the story of what happened: *I will narrate the story of 'The Pied Piper' while the rest of the class mime it.*
Word building: I **narrated**, I am **narrating** | Someone who narrates a story is a **narrator**.

narrative *(narra-tiv)*
writing which tells a story. See the 'Types of writing and speaking' table at the end of this book.

narrow
not wide.

nasty *(nar-stee)*
1. not pleasant: *I got a nasty fright when the big dog rushed at me.*
2. cruel or not kind: *Your nasty teasing has made my little sister cry.*
Word building: more nasty = **nastier**, most nasty = **nastiest**

nation *(nay-shon)*
a large group of people who have the same government and the same flag. A nation can be a large country, like Australia, a small part of a continent, like Switzerland, or a group of many islands, like Indonesia.

national *(nash-nal)*
Something is **national** if it belongs to or is part of a nation.

nationality *(nash-o-nal-i-tee)*
membership or connection that someone has with a country: *He has New Zealand nationality.*
Word building: For more than one we use **nationalities**.

national park

a natural area for everybody to use, where the environment is protected.

native *(nay-tiv)*

1. You are a **native** of a place if you were born there.

2. A plant or an animal is a **native** of a place if it belongs there: *This flower is a **native** of the rainforests of northern Queensland.*

natural *(nach-a-ral)*

not made by people or machines: ***Natural** materials like wool or cotton are comfortable to wear.*

Word use: The opposite of this is **artificial**.

nature *(nay-cher)*

1. everything in the world that was not made by people, such as the rocks, sea, sky, plants and animals.

2. the way a person or animal really is inside: *The little children enjoy riding the horse because it has a kind **nature**.*

naughty *(nor-tee)*

You are **naughty** when you're not behaving well.

Word building: more naughty = **naughtier**, most naughty = **naughtiest**

navy *(nay-vee)*

the fighting ships and sailors of a country.

Word building: For more than one we use **navies**. | Something to do with the navy or ships is **naval**.

near *(rhymes with **ear**)*

not far away.

nearby

not far away: *We could hear birds singing in a **nearby** tree. | I waved at Olivia, who was playing **nearby**.*

nearly

almost: *The train is **nearly** at the station.*

neat *(neet)*

tidy and in order: *Su-Li keeps her books in a **neat** pile so that she can easily find the one she wants.*

necessary *(ness-e-serry or ness-es-ree)*

Something is **necessary** if you really need it and if you can't do without it.

neck

the part of your body that joins your head to your shoulders.

necklace *(neck-less)*

a string of beads or other jewels that you wear round your neck.

nectar *(neck-ta)*

the sweet, sticky stuff that bees collect from flowers to turn into honey.

need

1. to have to get something important: *I **need** a new cable for my computer.*

2. to have to do something: *I **need** to clean my shoes after treading in all that mud.*

needle *(need-l)*

1. a small, thin piece of metal with a very sharp point at one end and a hole at the other end that you put thread through. You use it for sewing.

2. one of two short, thin rods you use for knitting.

3. a small, thin tube with a very sharp end that a doctor or nurse uses to give injections.

negative *(neg-a-tiv)*

saying or meaning no: *Sergio shook his head and gave a **negative** answer.*

Word use: The opposite of this is **positive**.

neglect *(ne-glect)*

to fail to look after something or someone properly: *If we **neglect** the garden the flowers might die.*

neigh *(nay)*
the sound that a horse makes.

neighbour *(nay-bor)*
someone who lives near you.
Word building: Your neighbours live in your **neighbourhood**.

neither *(ny-dher or nee-dher)*
not the one or the other: **Neither** of those CDs belong to me.

nephew *(nef-yoo)*
the son of your brother or sister.

nervous *(ner-vus)*
afraid of or excited about something: She was very **nervous** about singing in front of the whole school.

nest
a shelter that birds and some other small animals make for their babies.

net
1. a material made from pieces of string knotted together, with holes in between.
Word building: **Mosquito net**, **fishing net**, **butterfly net** are all sorts of nets.
2. the net, the system that links computers all around the world so that you can share information: I'll look up the address on **the net**.
Word building: This is a short way of saying **the internet**.
Word use: You can also write this as **the Net**.

netball
a ball game played by two teams. Players must not bounce the ball and they must try to get points by throwing the ball into a ring on top of a tall post.

network
many computers linked to each other.

never
not ever: I have **never** broken a bone in my life.

new
1. bought or made a short time ago: Be careful not to spill anything on the **new** couch.
2. not known before: We discovered a **new** way to Grandma's house today.

news
the important things you need to know about something that has just happened. You can hear the news on the radio, watch it on television or read about it in a newspaper or on the internet.

newsagency *(news-age-en-see)*
a shop where you can buy newspapers, pens, magazines and books.
Word building: Someone who runs a newsagency is called a **newsagent**.

newspaper *(news-pay-per)*
big sheets of paper folded over, with news and advertisements printed on them.

New Year
the time at the beginning of a year, when people celebrate the end of one year and the beginning of the next year.

next
1. straight after this one: Can I please have the **next** ride?
2. nearest: Come and sit at the desk **next** to mine.

nibble *(nibb-l)*
to eat something by taking a little bit at a time, like a mouse does.
Word building: I **nibbled**, I am **nibbling**

nice
1. pleasant: We have had a really **nice** day at the beach.
2. kind: It was **nice** of you to help me.
Word building: more nice = **nicer**, most nice = **nicest**

a
b
c
d
e
f
g
h
i
j
k
l
m
n
o
p
q
r
s
t
u
v
w
x
y
z

nickname *(nick-name)*
a name that people who know you sometimes use instead of your real name.

niece *(rhymes with geese)*
the daughter of your brother or sister.

night *(nite)*
the time when it is dark.

nil
nothing: *We won the game by three goals to nil.*

nit
the egg of a louse, which is an insect that can live in your hair and make your head itchy.

no
1. none or not at all: *There are no biscuits left. | Cats are no smarter than dogs.*
2. a word you use when you disagree, refuse to do something or forbid someone from doing something: *No, that's not right. | No, I won't do your homework for you. | No! You can't do that!*
Word use: The opposite of definition 2 is **yes**.

noble *(no-bl)*
1. Someone is **noble** if they are born into one of the old and important families that help to rule a country.
2. kind, generous and good.

nobody *(no-bod-ee)*
no person: *Nobody wants to come with me, so I will go by myself.*

nocturnal *(nok-ter-nal)*
An animal is **nocturnal** if it is active at night and asleep in the day: *Possums and bats are nocturnal animals.*

nod
to move your head slightly up and down to show that you agree with something: *I know you agree with what I said because I saw you nod.*
Word building: I **nodded**, I am **nodding**

noise *(noize)*
a sound, usually a very loud one or one you don't like.
Word building: Something that makes a loud noise is **noisy**.

none *(nun)*
1. not one: *None of my friends are coming.*
2. not any: *That's none of your business.*

nonfiction *(non-fic-shon)*
a story or book about people and things that happen which are real: *Books about sport are my favourite type of nonfiction.*

nonsense *(non-sense)*
words that are silly or that don't mean anything.

noodles *(noo-dls)*
a sort of pasta cut in long, thin strips.

noon
twelve o'clock in the middle of the day.
Word use: Another word that means the same is **midday**.

no-one *(no-wun)*
no person: *There is no-one at home.*

noose *(rhymes with goose)*
a loop you make in a rope, with a knot that slides along and makes the loop smaller when you pull the rope.

nor *(rhymes with saw)*
a word you use when you are talking about neither one thing or the other: *He can neither swim nor ride a bike.*

normal (*nor-mal*)
usual or ordinary.

Word building: If something is normal, then it's what you **normally** do.

north
the direction you will face if you are facing east and you turn to your left.

Word use: The opposite of this is **south**. The other directions are **east** and **west**.

nose
the part of your face that you use for smelling and for breathing.

nostril (*nos-tril*)
one of the two openings of your nose.

not
1. in no way similar, or the opposite of what is mentioned: *This is **not** blue, it is red. | This is **not** my car.*
2. a word you use when you disagree, refuse to do something or forbid someone from doing something: *That's **not** true. | I'm **not** doing your chores for you. | You are **not** to tease your little brother.*

note
1. a short letter.
2. a musical sound: *Hold onto the last **note** of the song for as long as you can.*

notebook
1. a book you can use for writing notes.
2. a small, light computer that can be carried around easily.

nothing
not anything: *I'm bored because I have **nothing** to do.*

notice (*no-tis*)
1. a short piece of writing that warns people or that tells them about something. You put it on a wall or a board for everyone to read.
2. to know about something because you have seen, heard, smelt or felt it.

Word building: I **noticed**, I am **noticing**

nought (*rhymes with* **sort**)
the sign '0' that we use for zero.

noun
a type of word which names something. Some nouns are **proper nouns**, like 'Australia' or 'Jane', and some nouns are **common nouns**, like 'beauty' or 'dog'.

novel (*nov-el*)
a story someone makes up that is so long it fills a whole book.

now (*rhymes with* **cow**)
at this time: *Don't wait till later, do it **now**!*

nowadays
in the times we are living now: *You won't find any dinosaurs around here **nowadays**.*

nowhere
not anywhere: *There's **nowhere** to ride my skateboard around here.*

nuclear (*new-clee-ar*)
having to do with a very strong energy, released when you split an atom, that can do things with great force and power.

Word building: Some things which use **nuclear power** to work are **nuclear bombs**, **nuclear reactors** and **nuclear weapons**.

nude (*nood* or *nyood*)
without any clothes on.

Word use: Another word that means nearly the same is **naked**.

nuisance (*new-sense*)
someone or something that makes you feel annoyed or that gives you trouble.

nulla-nulla (*null-a-null-a*)
a heavy, wooden stick traditionally used by Aboriginal people in fighting and hunting.

Word use: This word comes from the Dharug language of New South Wales. See the map of Australian Aboriginal languages at the end of this book.

numb *(num)*

You're **numb** if you can't feel anything: *My toes were **numb** with cold.*

numbat *(num-bat)*

a small Australian marsupial that eats termites. It has red and brown fur, and white strips on its back, a long, bushy tail, and a long, pointed nose. It is endangered. See the table at the end of this book.

Word use: This word comes from the Nyungar language of Western Australia. See the map of Australian Aboriginal languages at the end of this book.

number *(num-ber)*

1. one of the words or signs that we use to count: *Six is a **number** and so is 60.*
2. a group or a large amount of anything: *There are a **number** of presents I want to buy.*

nun

one of a group of women who choose to live together, help people who are poor or sick, teach young children or think about God or religion.

nurse *(nerse)*

1. someone whose job is to care for people who are sick or hurt.
2. to hold someone in your arms.

Word building: I **nursed**, I am **nursing**

nursery *(nerse-e-ree)*

a room or place for children.

nut

1. a dry fruit with the part that you can eat shut inside a hard shell.
2. an everyday word for someone you think is strange or silly.

nylon *(ny-lon)*

a strong material made from coal. It is used to make clothes or things like the bristles of a brush.

Oo

Owls observe ostriches in the orchard.

oak
a large tree with very hard wood.

oar *(rhymes with **saw**)*
a pole that is wide and flat at one end. You use it for rowing a boat.

oasis *(o-**ay**-sis)*
a place in a desert where there is water, so trees can grow.

Word building: For more than one we use **oases**.

obedient *(o-**bee**-dee-ent)*
You're **obedient** if you do the things you're told to do: *The **obedient** children finished their work and then went out to play.*

Word building: You are obedient if you **obey** and show **obedience**.

Word use: The opposite of this is **disobedient**.

object[1] *(**ob**-ject)*
something that you can touch or see: *What is that red **object** on the shelf?*

object[2] *(ob-**ject**)*
to say that you don't agree or that you don't like something.

Word building: If you object to something, then you have an **objection** to it.

oblong *(**ob**-long)*
a shape with two long sides and two short sides like a door has.

Word use: Another word that means nearly the same is **rectangle**.

observe *(ob-**zerv**)*
to watch something or someone carefully.

Word building: I **observed**, I am **observing** | If you observe something, you make an **observation**.

obstacle *(**ob**-sta-kl)*
something that is in your way.

obtain *(ob-**tane**)*
to get something: *Did you manage to **obtain** tickets for the show?*

obvious *(**ob**-vee-us)*
Something is **obvious** if it is easy to see or to understand: *The magic trick was **obvious** after the magician showed me how it was done.*

occasion *(o-**kay**-zhon)*
a special time or event: *New Year's Eve is one **occasion** when we are allowed to stay up very late.*

occur *(o-**kur**)*
1. to happen: *The eclipse will **occur** at midnight.*
2. occur to, to come into the mind of: *It **occurs to** me that we should have taken the bus.*

Word building: it **occurred**, it is **occurring** | If something occurs, it is an **occurrence**.

ocean *(o-shon)*
a large area of salt water: *The Indian Ocean stretches from Australia across to Africa.*

ocean liner *(o-shon line-er)*
a large ship that carries people or cargo long distances.

o'clock *(o-clock)*
by the clock: *It is three o'clock.*

octopus *(oct-o-puss)*
a sea animal with eight long arms.
Word building: For more than one we use **octopuses**.

odd
1. unusual or strange.
2. A number is **odd** if you can't divide it by two: *Three, five, seven and nine are odd numbers.*
3. made into a pair that doesn't match: *I had to wear odd socks because I couldn't find the two red ones.*
Word use: The opposite of definition 2 is **even**.

odour *(o-da)*
a smell.

of *(ov)*
a word you use when giving more information about something, such as its type, what causes it or what it belongs to: *This is a can of beans. | I feel like I will die of hunger! | That is one of Lisa's toys. | She is one of us.*

off
1. not connected or on top of something, or away from something: *The handle fell off the door. | Get off the roof! | My cat got scared and ran off.*
2. not being used or not turned on: *The television is off. | The lights are off.*
Word use: The opposite of this is **on**.

offer *(off-er)*
1. to hold out something for someone else to take.
2. to say that you will do something: *I would offer to take your photo, but the battery in my camera has run out.*

office *(off-iss)*
1. a place where people work, usually at desks.
2. a place where you go to buy tickets or get information.

officer *(off-iss-er)*
someone who is in charge of other people, especially someone in the army, navy, air force or police force.

official *(o-fish-al)*
1. someone with a rank or who has authority to do a particular job: *My aunty works as a government official.*
2. properly approved or arranged: *After the robbery, we gave an official statement to the police.*
Word building: If something is done in an official way, it is done **officially**.

often *(off-en or off-ten)*
many times: *We often go to the beach in summer.*

oil
1. a thick liquid that is used in machines and engines to make them run smoothly.
2. a slippery liquid from an animal or plant that is used in cooking.
Word building: Something that's covered with oil is **oily**.

ointment *(oint-ment)*
a soft grease that you put on cuts and sores to help them heal.

okay
all right: *Are you okay? | This sandwich is okay but it would be nicer with a bit of cheese.*
Word use: Some people spell this **OK**.

old

1. Someone or something is **old** if they have lived or existed for a long time.
2. not new: *I gave my little sister most of my old toys.*

old-fashioned (*old*-fash-end)

Something is **old-fashioned** if it comes from an earlier time: *Have you ever tried to write using an old-fashioned pen and a bottle of ink?*

olive (*ol*-iv)

a tree that has a strong-tasting fruit which can be eaten or crushed for its oil.

Olympic Games (o-*lim*-pic games)

a big sporting competition between most countries of the world held every four years in a different country.

omelette (*om*-let)

a food you make by mixing eggs together and frying them in a pan.

omit (o-*mit*)

to leave something out.

Word building: I **omitted**, I am **omitting**

on

1. connected to something or placed at the top of something: *Can you put the handle back on the door?* | *The cat is sleeping on the roof.*
2. being used or ready to be used: *The computer is on.* | *Turn on the lights.*

Word use: The opposite of this is **off**.

once (*wunce*)

1. a single time: *The postman comes once a day.*
2. at one time: *There were once trees where all these houses are now.*

Word use: If you do something **at once**, you do it immediately.

one (*wun*)

1. the first number, 1.
2. a single person or thing: *Put the eggs in the basket one at a time.*

onion (*un*-yen)

a round white vegetable that grows under the ground and has a very strong smell.

online (on-*line*)

1. directly linked to a computer.
2. connected to the internet: *It'll just take me a minute to get online.*
3. having a site on the internet: *Macquarie are online — have you checked out their site yet?*

only (*ohn*-lee)

1. alone: *There is only one mango left.*
2. no more than: *We need to do only a little bit more practice.*
3. but or except: *She would have sung in the concert, only she lost her voice.*

onto (on-*too*)

to a place on: *Put the box onto the table.*

ooze

to flow or leak out slowly.

Word building: it **oozed**, it is **oozing**

open (o-*pen*)

1. not shut or locked.
2. to undo or unlock something.

opening (*ope*-en-ing)

a hole or space in something: *My guinea pig escaped through an opening in the fence.*

opera (*op*-ra)

a play that is put to music, with the actors singing most of the words.

operation (op-e-*ray*-shon)

You have an **operation** when a doctor puts you to sleep and, usually using special cutting tools, fixes up part of your body which is sick or hurt.

Word building: When doctors do an operation, they **operate** on someone.

a b c d e f g h i j k l m n **o** p q r s t u v w x y z

opinion (o-**pin**-yen)
what you think about something: *My **opinion** is that a dog is a better pet than a cat.*

opponent (o-**pone**-ent)
someone who is on the opposite side to you in a competition.

opposite (**op**-o-sit)
1. completely different: *She turned the car around and drove off in the **opposite** direction.* | *Happiness and sadness are **opposite** feelings.*
2. Something or someone is **opposite** when they face you: *She lives in the house **opposite** mine.*

or (aw)
a word you use when you are talking about a choice of different things: *We could see a movie **or** we could go to the zoo.* | *Will you wear the red hat **or** the green hat?*

orange (**o**-rinj)
1. a round, juicy fruit with a thick skin.
2. Something is **orange** if it's the reddish-gold colour of this fruit.

orbit (**or**-bit)
the curved path or line something in space follows as it is moving around the earth or the sun: *The moon is in **orbit** around the earth.*

orchard (**or**-chid)
a garden or farm where fruit trees are grown.

orchestra (**or**-kes-tra)
a big group of people who play musical instruments together.

order (**or**-der)
1. to tell someone that they must do something.
2. to ask for something from a shop or restaurant.

ordinary (**or**-din-ree)
usual, normal or not special.

ore (or)
a rock in the ground that contains a valuable metal.

organ (**or**-gan)
a musical instrument with black and white keys like a piano, pedals you push with your feet and a lot of pipes.

organisation (or-gan-ize-**ay**-shon)
1. the arrangement or running of something: *This performance took lots of **organisation**.*
2. something which is run or managed, like a company or a charity.

organise (**or**-gan-ize)
1. to order or arrange neatly: *She likes to **organise** her medals along the shelf.*
2. to arrange or plan: *He will **organise** the excursion.*

original (o-**rij**-i-nal)
1. first or earliest: *The **original** road was a winding dirt track.*
2. newly invented and not copied from something else.

orphan (**or**-fan)
a child whose parents are dead.

ostrich (**os**-trich)
a large bird with long legs, that lives in Africa. It can run fast, but it can't fly.

other (rhymes with **brother**)
1. different from this one: *They had better games in the **other** shop.*
2. extra or more: *You and one **other** person have won the prize.*

otherwise
1. if things were different: *I spent all my money, **otherwise** I could lend you the bus fare.*
2. in other ways: *The weather was a bit chilly, but it was an **otherwise** lovely picnic.*

ought *(ort)*
should: *You **ought** to help Dad make the dinner.*

our *(rhymes with **flower**)*
a word you use when you are talking about something that belongs to yourself and another person or people: *These are **our** books.*

ours *(rhymes with **flowers**)*
a word you use when you are talking about something that belongs to yourself and another person or people: *These sandwiches are **ours**.*

ourselves *(**our**-selvz)*
a word you use when you are talking about yourself and others doing things to yourselves or doing something by yourselves without help: *We slipped in the mud and hurt **ourselves**. | Come on guys, we can do it **ourselves**!*

out
1. away from: *The family ran **out** of the burning house.*
2. so that it can be seen: *After the rain the sun came **out**.*
3. not alight or burning: *The fire was **out**.*
4. not switched on: *The lights were **out**.*

outback *(**out**-back)*
the part of the country that is far away from the cities and from the sea.

outdoors *(out-**doors**)*
outside, or out of a building such as a house: *We can't play **outdoors** when it is raining. | Let's go **outdoors** and have a walk.*
Word use: The opposite of this is **indoors**.

outer
further out, or on the outside: *Close the **outer** gate when you leave.*

outline *(**out**-line)*
a line that shows the shape of something: *We drew an **outline** of Australia.*

outside
1. the outer part or side: *This lolly has caramel on the inside and chocolate on the **outside**.*
2. outdoors, or to the outer part: *Let's go **outside** to play.*
Word use: The opposite of this is **inside**.

oval *(**o**-val)*
1. shaped like an egg. See the picture at the end of this book.
2. a field for playing sport on.

oven *(**uv**-en)*
the part of a stove where you bake or roast food.

over *(**o**-va)*
1. above: *Let's put some balloons **over** the door.*
2. around the top of: *I climbed **over** the fence.*
3. more than: *There were **over** 200 people at the wedding.*

overalls *(**o**-ver-alls)*
loose trousers with a high front to cover your chest, and shoulder straps. You can wear them over your other clothes.

overcoat *(**o**-ver-cote)*
a coat you wear over your ordinary clothes to keep you warm in cold weather.

overtake *(o-ver-**take**)*
to catch up with someone and go past them: *If you run as fast as you can, you can **overtake** the leader.*
Word building: I **overtook**, I have **overtaken**, I am **overtaking**

owe *(rhymes with **go**)*
to have to pay someone back: *I **owe** you the money I borrowed in the shop.*

owl *(rhymes with **growl**)*
a bird with large eyes, that hunts for small animals at night.

own *(rhymes with **bone**)*
1. to have something for yourself: *Does anyone here **own** this hat?*
2. If you do something on your **own** you do it alone, without help.
Word building: If you own something, then you are its **owner**.

ox
a strong animal of the cattle family that is used to pull carts.
Word use: For more than one we use **oxen**.

oyster *(**oy**-ster)*
a sea animal you can eat, that lives inside a pair of shells which you often find joined to rocks.

ozone layer *(**o**-zone **lay**-er)*
the outer area of the earth's atmosphere which protects the earth from the harmful rays of the sun.

Pp

Playful penguins paint prickly pineapples.

pace
1. one walking step.
2. the speed at which something moves.

pack
1. to put things into a bag or a box or something, so that you can move them.
2. a bag that you use to carry things on your back.
3. a group of animals that live together and find food together.
4. a set of things: *We need a **pack** of playing cards for this game.*

package *(pack-ij)*
something wrapped up in paper or cardboard, ready to be posted.

packet
a small package of anything.

pad
1. sheets of writing paper joined together at one edge.
2. a soft, thick lump of material that you use to protect something.

paddle[1] *(padd-l)*
a short oar that you use to make a canoe move through water.

paddle[2] *(padd-l)*
to walk in shallow water.
Word building: I **paddled**, I am **paddling**

paddock *(padd-ik)*
a large area of land with a fence around it and grass growing on it for sheep or cattle to eat.

padlock *(pad-lock)*
a lock with a metal loop that you can snap shut.

page
a sheet of paper in a book, magazine, newspaper or pad.

pain
the feeling you have when you are hurt.
Word building: If something causes you pain, it is **painful**.
Word use: Don't confuse **pain** with **pane**.

paint
liquid that you can brush on to change the colour of something.

painting *(paint-ing)*
a picture that you make using paint.

pair
two things of the same kind that go together.
Word use: Don't confuse this with **pear**.

palace *(pal-ess)*
a big house where a king, queen or some other very important person lives.

pale

Something is **pale** if it's nearly white or if it doesn't have much colour.

Word building: more pale = **paler**, most pale = **palest**

palm[1] *(parm)*

the inside of your hand, from your wrist to where your fingers start.

palm[2] *(parm)*

a tall plant with large leaves and no branches.

pan

1. a broad, shallow dish that you use for cooking.
2. any container shaped like this.

pancake *(pan-cake)*

a thin, flat cake made from flour, eggs and milk and fried in a pan.

pane

one sheet of glass in a window.

Word use: Don't confuse this with **pain**.

panic *(pan-ic)*

sudden fear that is so strong it makes you do things without thinking.

pants

1. trousers.
2. underpants.

paper *(pay-per)*

stuff made from straw, small bits of wood, rags and other things, pressed into thin sheets. We use it for writing and printing on, or for wrapping things in.

parachute *(pa-ra-shoot)*

a large umbrella-shaped piece of cloth tied to your back that unfolds and slows your fall when you jump out of a plane.

parade *(pa-rade)*

a group of people, often soldiers, marching along the street with a crowd watching them go past.

paragraph *(pa-ra-graf)*

a piece of writing about one thing. It starts on a new line.

parallel *(pa-ra-lel)*

Things are **parallel** if they are the same distance from each other all the way along: *A railway track is made up of two **parallel** lines.*

paralysed *(pa-ra-lized)*

not able to move: *His legs are **paralysed** and he has to use a wheelchair.*

Word building: If you're paralysed, you suffer from **paralysis** *(pa-**ral**-i-sis)*.

parcel *(par-sel)*

something wrapped up in paper, ready for posting or giving to someone.

pardon *(pard-n)*

to forgive someone and not punish them.

parent *(pair-rent)*

a person who has children.

park

1. a piece of land for everybody to use.
2. to put or leave your car or bicycle somewhere.

parliament *(par-la-ment)*

the group of people we choose to make our laws.

parrot *(pa-rot)*

a bird with brightly coloured feathers and a curved beak. You can teach some parrots to talk.

parsley *(parce-lee)*

a plant used in cooking or for making food look nice.

part

a bit of anything, not the whole thing.

Word building: If part of something has been taken, then it's **partly** gone.

particular *(par-**tick**-yoo-lar)*

1. one single thing out of many: *I am looking for a **particular** book by this author.*
2. more than usual or special: *Pay **particular** attention to the first part of the film.*

Word building: If something is of particular interest to you, it is **particularly** interesting.

partner *(**part**-ner)*

someone who shares or does something with you.

party *(**par**-tee)*

a group of people who have come together to enjoy themselves or to celebrate something: *I'm going to invite you to my birthday **party**.*

Word building: For more than one we use **parties**.

pass *(parce)*

1. to go by someone or something: *We always **pass** them on the way to school.*
2. to succeed in something you try to do: *I'm sure I'll **pass** the test.*
3. to put something into someone's hand: ***Pass** me the salt please.*

passage *(**pass**-ij)*

a way of going from one room or place to another one, like a corridor.

passenger *(**pass**-en-jer)*

someone, not the driver, who travels in a car or on a ship, bus or plane.

passer-by

someone who passes by: *A kind **passer-by** helped Dad start the car.*

Word building: For more than one we use **passers-by**.

passionfruit *(**pash**-on-froot)*

a small fruit with purple skin. It has a soft yellow part inside and black seeds that you can eat.

password *(**parce**-werd)*

a secret group of letters or numbers you use to show who you are when you are doing something like logging on to your computer.

past *(rhymes with **last**)*

1. time that has gone by: *I walk to school now, but in the **past** Mum or Dad always drove me.*
2. right by you: *We watched the parade go **past**.*

pasta *(**pars**-ta or **pas**-ta)*

a food made from flour, water and sometimes egg as well. Spaghetti and macaroni are two sorts of pasta.

paste *(payst)*

1. flour and water mixed together and used for sticking paper onto things.
2. something that has been made very soft and smooth like toothpaste.

pastry *(**pay**-stree)*

a mixture of flour, water and fat that you cook as a crust for pies and tarts.

pasture *(**parce**-cher)*

land with plenty of grass for feeding cattle or sheep.

patch

1. anything you use to mend a hole or a weak part of something: *I'll sew a **patch** on your jeans.*
2. a small piece of something: *I'll use this **patch** of garden to grow vegetables.*

Word building: For more than one we use **patches**.

patent *(pay-tent)*
permission given by the government to be the only person allowed to make or sell an invention.

path *(parth)*
a narrow way for walking from one place to another.

patient *(pay-shent)*
1. someone who is being looked after by a doctor.
2. You are **patient** if you can wait for a long time without getting cross.
Word building: If you are patient, you have a lot of **patience**.

patio *(pat-ee-o or pay-shee-o)*
an open part of your house with a floor of cement, bricks or tiles, where you can eat outside.
Word building: For more than one we use **patios**.

patrol *(pa-trol)*
to go around a place at special times to make sure there is no trouble: *The police patrol this street twice each night.*
Word building: I **patrolled**, I am **patrolling**

pattern *(patt-n)*
a drawing someone does on something to make it look nice. The shapes they use are often repeated over and over again.

pause *(porze)*
a short rest or stop.

pavlova *(pav-lo-va)*
an Australian dessert made of a large, round meringue, and usually topped with cream and fruit.

paw *(por)*
the foot of an animal with nails or claws.
Word use: Don't confuse this with **pour**, **poor** or **pore**.

pay
to give money to someone when they give you something in return.
Word building: I **paid**, I am **paying** | When you pay for something, you make a **payment**.

PE *(pee ee)*
sport and other forms of exercise, usually done at school.
Word building: This is a short way of saying **physical education**.

pea *(pee)*
a small, round, green vegetable which grows in a pod.

peace *(peece)*
1. a time when there is no war.
2. a time when everything is quiet and still.
Word building: If there is peace, then everything is **peaceful**.
Word use: Don't confuse **peace** with **piece**.

peach *(peech)*
a round, sweet fruit with furry skin and one large seed.
Word building: For more than one we use **peaches**.

peacock *(pee-cock)*
a large male bird with long, brightly coloured feathers in its tail which it can open up like a fan.
Word building: The female is a **peahen**.

peak
the pointed top of a mountain.

peanut *(pee-nut)*
a small nut which you can eat, that grows under the ground.

pear *(rhymes with care)*
a juicy fruit with thin, green or brown skin. It is round at the bottom and gets smaller near its stalk.
Word use: Don't confuse this with **pair**.

pearl *(perl)*
a hard, shiny, white ball that grows inside the shell of some oysters. We use pearls in jewellery.

pebble *(pebb-l)*
a small, smooth, round stone.

peculiar *(pe-kew-lee-ar)*
strange or odd.

pedal
1. a lever that you use with your foot: *The pedal on my bike needs to be fixed.* | *Dad showed me how to work the pedal on our sewing machine.*
2. to use a pedal to make something move or work: *Pedal harder, we're almost at the top of the hill!*
Word building: I **pedalled**, I am **pedalling**

pedestrian *(pe-dess-tree-an)*
someone who walks somewhere in a town or city: *The pedestrian looked to the right and then to the left before crossing the busy street.*

peep
to look quickly from the place where you're hiding or to look through a small hole: *Peep out from behind the bush, but don't let them see you.* | *They tried to peep through the keyhole but they couldn't see anything.*

pelican *(pel-i-can)*
a large bird that swims in the sea. It has a pouch hanging under its bill for holding the fish it catches.

pen¹
an object like a pencil that you use for writing and drawing with ink.

pen²
an area surrounded by a fence or a wall for animals on a farm: *I help clean out the pens every morning.*

penalty *(pen-al-tee)*
what you have to pay for doing something wrong.
Word building: For more than one we use **penalties**.

pencil *(pen-sil)*
a thin, pointed piece of wood with a black or coloured centre. You use it for writing or drawing.

penguin *(pen-gwin)*
a type of bird that lives near the South Pole. It swims in the sea but it can't fly.

penny
a coin that is worth only a small amount. It used to be used in Australia and still is in some other countries.
Word building: For more than one we use **pennies**.

people *(pee-pl)*
humans like you and me.

pepper *(pepp-er)*
a black or a white powder with a hot taste, that you use in cooking or sprinkle on your food. It can make you sneeze.

per cent
in every hundred: *We worked out that ten per cent of 200 is 20.*
Word use: Some people write this as **percent**.

perch
a rod for birds to rest on.
Word building: For more than one we use **perches**.

perfect *(per-fect)*
Something is **perfect** if it's the very best it can be and if there is nothing wrong with it.
Word building: Anything that is perfect has **perfection**.

a
b
c
d
e
f
g
h
i
j
k
l
m
n
o
p
q
r
s
t
u
v
w
x
y
z

perform *(per-form)*
to do something in front of a group of people.

Word building: If you perform, then you are a **performer** and you give a **performance**.

perfume *(per-fume)*
a liquid with a sweet smell, that people put on their skin.

perhaps
maybe or possibly: *Perhaps Jack can help you with your homework.*

period
1. any portion or part of time: *After all our hard work, we enjoyed a period of rest and relaxation.*
2. a particular time in history: *I'm interested in the ancient Roman period.*

permanent *(per-ma-nent)*
Something is **permanent** if it lasts for a very long time or all the time: *My sister doesn't need pocket money anymore — she's got a permanent job at the bank.*

Word use: The opposite of this is **temporary**.

permit *(per-mit)*
1. to let someone do something: *Will your parents permit you to stay the night at my house?*
2. *(per-mit)* a special piece of paper that allows you to do something: *This permit lets me park in the school grounds.*

Word building: I **permitted**, I am **permitting** | If you permit someone to do something you give them **permission**.

persist *(per-sist)*
to keep doing something, even though it may be difficult: *I'll persist with this puzzle until I solve it.*

Word building: If you persist, then you're **persistent** and you have a lot of **persistence**.

person *(per-son)*
a human like you or me.

personal
1. private or having to do with a particular person: *She keeps her personal possessions in the top drawer.* | *I have a personal matter that I need to speak to you about.*
2. directed to a particular person in a rude way: *You shouldn't make personal remarks during a debate.*

personal best
an athlete's best performance: *That swimming race was a personal best for Josie.*

persuade *(per-swade)*
to get someone to do or to believe something: *Try to persuade him to come too.*

Word building: I **persuaded**, I am **persuading** | When you persuade someone, then you use your power of **persuasion** *(per-sway-zhon)*.

Pesach *(pay-sahk)*
a festival when Jewish people celebrate the saving of their people in ancient times. It is also called **Passover**.

pest
someone or something that annoys or hurts you.

pet
1. an animal that lives with you and that you love.
2. an everyday word for someone who is given special attention: *I think Maurice is the teacher's pet.*

petal *(pet-l)*
any of the soft, coloured parts of a flower.

petrol *(pet-rol)*
the liquid made from oil that is often used to make a car's engine run.

Word building: The place where you buy petrol is called a **petrol station**.

phone *(fone)*
a short way of writing **telephone**.

photograph *(fo-ta-graf)*
a picture you take with a camera.
Word building: This word is often shortened to **photo**.

phrase
a small group of words that go together, but do not form a complete sentence. In the sentence 'We camped by the river', 'by the river' is a phrase.

physical *(fiz-i-cal)*
Something is **physical** if it has to do with your body: *Running is hard physical exercise.*

physics *(fiz-ics)*
the science of heat, light, electricity, movement and other forms of matter and energy.
Word building: Someone who studies physics is a **physicist**.

piano *(pee-an-o)*
a large musical instrument you play by pressing down the white or black keys with your fingers.
Word building: Someone who plays the piano is a **pianist**.

pick
1. to choose or to decide on someone or something: *Pick me to be your partner.*
2. to take or gather something: *As soon as they are ripe, we can pick those cherries.*

picnic *(pic-nic)*
a trip to the beach or a park, to have a meal in the open air.

picture *(pic-cher)*
a drawing, a painting or a photo.

pie
fruit, vegetables or meat covered with pastry and baked in an oven.

piece *(peece)*
a bit or part of something.
Word use: Don't confuse this with **peace**.

pierce *(rhymes with fierce)*
to go into or through something sharply: *Don't let the pin pierce the balloon.*
Word building: it **pierced**, it is **piercing**

pig
1. a farm animal with a flat nose, called a snout, and a curly tail.
2. an everyday word for someone who is dirty, selfish or greedy.
Word building: A young pig is a **piglet**.
Word use: The male is a **boar** and the female is a **sow**.

pigeon *(pij-en)*
a plump bird that some people keep to fly in races.

pikelet *(pike-let)*
a small, sweet pancake.

pile
a lot of things lying one on top of the other.

pillar *(pill-ar)*
a long, thin support for holding up part of a building.

pillow *(pill-oe)*
a soft cushion you rest your head on when you're in bed.

pilot *(py-lot)*
someone who flies a plane.

pimple *(pim-pl)*
a small, red or white spot on someone's skin.

pin
1. a thin piece of metal with a pointed end that you use to join things together.
2. to fasten or hold securely in position: *I will pin this label onto your jacket. | If that branch falls, it could pin you to the ground.*
Word building: I **pinned**, I am **pinning**

PIN *(pin)*

a group of numbers or letters you use to show who you are when you are doing something like getting money from an ATM.

Word use: Another way of saying this is **PIN number**, although **PIN** actually stands for **Personal Identification Number**.

pinch

1. to squeeze someone's skin so tightly between your finger and thumb that you hurt them.
2. an everyday word which means to steal something.

pine[1]

a tree with leaves that are like green needles and cones instead of flowers.

pine[2]

to want something very much: *The children began to pine for all their friends at home.*

Word building: I **pined**, I am **pining**

pineapple *(pine-ap-l)*

a large, yellow fruit with a rough skin and a sweet, juicy part inside. It grows in hot places.

ping-pong

a game like tennis that you play indoors on a table, using small bats and a very light plastic ball.

Word use: Another name for this is **table tennis**.

pink

pale red.

pioneer *(py-o-near)*

the first person to explore or live in a place and to make it safer for other people to follow.

pipe

1. a tube for taking water or gas from one place to another.
2. a small bowl with a tube joined to it for smoking tobacco.

pirate *(pie-rat)*

1. a robber who attacks ships at sea and steals their cargo.
2. to make a copy of something such as a DVD, computer game, CD or video when you don't have permission from its maker to do so.

Word building: I **pirated**, I am **pirating** | If you are a pirate, or if you pirate something, you can get in trouble for **piracy**.

pistol *(pist-l)*

a small gun that can be fired with one hand.

pitch *(pich)*

1. to throw or toss something: *Pitch the ball to the person batting.*
2. a piece of ground marked out for a game such as cricket or football.

pity *(pit-ee)*

the feeling of sorrow you have for people who are sad or in trouble or pain.

pizza *(peet-sa)*

a piece of round, flat dough covered with tomato, sausage or cheese and baked in an oven.

place

1. the spot to put something: *Have I put the cursor in the right place?*
2. where you come in a race or a competition: *I got second place in my heat.*

plague *(playg)*

an illness that can kill people and which spreads very quickly.

plain

1. easy to see, to hear or to understand.
2. simple or ordinary: *I'm going to wear plain white socks.*
3. a large, flat piece of land.

Word use: Don't confuse this with **plane[1]** or **plane[2]**.

plait *(plat)*
to twist together three or more pieces of something so that they cross over and under each other: *Will you **plait** my hair for me, please?*

plan
an idea or drawing for how something should be done or made: *I have thought of a **plan** for our next holiday.* | *Has the architect finished the **plan** for your new kitchen?*

plane[1]
a machine with wings and propellers or jet engines, which flies through the air.
Word building: This word is a short way of saying **aeroplane**.
Word use: Don't confuse this with **plain** or **plane**[2].

plane[2]
a tool you use to make wood smooth.
Word use: Don't confuse this with **plain** or **plane**[1].

planet *(plan-et)*
any of the large objects in space that move around the sun like the earth does.

plant
a living thing which grows in the ground the way a tree or a flower does.

plaster *(plar-ster)*
a mixture of water and white powder used to cover and hold in place a broken bone. Sometimes sand is added to the mixture and it is used to cover walls and ceilings. It is soft when you spread it but it goes hard as it dries.

plastic *(plas-tic)*
a material that is made in a factory and can be pulled into many different shapes while it is still soft.

plate
a round, flat dish for holding food.

platform *(plat-form)*
1. a raised floor, such as a stage in a hall or a theatre.
2. the part of a railway station next to, but higher than, the tracks.

platypus *(plat-a-pus)*
an Australian animal with fur and with feet and a bill like a duck's. The mother platypus lays eggs like a duck and feeds its babies with its own milk like a cat.
Word building: For more than one we use **platypuses**.

play
1. to do something you enjoy or to take part in a game: *I love to **play** elastics at lunchtime.*
2. to perform on a musical instrument: *I **play** the flute.*
3. a story that people act out, often in a theatre.
Word building: If a person plays, they are a **player**, and if they like to play, then they are **playful**. People who play together are **playmates**.

playground *(play-grownd; the last part rhymes with **round**)*
a place outside with swings and other things like that, where children can play.

pleasant *(plez-ant)*
Something is **pleasant** if you enjoy it or if it pleases you.

please *(pleeze)*
1. to make someone happy or content.
2. a polite way of asking someone to do something: *Come over here, **please**.*
Word building: I **pleased**, I am **pleasing** | If something pleases you, you are **pleased**.

pleasure *(plezh-er)*
a feeling of happiness or enjoyment.

165

a
b
c
d
e
f
g
h
i
j
k
l
m
n
o
p
q
r
s
t
u
v
w
x
y
z

a
b
c
d
e
f
g
h
i
j
k
l
m
n
o
p
q
r
s
t
u
v
w
x
y
z

plenty *(plen-tee)*
a large amount or more than enough of something: *I'll give you some of the peaches from our tree because we have* **plenty**.

plough *(rhymes with* **cow***)*
a machine that a farmer uses for digging the soil.

pluck
to play the notes on the strings of a musical instrument like a guitar or a harp by pulling at them with your fingers.

plug
1. something you use to stop the water from running out of the hole in a bath or basin.
2. the part at the end of an electric wire that fits into the place on the wall where electricity can go through it.

plum
a soft fruit with a smooth skin and one hard seed inside.

plumber *(plumm-er)*
someone whose job is to put in the pipes that carry water and waste around a building and who comes to fix them when something goes wrong.

plump
rather fat, with a round body.

plunge *(plunj)*
to dip or dive suddenly into something, usually into water.
Word building: I **plunged**, I am **plunging**

plus
add: *9* **plus** *1 is 10.*
Word use: The opposite of this is **minus**.

pocket *(pock-et)*
a part like a small bag or pouch, sewn into some clothes. You use it for keeping things in.

pocket money
1. a small amount of money that is given weekly to a child by their parent or someone who looks after them.
2. spending money.

pod
a long seed case on some plants, that has seeds like peas or beans inside.

poem *(po-em)*
a piece of writing set out in a special way. It often has lines that are the same length and end in words that rhyme.
Word building: A poem is written by a **poet**.

poetry *(poe-e-tree)*
writing which expresses feelings and thoughts about people and things that happen, especially your own thoughts. See the 'Types of writing and speaking' table at the end of this book.

point
1. a sharp end: *Push the* **point** *of the needle through the cloth.*
2. a mark you use to keep the score in a game.
3. to show where something is using your finger or a sign: **Point** *to the part of your arm that's hurting.*
4. to aim a weapon at something or someone.

poison *(poy-zon)*
something that can kill you or make you very ill if you swallow it.
Word building: Anything that contains poison is **poisonous**.

poke
to push something quite hard: **Poke** *the fire with that stick.*
Word building: I **poked**, I am **poking**

pole[1]
a long, thin piece of wood or metal: *A flag flies from that* **pole**.

pole²
one of the two ends of the earth. The **North Pole** is at the top and the **South Pole** is at the bottom.

Word building: Anything to do with one of the Poles is **polar**.

police *(po-leece)*
the people whose job is to prevent crime.

polish *(pol-ish)*
to make something shiny by rubbing it, often with a special liquid or wax.

polite *(po-lite)*
You are **polite** if you behave in a thoughtful way towards other people: *The **polite** child stood up and let the old person sit down.*

Word building: When you are polite, you behave **politely** and with a lot of **politeness**.

Word use: The opposite of this is **rude**.

politician
someone who works in politics.

politics
the leading and managing of a country or a state: *My cousin has a job in state **politics**.*

Word building: Something that happens in politics is **political**.

pollen *(poll-en)*
the yellow seed dust in flowers.

pollute *(po-loot)*
to spoil something or make it dirty: *The fumes of petrol from cars **pollute** the air.*

Word building: it **polluted**, it is **polluting**

pollution *(pol-oo-shun)*
something that pollutes the environment, spoiling it and making it dirty: ***Pollution** from the factory has spoiled the water in the river.*

pond
an area of water that's smaller than a lake.

pool
a small area of water, especially one for swimming in.

poor *(por)*
1. You are **poor** if you don't have much money.
2. not very good: *This jacket is of very **poor** quality — you should return it to the shop.*

Word use: Don't confuse this with **paw**, **pour** or **pore**.

pop¹
1. to make a short, loud sound: *That balloon is going to **pop**!*
2. to come, go or put something quickly or suddenly: *I'm just going to **pop** out to the post office.* | ***Pop** the book on the table.*

Word building: I **popped**, I am **popping**

pop²
music that is very popular at a particular time, especially among young people.

popular *(pop-yu-lar)*
Something or someone is **popular** if many or most people like them.

population *(pop-yu-lay-shon)*
the people living in a place: *Most of Australia's **population** live in cities.*

porch
the covered part at the door of a building.

Word building: For more than one we use **porches**.

pore *(por)*
one of the tiny openings in your skin.

pork
the meat from a pig.

porridge *(po-rij)*
a hot food that you eat for breakfast, made from oats cooked in water or milk.

port
a harbour where ships load and unload.

portrait *(por-trit)*
a picture of someone.

position *(po-**zish**-on)*
1. a place: *Plant these flowers in a sunny position.*
2. the way you arrange your body: *I could not get into a comfortable position on the hard seat.*

positive *(**poz**-i-tiv)*
1. very sure or certain: *I am positive that this is the right street.*
2. saying or meaning yes: *Just nod your head to give a positive answer.*
Word use: The opposite of definition 2 is **negative**.

possess *(po-**zess**)*
to have or own.
Word building: If you possess something, then it is your **possession**.

possible *(**poss**-i-bl)*
Something is **possible** if it can happen or can be done: *Would it be possible for you to finish your homework before dinner?*
Word building: Something that is possible will **possibly** happen.
Word use: Don't confuse **possible** with **probable**, which means *likely* to happen rather than simply *able* to happen. There is a stronger chance of something happening if it's **probable**.

possum *(**poss**-um)*
an Australian animal with a long tail, that lives in trees and feeds at night. The female has a pouch to carry her babies.

post[1] *(rhymes with **most**)*
a pole of wood or metal with one end stuck into the ground.

post[2] *(rhymes with **most**)*
1. to send a letter, parcel or card to someone.
2. to send a message over the internet or put something on the internet for other people to see: *I'm going to post my comments on the web page.*

postbox
a letterbox in a public place where you can post mail.

postcard *(**post**-card)*
a card that you post, which has a picture on one side and a space on the other side for you to write on.

poster *(**post**-er)*
a large picture or notice printed on paper and put on a wall where people can see it.

post office
a building where you can post letters and parcels and buy the things you need to package and post things.

postpone *(post-**pone**)*
to put something off until a later time: *We will have to postpone the sports day if it rains.*
Word building: I **postponed**, I am **postponing**

pot
1. a round, deep container: *Cook the spaghetti in the pot.* | *I moved the flower pot into the shade.*
2. to put or plant in a pot: *You need to pot those plants before they grow too big.*
Word building: I **potted**, I am **potting**

potato *(po-**tay**-toe)*
a vegetable that is white inside and which grows under the ground.
Word building: For more than one we use **potatoes**.

potoroo *(pot-o-roo)*
a small, long-nosed animal with a pointed head that lives in thick grass. It sleeps during the day and comes out at night. It is endangered. See the table at the end of this book.
Word use: This word comes from the Dharug language of New South Wales. See the map of Australian Aboriginal languages at the end of this book.

pouch *(powch)*
1. a small bag.
2. a pocket of skin that some animals have on their bodies. Female kangaroos and other marsupials have a pouch to carry their babies.
Word building: For more than one we use **pouches**.

poultry *(pol-tree)*
birds that are kept for their eggs or meat, such as chickens, ducks and turkeys.

pounce *(pownce)*
to jump on something or someone suddenly.
Word building: I **pounced**, I am **pouncing**

pound[1] *(rhymes with round)*
to hit something hard many times: *The angry man began to pound on the door with his hand.*

pound[2]
1. an old-fashioned measure of how heavy things are. One pound is just under half a kilogram.
2. a type of money that was once used in Australia and is still used in some other countries.

pour *(por)*
1. to tip or flow from one place to another place: *Pour some water into this bucket.*
2. to rain very hard.
Word use: Don't confuse this with **paw**, **poor** or **pore**.

powder *(pow-der)*
something that is made up of many tiny, loose, dry bits.

power *(pow-er)*
1. strength: *Some people have great power in their arms and can lift heavy things.*
2. If you have **power**, you are able to do something because you've been given the authority to do it: *A judge has the power to send a criminal to jail.*
Word building: Someone or something that has power is **powerful**.

practical
1. interested in and good at useful work: *Charlie will help us, he's a very practical person.*
2. sensible and realistic: *That's not a very practical way to solve the problem.*
Word building: If you talk about whether something is practical or not, you talk about its **practicality**.

practice *(prac-tiss)*
something that you do many times so that it gets better: *We have choir practice every Friday afternoon.*
Word use: Don't confuse this with **practise**.

practise *(prac-tiss)*
to do something over and over again so that you get better at doing it: *If I want to get better at playing the piano I must practise more.*
Word building: I **practised**, I am **practising**
Word use: Don't confuse this with **practice**.

praise *(praze)*
to say that you think something is very good.
Word building: I **praised**, I am **praising**

prance *(rhymes with dance)*
to leap about.
Word building: I **pranced**, I am **prancing**

prawn *(rhymes with **horn**)*
a small sea animal that you can eat. Its body is covered by a soft shell.

pray
to talk to God.
Word building: When you pray, you are saying a **prayer** *(rhymes with **care**)*.
Word use: Don't confuse **pray** with **prey**.

preach *(preech)*
to give a talk about something serious to people, often in a church.

precious *(**presh**-us)*
very special or valuable: *That vase is **precious** so you must be careful not to knock it over.*

predator *(**pred**-a-ter)*
an animal that hunts other animals for food.
Word building: If something is a predator, it is **predatory**.

predict *(pre-**dict**)*
to say what will happen in the future.
Word building: If you predict something, then you make a **prediction**. If it's easy to see what will happen, it's **predictable**.

prefer *(pre-**fer**)*
to like one thing more than another thing: *I **prefer** swimming to playing tennis.*
Word building: If you prefer something, then you have a **preference** for it and you think it's **preferable** *(**pref**-ra-bl)*.

pregnant *(**preg**-nant)*
A female is **pregnant** if she is going to have a baby.

prehistoric *(pree-his-**torric**)*
from a time before history was written.

premier *(**prem**-ee-er)*
1. first or best.
2. the leader of a State's government.
Word use: Don't confuse this with **premiere**.

premiere *(prem-ee-**air**)*
the first time something is shown or done: *Many famous people came to the **premiere** of the film.*
Word use: Don't confuse this with **premier**.

prepare *(pre-**pair**)*
to make something ready.
Word building: I **prepared**, I am **preparing** | When you prepare for something, you make **preparations** for it.

preposition *(prep-o-**zish**-on)*
a word such as 'to' or 'in' that you place before a noun to show its relationship to other words in the sentence.

preschool *(pre-skool)*
a place some young children go for a year or so before they start primary school.

prescription *(pre-**skrip**-shon)*
the instruction a doctor writes to a chemist for a medicine.

present[1] *(**prez**-ent)*
1. now or at this time: *She is out at **present**, but I'll give her the message as soon as she comes home.*
2. here: *Is everyone **present**?*

present[2] *(**prez**-ent)*
1. a gift or something special that you give to someone: *Here's your birthday **present**.*
2. *(pre-**zent**)* to give something in a formal way: *Our school principal **presented** the prizes.*

preserve *(pre-**zerv**)*
1. to keep something safe.
2. to do something to food to stop it from going bad.
Word building: I **preserved**, I am **preserving**

president *(**prez**-i-dent)*
1. someone elected to rule a country that does not have a king or queen.
2. someone who is in charge of a business company or a club.

press
1. to push on something: *If you **press** the black button the doorbell will ring.*
2. to use an iron to make clothes flat and smooth.

pressure *(presh-er)*
the force that you use to press down on something.

pretend *(pre-tend)*
to make it seem as if something is real when it isn't: *If they come in you could **pretend** to be asleep.*

pretty *(pritt-ee)*
pleasant to look at: *Aya's dress is very **pretty**.*
Word building: more pretty = **prettier**, most pretty = **prettiest**

prevent *(pre-vent)*
to keep something from happening: *There is a fence along the top of the cliff to **prevent** people from falling off the edge.*

preview *(**pree**-vew; the last part rhymes with **new**)*
a special look at something before everyone else: *The newspaper reporter was invited to a **preview** of the new film.*

prey *(pray)*
any animal that is hunted and eaten by another animal.
Word use: Don't confuse this with **pray**.

price
the amount of money that you have to pay for something.

prick
to make a small hole with a sharp point: *Be careful that you don't **prick** your finger with that needle.*

prickle *(prik-l)*
something with a sharp point, such as a thorn.

pride
the good feeling you have when you've done something well: *I was full of **pride** when the teacher praised my work.*

priest *(preest)*
a person who teaches people about their religion.

primary *(**prime**-ree or **prime**-a-ree)*
Something is **primary** if it is first. A primary school is the first school you go to, until you're about twelve. Then you go to secondary school.

prime minister *(prime **min**-i-ster)*
the leader of the government in some countries, including Australia.

prince
the son of a king or queen.

princess *(**prin**-sess)*
the daughter of a king or queen.

principal *(**prin**-si-pl)*
1. main or most important.
2. the person in charge of a school.
Word use: Don't confuse this with **principle**.

principle *(**prin**-si-pl)*
a rule: *They follow the **principle** of always trying to help others.*
Word use: Don't confuse this with **principal**.

print
to write with letters that are not joined together.

printer *(**print**-er)*
a machine that is attached to your computer and prints what is on your computer screen so that you can read it on paper.

prison *(**priz**-en)*
a place where people who have broken the law are kept locked up as a punishment.
Word building: Someone who is kept in a prison is **imprisoned**, and is a **prisoner**.
Word use: Another word that means the same is **jail**.

private (*pry*-vit)
Something is **private** if it belongs to somebody and not to everybody: *Keep out! This is **private** land.*

prize
a reward you get when you win something.

probable (*prob*-a-bl)
likely or expected to happen: *It is **probable** that we will go to the beach tomorrow if it is a hot day.*

Word building: If something is probable, then it will **probably** happen.

Word use: Don't confuse **probable** with **possible**, which simply means *able* to happen rather than *likely* to happen. There is a greater chance of something happening if it is **probable**.

problem (*prob*-lem)
something that makes you worried because it is difficult to understand or to do.

procedure (pro-*seed*-yer)
1. the way of doing something: *What is the **procedure** for listening to voicemail messages on this phone?*
2. writing which tells how to do or make something. See the 'Types of writing or speaking' table at the end of this book.

proceed (pro-*seed*)
to go on: *If you **proceed** along this road you will come to a bridge.*

procession (pro-*sesh*-on)
a group of people or cars moving along in a line.

prod
to push someone or something with a finger or a stick.

produce (pro-*duce*)
1. to make something: *They **produce** computers in that factory.*
2. to pull out something and show it: *I hope the magician can **produce** a rabbit from a black hat.*

Word building: I **produced**, I am **producing** | Something that you can produce is a **product**.

professor (pro-*fess*-er)
a university teacher of the highest rank.

profit (*prof*-it)
the extra money that you get when you sell something for more than it cost you to make or to buy: *If you buy that for $8 and then sell it for $10 you will make a **profit** of $2.*

Word use: Don't confuse this with **prophet**.

program (*pro*-gram)
1. a show on television or radio.
2. a list for the audience at a play or concert telling them about the performers and what they will do.
3. a set of stored instructions inside a computer that tells the computer how to do things.

Word building: Someone whose job it is to write programs for a computer is called a **computer programmer**.

Word use: Another spelling for definitions 1 and 2 is **programme**.

progress (pro-*gress*)
to move forward or ahead.

prohibit (pro-*hib*-it)
to say that something must not be done: *There is a law to **prohibit** people from smoking on trains.*

project (*pro*-ject)
a special piece of work that you do for school where you find out as much as you can about something.

projector (pro-**ject**-or)
a machine for showing pictures or written information on a large screen.

promise (**prom**-iss)
to say that you will do something.
Word building: I **promised**, I am **promising**

pronoun (**pro**-nown)
a word which stands for a noun, such as 'we', 'her', 'they', 'it', 'that' or 'who'.

pronounce (pro-**nounce**)
to make the sound of a word: *You can* **pronounce** *'dance' in two ways.*
Word building: I **pronounced**, I am **pronouncing** | The way a word is pronounced is its **pronunciation** (pro-nun-see-**ay**-shon).

proof
something that shows you that a thing is true or real: *The muddy footprints on the carpet were* **proof** *that someone had been in the house.*

propeller (pro-**pell**-er)
a set of blades that spin around to move something through air or water. Planes and helicopters use propellers to move through air. Ships and boats use propellers to move through water.

proper (**prop**-er)
right or correct: *If you put your things in their* **proper** *place, then you'll always be able to find them.*

property (**prop**-er-tee)
1. something that is owned by someone: *These books are the* **property** *of the library, but we may borrow them.*
2. land or buildings owned by someone: *My grandparents live on a sheep* **property**.
Word building: For more than one we use **properties**.

prophecy (**prof**-a-see)
a prediction of what will happen: *The wizard made a* **prophecy** *about the future of the kingdom.*
Word building: For more than one we use **prophecies**.
Word use: Don't confuse this with **prophesy**.

prophesy (**prof**-a-suy)
to make a prophecy, or to predict: *She will* **prophesy** *a terrible battle.*
Word building: I **prophesied**, I am **prophesying**
Word use: Don't confuse this with **prophecy**.

prophet (**prof**-it)
someone who says what will happen in the future.
Word use: Don't confuse this with **profit**.

prosecute (**pros**-e-cute)
to make someone go to a court of law because you believe that they have done something wrong.
Word building: I **prosecuted**, I am **prosecuting**

prosperous (**pros**-pe-russ)
rich and successful, especially in business.

protect (pro-**tect**)
to keep something safe from harm: *It is important to wear a hat at the beach to* **protect** *your face from the sun.*
Word building: Something that protects you gives you **protection**.

protest (pro-**test** or **pro**-test)
to say or show that you disapprove of something: *Many people went to the meeting to* **protest** *about the new freeway.*

prototype (**pro**-to-type)
the first of something; especially something from which many things are copied.

proud (prowd)
You feel **proud** when you or others have done something well: *We are **proud** of our team because they tried hard and did their best.*

prove (proov)
to show that something is true or real.
Word building: I **proved**, I am **proving**

provide (pro-**vide**)
to give something that's needed: *You bring the drinks and I'll **provide** the sandwiches.*
Word building: I **provided**, I am **providing**

prowl
to move about quietly, like an animal hunting for prey.

prune¹
a dried plum.

prune²
to cut twigs and branches from a tree or a bush to make it grow better.
Word building: I **pruned**, I am **pruning**

public (**pub**-lic)
Something is **public** if it's for everyone's use: *You can't stop us walking here — this is a **public** path!*

publish (**pub**-lish)
to print a book or other writing for sale to the public.

pudding (**pood**-ing; *the first part rhymes with **wood***)
a soft, sweet, cooked food people eat after the main part of their meal.

puddle (**pudd**-l)
a small shallow pool of water.

puff
a small amount of air or smoke: *Suddenly there was a **puff** of wind and my hat blew off.*

pull
to move something by holding on to it and making it come towards you: *Can you help me **pull** the canoe onto the beach?*

pulse (pulce)
the throbbing that you can feel when you put your fingers on your wrist. It is made by your heart pumping blood around your body.

pump
1. a machine that pushes liquid or air in or out of something.
2. to push liquid or air in or out of something: *They **pump** water from the river to spray onto their vegetable garden.*

pumpkin (**pump**-kin)
a large round vegetable with a hard skin. The part you eat is orange but the skin is often green.

punch
to hit something hard with your fist.

punctual (**punk**-choo-al)
You are **punctual** if you are on time.

punctuation (punk-choo-**ay**-shon)
the marks you put next to some words when you write. They show things such as where a sentence ends or if someone is speaking.

puncture (**punk**-cher)
a small hole made in something: *The tyre on my bike is flat because it has a **puncture** from some broken glass.*

punish (**pun**-ish)
to make someone suffer because they have done something wrong.
Word building: Something that is done to punish is a **punishment**.

pupil[1] *(pew-pil; the first part rhymes with new)*
someone who is being taught.

pupil[2] *(pew-pil; the first part rhymes with new)*
the small, dark spot in the middle of your eye.

puppet *(pupp-et)*
a doll with strings on its arms and legs that you can pull to make it move, or which is made in the shape of a glove that you can move with your fingers.

puppy
a young dog.
Word building: For more than one we use **puppies**.

pure *(pyoo-a)*
Something is **pure** when it has nothing else mixed with it: *This jumper is made of pure wool.*
Word building: more pure = **purer**, most pure = **purest**

purple *(per-pl)*
Something is **purple** if it's the reddish-blue colour of a plum's skin.

purpose
1. the reason something is done or made: *The purpose of exercise is to keep you fit and healthy.*
2. If you do something on **purpose**, you mean to do it: *Did you miss the bus this morning on purpose?*

purr *(per)*
the low sound that a cat makes when it is happy.

purse *(perse)*
a small bag for carrying money.

pursue *(per-syoo)*
to chase someone: *The police officer hurried to her car to pursue the criminals.*
Word building: When you pursue something you are in **pursuit** of it.

push *(rhymes with bush)*
to move something away from you by pressing hard against it: *I think I can push a few more socks into the drawer.*

put *(rhymes with foot)*
to place something somewhere: *She put the plate on the shelf.*
Word building: I **put**, I am **putting**
Word use: If you **put up with** something, then you allow it to happen to you for a long time.

puzzle *(puzz-l)*
1. a game or question that is fun to do but that you must think hard about before you work it out.
2. something that is difficult to understand.

pygmy *(pig-mee)*
any group of people, animals or plants that are small in size.
Word use: Another spelling is **pigmy**.

pyjamas *(pa-jar-maz)*
the loose pants and shirt that you wear to bed.

pylon *(py-lon; the first part rhymes with eye)*
a strong tower built to support something.

pyramid *(pirra-mid)*
a shape with a square bottom and sides that join together in a point at the top. The Egyptians long ago used to build pyramids out of stone blocks to hold the body of a dead king or queen. See the picture at the end of this book.

python *(py-thon; the first part rhymes with eye)*
a very large, very strong snake that crushes its prey by winding its body around it.

Qq

Quolls and quokkas quarrel with a queen.

quack *(kwack)*
the sound a duck makes.

quail *(kwail)*
a small bird that builds its nest on the ground.

quake *(kwake)*
to tremble or shake: *I began to quake with fear as I heard the moaning.*
Word building: I **quaked**, I am **quaking**

quality *(kwol-i-tee)*
how good a thing is: *This silk is of the best quality.*

quantity *(kwon-ti-tee)*
an amount or measure of something: *What quantity of jam does this jar hold?*
Word building: For more than one we use **quantities**.

quarrel *(kwo-rel)*
to argue or not agree with someone: *Toss a coin, rather than quarrel about who'll bat first.*
Word building: I **quarrelled**, I am **quarrelling** | If you often quarrel, then you're **quarrelsome**.

quarter *(kwor-ter)*
one of the four equal parts you can split something up into.

quay *(kee)*
a place where you can get on or off a ship or a ferry.

queen *(kween)*
1. a woman who is born to be the ruler of her country.
2. the wife of a king.
Word use: Compare this with **king**.

queer *(kweer)*
strange or not usual: *I had a queer dream last night — everyone walked on their hands.*

question *(kwes-chen)*
what you ask someone.

queue *(kyoo)*
a line of people or cars.

quick *(kwick)*
Something is **quick** if it happens in a short time.

quicksand *(kwick-sand)*
wet sand which traps people who fall into it so that they can't escape.

quiet *(kwy-et)*
1. silent or without any sound.
2. peaceful or with nothing much happening: *We'll spend a quiet weekend at home.*
Word building: When you are quiet, you are doing something **quietly**. When you make something or someone quiet, you **quieten** them.

quilt *(kwilt)*
a light, warm cover for a bed.

quit *(kwit)*
to stop or leave something: *You should* **quit** *smoking.* | **Quit** *the program and turn off the computer.*
Word building: I **quit**, I am **quitting**

quite *(kwite)*
1. totally or wholly: *I'm* **quite** *sure I know where that country is because I looked it up in the atlas.*
2. sort of, more or less: *He's* **quite** *clever, but his sister is very clever.*

quiver *(kwiv-er)*
to tremble or shake gently: *The kitten began to* **quiver** *with fear when I picked it up.*

quiz *(kwiz)*
a test to see who knows the most about something.
Word building: For more than one we use **quizzes**.

quokka *(kwok-a)*
a small wallaby, just larger than a cat, with round ears and a short face. It is vulnerable. See the table at the end of this book.
Word use: This word comes from the Nyungar language of Western Australia. See the map of Australian Aboriginal languages at the end of this book.

quoll *(kwoll)*
a marsupial with a long tail and spots, about the size of a cat. It is endangered. See the table at the end of this book.
Word use: Another word for this is **native cat**. The word **quoll** comes from the Guugu Yimidhirr language of Queensland. See the map of Australian Aboriginal languages at the end of this book.

quotation *(kwo-**tay**-shon)*
a part of a book or of a speech that someone copies and repeats somewhere else.
Word building: If someone uses a quotation, then they **quote** what another person has said.

a
b
c
d
e
f
g
h
i
j
k
l
m
n
o
p
q
r
s
t
u
v
w
x
y
z

Rr

Reindeers on rollerblades raid refrigerators.

rabbi (*rab* cyc)
a leader or a priest of the Jewish religion.

rabbit (*rabb*-it)
a small animal with long ears, that lives in a burrow.

race¹
a contest to see who is the fastest.

race²
all the people who have the same ancestors or the same way of doing things.

rack
a frame or set of bars to put things on or lock things to: *Hang your hat on the hat rack.* | *Is there a bike rack there where I can leave my bike?*

racket (*rack*-et)
loud, mixed-up noise.

racquet (*rack*-et)
a long-handled bat with strings stretched across a frame.
Word use: Another spelling is **racket**.

radar (*ray*-dar)
a machine that can tell where things like ships or planes are.

radiator (*ray*-dee-ay-tor)
1. something that you can plug into the electricity and use to heat a room.
2. a part of a car which is filled with water to keep the engine cool.

radio (*ray*-dee-o)
a machine you can use to listen to music or people talking.
Word building: For more than one we use **radios**.

radius (*ray*-dee-us)
a straight line going from the centre of a circle to its edge.
Word building: For more than one we use **radii** (*ray*-dee-eye).

raft (*rarft*)
a piece of wood or some logs tied together, for carrying people or things over the water.

rage
very great anger.

raid
a sudden attack that nobody is expecting: *There was a police raid on the house.*

rail
1. a rod or a bar used to hold something up or to keep something out.
2. one of the metal bars that a train runs on.

railway *(rail-way)*
train tracks and trains that run on them.

rain
the water that falls out of the sky.
Word use: Don't confuse this with **reign** or **reins**.

rainbow *(rain-boe)*
the curved line of colours that you can often see in the sky when the sun starts shining after rain.

raincoat
a waterproof coat you wear in the rain.

rainforest *(rain-fo-rest)*
the thick forest that grows in hot places where it rains a lot.

raise *(raze)*
to lift something up to a higher place: *Can you **raise** your arms above your head?*
Word building: I **raised**, I am **raising**
Word use: The opposite of this is **lower**.

raisin *(ray-zin)*
a sweet grape that has been dried.

rake
a garden tool with a long handle that you use for gathering grass and leaves.

ram
1. a male sheep.
2. to hit something very hard.
Word building: it **rammed**, it is **ramming**
Word use: The female of definition 1 is a **ewe**.

Ramadan *(ram-a-darn)*
the special time for Muslims when they don't eat from sunrise to sunset.

ranger *(rain-jer)*
someone who looks after one of the large parks the government owns.

rank
1. the level of importance that someone reaches in their job: *My mother has reached the **rank** of professor at the university.*
2. a row or line of people: *The soldiers stood in **rank**.*

rap
a type of music that has strong rhythms in which the words rhyme and are spoken, not sung.

rapid *(rap-id)*
able to go fast.

rare *(rair)*
not very common.
Word building: more rare = **rarer**, most rare = **rarest**

rascal *(rars-kal)*
a child who's always playing naughty tricks.

rash
red spots or patches on your skin.

rat
a small animal with a long tail, similar to a mouse but bigger.

rather *(rardh-er)*
1. quite, or sort of: *I'm **rather** good at the piano but I need to practise harder.*
2. to want to do one thing more than another: *I thought you'd **rather** watch TV than go to bed.*

rattle *(ratt-l)*
1. to make short, sharp noises: *The windows started to **rattle** as the wind blew harder.*
2. a baby's toy which you shake to make a noise.
Word building: I **rattled**, I am **rattling**

raw *(ror)*
not cooked at all.
Word use: Don't confuse this with **roar**.

ray
a thin line of light: *A **ray** of sunshine shone through the curtain.*

reach *(reech)*
1. to get to a place: *When will the train **reach** our station?*
2. to manage to stretch up or out and touch something: *Now that I'm taller, I can **reach** that high shelf.*

read *(reed)*
1. to look at words and understand what they mean: *I can **read** that sign now — it says 'Stop'.*
2. to be able to be translated and understood: *Can the computer **read** that disk?*
Word building: I **read** *(red)*, I am **reading**

ready *(red-ee)*
1. able to do something straight away: *I'm **ready** to go out now.*
2. able to be used straight away: *Come and sit down quickly because dinner is **ready**.*

real *(reel)*
Something is **real** if it's true and not made up: *What is the **real** reason you're late?* | *Adventures like that happen in fairytales, not in **real** life.*
Word building: When you find out the real reason for something, you find out what **really** happened.
Word use: Don't confuse **real** with **reel**.

realise *(ree-a-lize)*
to come to understand something: *I don't think they **realise** that Satoshi's really my brother.*
Word building: I **realised**, I am **realising**

rear[1] *(rhymes with **ear**)*
the back of anything: *There's a beautiful view from the **rear** of the house.*

rear[2] *(rhymes with **ear**)*
1. to look after children or young animals until they are big enough to take care of themselves: *I'd like to **rear** this lamb myself as its mother is dead.*
2. to stand up on its back legs: *This horse will **rear** if it sees a snake.*

reason *(ree-zen)*
anything that explains why someone has acted in some way or why something has happened: *The **reason** I didn't come was that I wasn't invited.*

receipt *(re-seet)*
a piece of paper that shows that you have paid for something.

receive *(re-seeve)*
to get or be given something: *You'll **receive** your presents tomorrow morning.*
Word building: I **received**, I am **receiving**

recent *(ree-sent)*
Something is **recent** if it happened a short time ago.
Word building: When anything is recent, then it happened **recently**.

recipe *(res-i-pee)*
a list of all the things you need for cooking something, and the instructions telling you how to use them.

recite *(re-site)*
to say the words of something without looking at them: *I'd like to **recite** this poem at our class concert.*
Word building: I **recited**, I am **reciting**

reckon *(reck-on)*
1. to count up or to work out how much or how many you have: *I **reckon** we made $20 at our sweet stall.*
2. to say what you think or believe: *I **reckon** she is very clever.*

recognise *(rek-og-nize)*
to know someone or something when you see them again.
Word building: I **recognised**, I am **recognising**

record *(re-cord)*
1. to write down important facts so that everyone can remember them: *I'd better record the details of our talk.*
2. to put music or other sounds onto a tape recorder, computer or some other machine.
3. *(rek-ord)* the best that anyone has ever done in a sport: *Jo broke the record for running 100 metres.*

recorder
1. a machine for recording sound or pictures.
2. a type of wooden or plastic flute with a soft sound.

recount *(ree-count)*
writing which explains exactly how things happened. See the 'Types of writing and speaking' table at the end of this book.

recover *(re-cuv-er)*
to get well again after you've been sick: *She should recover from the flu in a few days.*
Word building: When you recover, you make a **recovery**.

recreation *(rek-ree-ay-shon)*
a game, a hobby or a sport.

rectangle *(rek-tang-gal)*
a shape with four straight sides and four straight corners. See the picture at the end of this book.
Word use: An **oblong** is a kind of rectangle, and so is a **square**.

recycle *(ree-sy-kl)*
to use again, usually in a different way: *At home we recycle paper, glass, cans and as many plastic things as we can.*
Word building: I **recycle**, I am **recycling**

red
the colour of a ripe tomato.
Word building: If something turns red, it **reddens**.

reduce *(re-duce)*
to make something lower or smaller: *The sign says, 'reduce speed now'.* | *We need to reduce the number of plastic bags we use.*
Word building: I **reduced**, I am **reducing** | If you reduce something, you make a **reduction**.

reed
a kind of tall grass that grows in wet places.
Word use: Don't confuse this with **read**.

reef
a strip of rock, sand or coral near the surface of the sea.

reel
a round piece of wood or metal that you can wind something onto.

refer *(re-fer)*
to speak or write briefly about something: *I'd like to refer to last week's test before we start work.*
Word building: I **referred**, I am **referring**

referee *(ref-e-ree)*
someone in charge of a game who makes sure it's played according to the rules.
Word use: Another word that means nearly the same is **umpire**.

reference (ref-rence)

1. a book or a place in a book or other writing where you look to find information.
2. a letter that describes a person's character and abilities.

reflect (re-flect)

to throw back light or heat: *Look at the way the shining waves reflect the sun.*

Word building: When light is reflected, you might see a **reflection**.

refresh (re-fresh)

to make someone who is tired feel strong and full of energy again.

Word building: Something that refreshes is a **refreshment**.

refrigerator (re-frij-e-ray-tor)

a container with shelves and a door, for keeping food and drink cold.

Word building: This word is often shortened to **fridge**.

refugee (ref-yoo-jee)

a person who has left their original country because of danger and is living in a new country.

refund (ree-fund)

money that you get back from a shop when you return something you've bought, usually because there is something wrong with it: *Mum got a refund when she took back the new tent, because it had a hole in it.*

refuse (re-fuze)

to say you won't do something: *They refuse to give me back my money.*

Word building: I **refused**, I am **refusing** | If you refuse something, you state your **refusal**.

regard

1. to think of or consider: *I regard Sanjay as a true friend.*
2. to look at or observe: *The cat regarded us with its yellow eyes.*
3. thought or attention: *They gave no regard to the trouble I went to for them.*

Word building: If you do something without regard for what somebody says or thinks, you do it **regardless** of that person.

regret (re-gret)

to feel sorry or sad about something: *I regret shouting at you this morning.*

Word building: I **regretted**, I am **regretting**

regular (reg-yoo-lar)

1. usual or ordinary: *Let's go home the regular way and stop at the shops like we always do.*
2. Something is **regular** if it always happens at the same time: *We have three regular meals each day.*

Word building: When something is regular, then it happens **regularly**.

rehearse (re-herse)

to do something many times by yourself to make it good for other people to see or hear.

Word building: When you rehearse something, you have a **rehearsal**.

reign (rain)

to rule over a country and its people the way a king or a queen does.

Word use: Don't confuse this with **rain** or **reins**.

reindeer (rain-deer)

a kind of deer that lives in cold countries near the North Pole.

Word building: For more than one we use **reindeer**.

reins *(rains)*
the long, thin straps that a rider uses to guide a horse.
Word use: Don't confuse this with **rains** or **reigns**.

reject *(re-**ject**)*
to say that you won't take or use something: *I'll have to **reject** your work — it's too messy.*
Word use: The opposite of this is **accept**.

rejoice *(re-**joice**)*
to be glad or very pleased about something.
Word building: I **rejoiced**, I am **rejoicing**

relation *(re-**lay**-shon)*
anyone who is part of your family.
Word use: Another name for this is **relative**.

relationship
1. a connection between people or things: *Do you have a good **relationship** with your boss? | What is the **relationship** between the time of day and the amount of traffic on the roads?*
2. a family connection.
3. a special connection between two people who are in love with each other.

relax *(re-**lax**)*
1. to make something loose: ***Relax** your arms and let them swing by your sides.*
2. to rest and make yourself comfortable.
Word building: When you have relaxed, you're in a state of **relaxation**.

release *(re-**leese**)*
to let something or someone go free.
Word building: I **released**, I am **releasing**

reliable *(re-**ly**-a-bl)*
You are **reliable** if people can trust you to do things.

relief *(re-**leef**)*
the feeling you have when your pain, worry or sadness goes away: *We felt such **relief** when they returned safely.*
Word building: You feel relief and you're very **relieved** when something **relieves** you.

religion *(re-**lij**-en)*
what people believe about God, or their set of special beliefs about how to live their lives and how to be a good person.
Word building: Something that has to do with religion is **religious**.

remain *(re-**main**)*
1. to stay somewhere: *I'd rather **remain** at home while you go to the museum.*
2. to be left after other parts or other people have gone: *These are the only pieces of the puzzle that **remain**.*

remark *(re-**mark**)*
1. to say what you think or notice about something.
2. the thing that is said.

remember *(re-**mem**-ber)*
to bring something back into your mind: *Can you **remember** what that girl's name is?*
Word use: The opposite of this is **forget**.

remind *(re-**mind**)*
to make someone remember something: *I always have to **remind** you to clean your teeth.*

remote *(re-**mote**)*
far away: *The centre of Australia is very **remote**.*

remote control
a small gadget with buttons that you can use to change the settings on a machine such as a television or DVD player from across the room. You hold it in your hand and can carry it around.

a b c d e f g h i j k l m n o p q **r** s t u v w x y z

remove *(re-moov)*
to take something away from somewhere.
Word building: I **removed**, I am **removing** | If you remove something, then you are responsible for its **removal**.

rent
the money you pay for a house or a flat that you live in but that you don't own.

repair *(re-pair)*
to make something work as well as it did when it was new.

repeat *(re-peet)*
to say or do something again.

replace *(re-place)*
1. to take the place of someone else: *James will **replace** the sick player today.*
2. to put something back in its place: *I'll **replace** the tools now that I've finished.*
Word building: I **replaced**, I am **replacing**

reply *(re-ply)*
to give an answer to someone.
Word building: I **replied**, I am **replying**

report *(re-port)*
1. the news about something.
2. a letter your teacher writes saying how good your work is.

reporter *(re-port-er)*
someone whose job is to gather news for radio, television or for a newspaper.

represent *(rep-re-zent)*
1. to stand for or mean: *The colour red often **represents** danger.*
2. to say or do something in place of a group to which you belong: *Tan will **represent** the school at the district swimming carnival.* | *Our school captain **represents** the wishes of the students at the school council meetings.*
Word building: If you represent something, you are **representative** and you provide **representation**.

reptile *(rep-tile)*
a crawling animal such as a lizard, snake, turtle or alligator.

republic *(re-pub-lic)*
a nation which has an elected president, not a king or queen.

request *(re-kwest)*
to ask for something in a polite way.

require *(re-kwire)*
to need something: *I **require** a new mouse for my computer.*
Word building: I **required**, I am **requiring**

rescue *(res-kew)*
to save someone from the danger they're in.
Word building: I **rescued**, I am **rescuing**

research *(re-search)*
careful and detailed study to find new facts or learn more about something.

resemble *(re-zem-bl)*
to be like: *Do you **resemble** your sister?*
Word building: If you resemble something, you have a **resemblance** to it.

reserve *(re-zerv)*
to ask for something to be kept for you to use at a later time: *I can **reserve** books on the library's website.*
Word building: I **reserved**, I am **reserving** | When you reserve something, you make a **reservation**.
Word use: Don't confuse **reserve** with **reverse**.

reservoir *(rez-ev-wah)*
a place where a lot of water is kept until it is needed.

resource *(re-zorce or ree-sorce)*
something very useful, such as natural materials like water, minerals and sunlight: *Our natural **resources** are running out.*

respect (re-**spect**)
the feeling you have for someone you admire and think good things about.

responsible (re-**spons**-si-bl)
1. You are **responsible** for something if you must look after it.
2. You are **responsible** for something that goes wrong if it was your fault.
3. You are a **responsible** person if you can be trusted to do things properly.

rest[1]
to sleep or relax when you're tired or when you've been busy.

rest[2]
everyone or everything left: *The **rest** of the children have gone home.*

restaurant (**rest**-a-ront or **rest**-ront)
a place where you can buy a meal and eat it.

result (re-**zult**)
1. anything that happens when you do something or after something takes place: *The **result** of my kindness to her was that we became friends.*
2. the answer to a sum.

retire (re-**ty**-er)
to leave work because you're getting old or because you're sick.
Word building: I **retired**, I am **retiring**

retreat (re-**treet**)
to go back because you see that there is danger ahead: *The soldiers will have to **retreat** because the enemy is too strong for them.*

return (re-**tern**)
1. to go or come back: *We must **return** home now.*
2. to give or send something back: *If you lend me your jumper, I'll **return** it tomorrow.*

reusable (ree-**yooz**-a-bl)
Something is **reusable** if you can use it more than once: ***Reusable** materials are better for the environment than materials you use once and then throw away.*

reveal (re-**veel**)
to show or tell something: *I lifted the rug to **reveal** the stain on the carpet.* | *Don't **reveal** my secret to anyone.*

revenge (re-**venj**)
anything bad you do to someone in return for the bad things they have done to you.

reverse (re-**verse**)
1. the opposite of anything: *I don't believe you — I think the **reverse** is true.*
2. to drive a car backwards: *I'll try to **reverse** into the garage.*
Word building: I **reversed**, I am **reversing**
Word use: Don't confuse this with **reserve**.

review (re-**vyoo**)
1. a newspaper or magazine article which describes and gives you an opinion of a book, a film, a performance or an art exhibition.
2. an inspection or examination: *Your behaviour is under **review**.*
3. to write about: *Why don't you **review** this film for your school magazine?*
Word building: If you review something, you are a **reviewer**.

revise (re-**vize**)
to go back over something so that you'll learn it: *I'm trying to **revise** my maths for the exam.*
Word building: I **revised**, I am **revising** | If you revise something, you're doing **revision**.

revolution *(rev-er-**loo**-shun)*
1. a complete change: *My invention will cause a **revolution** in space travel.*
2. one complete turn, usually in a circle: *The car tyre made wobbly **revolutions** as it rolled down the hill.*
Word building: If you cause a revolution, you **revolutionise**.

revolver *(re-**vol**-ver)*
a small gun that you can fire several times without reloading.

reward *(re-**ward**; the last part rhymes with **lord**)*
something you get in return for doing good work.

rhinoceros *(ry-**noss**-e-ross)*
a large animal with a thick skin and with horns on its nose.
Word building: For more than one we use **rhinoceroses**.

rhyme *(rime)*
a likeness in the sounds at the end of words such as 'cat' and 'bat' or 'lion' and 'iron'.

rhythm *(ridh-m)*
the pattern of strong and weak sounds you can hear in music or when someone is reading a poem.

ribbon *(ribb-n)*
a band of thin material you use for tying things up or to make something look pretty.

rice
white or brown seeds from a plant that people cook and eat.

rich
You are **rich** if you have a lot of money.
Word use: The opposite of this is **poor**.

riddle *(ridd-l)*
a question with clever words, that you ask someone as a joke.

ride
to sit on or in something and go along.
Word building: I **rode**, I have **ridden**, I am **riding** | If you ride something, you are a **rider**.

ridge *(rij)*
any long, narrow strip that's higher than what is around it: *We walked along the **ridge** of earth left by the plough.*

ridiculous *(ri-**dik**-yu-lus)*
Something is **ridiculous** if it's funny or if it makes people laugh.

rifle *(**ry**-fel)*
a long gun.

right *(rite)*
1. correct: *I got six sums **right** and two wrong.*
2. fair and good: *It was **right** to give the money we found in the playground to the teacher.*
3. the opposite of **left**.
Word use: The opposite of definitions 1 and 2 is **wrong**.

rim
the outside edge of a round thing: *She has left a smudge of lipstick on the **rim** of the cup.*

rind *(rhymes with **dined**)*
the thick, hard skin that you find on things like bacon or an orange.

ring[1]
1. a circle of thin metal that you wear on your finger.
2. anything that has the shape of a circle.

ring[2]
1. to make a sound like a bell.
2. to telephone someone: *I must **ring** my mother.*
Word building: I **rang**, I have **rung**, I am **ringing**

rinse
to wash something in clean water to get off the soap or dirt.
Word building: I **rinsed**, I am **rinsing**

riot *(ry-ot)*
many people shouting and fighting and making a lot of noise and trouble.

rip
to tear something in a rough way.
Word building: I **ripped**, I am **ripping**

ripe
ready to be picked or eaten: *A tomato is ripe when it turns red.*
Word building: more ripe = **riper**, most ripe = **ripest**

rise *(rize)*
1. to go upwards: *The kite began to rise into the air.*
2. to stand up: *Please rise for the national anthem.*
Word building: I **rose**, I have **risen**, I am **rising**

risk
the chance that something might go wrong or might hurt you: *We didn't use the old bridge because of the risk that it might not be safe.*

river *(riv-er)*
a large stream of water.

road *(rode)*
a path for cars to go along.

roam *(rhymes with home)*
to walk or travel about without really trying to get anywhere: *It's such a lovely day, let's roam in the park.*

roar *(ror)*
to make a loud sound: *The wind began to roar as the storm got closer.*
Word use: Don't confuse this with **raw**.

roast
to cook food over a fire or in an oven.
Word use: Another word that means nearly the same is **bake**.

robbery *(robb-e-ree)*
stealing from someone: *There's been another robbery at our bank.*

robot *(roe-bot)*
a machine that can move about and do a job usually done by a person.

rock[1]
a large piece of stone.

rock[2]
1. to move from side to side: *The waves made the little boat rock.*
2. a type of popular music with strong rhythms played on drums and electric guitars. It is usually played very loud.
Word building: Definition 2 is a short way of saying **rock 'n' roll**.

rock art
a picture made on a rock surface: *This Aboriginal rock art is sacred.*

rocket *(rock-et)*
a machine for travelling in space. It shoots up into the air when hot gas rushes out from its bottom end.

rod
a long stick of wood or metal.

role
1. the part or character that an actor plays: *I want the role of Robin Hood in the play.*
2. the particular part that you play in life: *A parent's role is to set a good example for their children. | A friend's role is to be a good listener.*
Word use: Don't confuse this with **roll**.

roll *(rhymes with **pole**)*
1. to move along by turning over and over: *If you drop that ball it will **roll** down the hill.*
2. something that is made into the shape of a tube: *He spread out the **roll** of carpet to show us the colour.*
3. a list of names: *The teacher has to tick off your name on the **roll**.*
4. a small, round piece of bread.
Word use: Don't confuse this with **role**.

rollerblade *(roll-er-blade)*
1. a type of rollerskate with narrower wheels that are positioned in a straight line from the front of the sole to the back of the sole.
2. to move swiftly on the ground, wearing rollerblades.
Word building: I **rollerblade**, I am **rollerblading**
Word use: Another word for this is **in-line skate**.

rollerskate *(roll-er-skate)*
1. a special boot with two wheels on the front of the sole and two wheels on the back of the sole.
2. to move swiftly on the ground, wearing rollerskates.
Word building: I **rollerskated**, I am **rollerskating** | This word is often shortened to **skate**.

roof
the covering on the top of a building or a car.
Word building: For more than one we use **roofs** *(roovz)*.

room
1. a part of a building with walls around it.
2. space: *Is there enough **room** on your desk for a bigger monitor?*

rooster *(roo-ster)*
the male bird you keep with the hens, that crows early in the morning.

root *(rhymes with **boot**)*
the part of a plant that grows down into the soil.
Word use: Don't confuse this with **route**.

rope
a thick string made of many long, strong threads twisted together.

rose *(roze)*
a bush with thorns and beautiful flowers.

rosella *(roe-zell-a)*
a parrot with brightly coloured feathers, common in Australia.

Rosh Hashana *(rosh ha-shah-na)*
a two-day Jewish holiday, usually in September or October, that marks the Jewish New Year.

rotten *(rott-n)*
Something is **rotten** if it has gone bad or if it's falling apart: *We found a **rotten** apple that had been behind the cupboard for a month. | The wharf is not safe to walk on because the wood is **rotten**.*

rough *(ruff)*
1. not smooth or even: *I scraped my knee when I fell on the **rough** road. | He spoke with a **rough**, unpleasant voice.*
2. wild or not calm or gentle: *The storm made the sea **rough**. | He grabbed the boy by the collar and pulled him out of the chair in a very **rough** way.*

round
shaped like a circle or a ball.

route *(rhymes with **boot**)*
the road or way that you take to go from one place to another place.
Word use: Don't confuse this with **root**.

row[1] *(rhymes with **go**)*
a line of people or things.

row² *(rhymes with go)*
to make a boat move along by using oars.

row³ *(rhymes with now)*
a very noisy fight.

royal *(roy-al)*
Something is **royal** if it has to do with a king or a queen.

rub
to move something backwards and forwards against something else.
Word building: I **rubbed**, I am **rubbing**

rubber *(rubb-er)*
1. a material that you can stretch. We use it to make things like car tyres, bouncing balls and elastic bands.
2. a small piece of soft rubber that you can use to clean off pencil marks.

rubbish *(rubb-ish)*
anything that you can't use or that's broken and you have to throw away.

rudder *(rudd-er)*
a flat board at the back of a boat that you use to steer the boat.

rude *(rood)*
You are **rude** if you behave in a careless way towards other people: *It was **rude** of them to go home without saying goodbye.*
Word use: The opposite of this is **polite**.

rug
1. a thick blanket.
2. a small carpet.

Rugby League
a type of football played by teams of 13 players. It is similar to the game of Rugby Union, but has some different rules.
Word building: This is sometimes shortened to **League**.

Rugby Union
a type of football played by teams of 15 players. It is similar to the game of Rugby League, but has some different rules.
Word building: This is sometimes shortened to **Union**.

ruin *(roo-in)*
to spoil or wreck something.

rule *(rhymes with cool)*
1. a law or instruction that you should obey.
2. to control or to be in charge of something.
Word building: I **ruled**, I am **ruling**

ruler *(rool-er)*
1. a strip of wood or plastic with a straight edge, that you use for drawing or measuring lines.
2. someone who rules a country or an empire.

rumble *(rum-bl)*
a long loud sound, like the sound of thunder.

rumour *(roo-mer)*
something that a lot of people are saying about someone or something even though it might not be true.

run
to move quickly using your legs.
Word building: I **ran**, I am **running**

rung
one of the steps of a ladder.

runway *(run-way)*
the strip of land that an aeroplane takes off from and lands on.

rush
to do something in a hurry.

rustle *(russ-l)*
the sound that grass or leaves make when they are blown by the wind.

Ss

Sharks on surfboards see a sinking ship.

sack
a large bag made out of strong material.

sacred *(sake-red)*
important and special because it has to do with religion.

sad
You are **sad** if you don't feel pleased or glad or if you're sorry about something: *I'm **sad** that my friend has gone away.*
Word building: more sad = **sadder**, most sad = **saddest**
Word use: The opposite of this is **happy**.

saddle *(sadd-l)*
a seat that you tie onto a horse's back when you want to ride it.

safari *(sa-far-ree)*
a long journey made by a group of people who want to watch or hunt wild animals.
Word building: For more than one we use **safaris**.

safe
1. free from danger: *It is **safe** to cross the road here.*
2. a strong box where you can keep money, jewels or other valuable things.
Word building: more safe = **safer**, most safe = **safest** | If you talk about how safe something is, you talk about its **safety**.

sail
1. a large piece of strong material on a boat, that catches the wind. The wind then makes the boat move across water.
2. to travel across water.
Word building: Someone who sails in ships is a **sailor**.
Word use: Don't confuse **sail** with **sale**.

salad *(sal-ad)*
a mixture of vegetables that you eat raw.

salamander *(sal-a-man-der)*
a type of amphibian with a tail, which lives in the water when very young, but later lives on land.

salary *(sal-a-ree)*
the regular money paid to someone each week or each month for the work they do in their job.
Word building: For more than one we use **salaries**.

sale
1. the selling of something: *I got $50 from the **sale** of my bike.*
2. a special time when things are sold at a lower price than usual.
Word use: Don't confuse this with **sail**.

salmon *(sam-on)*
a fish with pink flesh that you can eat.

salt *(solt)*
a white powder that comes from sea water.

salute *(sa-**loot**)*
to touch the side of your forehead with your right hand as a way of showing respect for someone: *The soldiers stood in a line to **salute** the prince.*

Word building: I **saluted**, I am **saluting**

same
Something that is the **same** as something else is like it in every way: *Your watch is the **same** as mine.*

sample *(**sam**-pl or **sarm**-pl)*
a small piece that shows what something is like: *We tasted a **sample** of each chocolate before we decided which one we wanted to buy.*

sand
the tiny bits of worn-down rock that cover the beach and the desert.

sandal *(**sand**-l)*
a kind of light shoe with straps, that you wear in summer.

sandshoe *(**san**-shoo)*
a canvas shoe with a rubber bottom, that you wear when you play sport.

sandwich *(**san**-wich)*
two slices of bread with food in between.
Word building: For more than one we use **sandwiches**.

sane
You are **sane** if you have a normal and healthy mind.
Word building: more sane = **saner**, most sane = **sanest**

sap
the juice that carries food and water around a plant.

sapling *(**sap**-ling)*
a young tree.

sarcastic *(sar-**kas**-tic)*
You are **sarcastic** when you say ordinary things in a way that will hurt or tease someone: *'You're up early', she said in a **sarcastic** voice, 'it's not even lunchtime yet'.*

sardine *(sar-**deen**)*
a young fish cooked in oil and tinned ready for eating.

sash
a strip of material that you wear over one shoulder or around your waist.
Word building: For more than one we use **sashes**.

satay *(**sar**-tay)*
cubes of meat or vegetables cooked on a stick and covered with hot peanut sauce.

satchel *(**sach**-l)*
a school bag with straps, that you carry on your back.

satellite *(**sat**-e-lite)*
something in space, such as the moon, that goes around and around a larger thing, such as the earth.

satin *(**sat**-n)*
cloth that is smooth and silky.

satisfy *(**sat**-is-fy)*
to please someone or make them happy: *To **satisfy** my mother I did my homework before I watched television.*
Word building: I **satisfied**, I am **satisfying** | If you satisfy someone, you give them **satisfaction** and you have behaved in a **satisfactory** way.

sauce *(rhymes with **horse**)*
a thick liquid that you put on food to make it taste better.
Word use: Don't confuse this with **source**.

saucepan *(sorce-pan)*
a pot with a lid and a handle. You use it for cooking.

saucer *(sorce-a)*
a small plate that you put under a cup.

sausage *(soss-ij)*
chopped-up meat inside a thin skin.

sausage roll *(soss-ij **roll**)*
a roll of baked pastry filled with sausage meat.

save
1. to rescue something or someone from danger.
2. to keep something so that you can use it later: *We **save** bits of bread for the hens. | I am going to **save** my pocket money until I have enough to buy new rollerblades.*
3. to store a file in the memory of a computer: *You must **save** it before you exit.*
Word building: I **saved**, I am **saving**

saw *(sor)*
a tool which has a blade with a sharp, jagged edge that you move backwards and forwards across a piece of wood to cut it.
Word use: Don't confuse this with **soar** or **sore**.

say
to tell something with words: *I'll ring Mum to **say** that I'll be home late. | What does it **say** in the paper about tomorrow's weather?*
Word building: he **says** *(sez)*, he **said** *(sed)*, he is **saying**

scab
the hard, dry crust that forms on the surface of a sore or abrasion when it begins to heal.

scald *(scorld)*
to burn something with very hot liquid.

scale
one of the thin, hard, flat pieces of skin that cover the outside of fish and some other animals.
Word building: Anything that's covered with scales is **scaly**.

scales
a machine that you use to find out how much something weighs.

scallop *(skoll-op)*
a soft sea animal that lives inside two flat shells. It is good to eat.

scalp
the skin on your head under your hair.

scamper *(skamp-er)*
to run about quickly: *The puppy loves to chase waves and **scamper** on the beach.*

scanner *(skann-er)*
a machine that looks at written information and puts it directly into a computer.

scar
the mark left on your skin after a sore or a burn has healed.

scarce *(skairce)*
1. not as much as is needed: *Water is **scarce** during a drought.*
2. not seen very often: *Trees are **scarce** in our city.*

scare *(scair)*
to frighten someone.
Word building: I **scared**, I am **scaring**

scarecrow *(scair-croe)*
something made to look like a person, that a farmer puts in a field to scare birds away from crops.

scarf
a piece of cloth that you wear around your head or neck.

Word building: For more than one we use **scarves**.

scarlet (*skar*-let)
bright red.

scatter (*skatt*-er)
to throw things through the air so that they land in many different places.

scene (*seen*)
1. a place where something has happened: *The ambulance raced to the scene of the accident.*
2. a part of a play: *The first scene takes place in the queen's bedroom.*

scenery (*seen*-e-ree)
the natural things that you see all around you when you're in the country, such as trees, rivers and hills.

scent (*sent*)
1. a sweet smell that people like.
2. the smell of an animal: *The dogs followed the scent of the rabbit until they found the burrow.*

Word use: Don't confuse this with **cent** or **sent**, which is a form of the word **send** (*I sent the letter yesterday*).

scheme (*skeem*)
a plan of how to do something: *I've thought of a scheme to get money for the books we need.*

school (*skool*)
the place where children go to learn.

science (*sy*-ense)
the way we study the world around us and the things we discover about it by doing tests and experiments and by measuring things.

Word building: Someone who studies science is a **scientist**.

scissors (*sizz*-ez)
a tool with two blades joined together, that you use for cutting things like paper or cloth.

Word use: Some people say **a pair of scissors**.

scold (*skold*)
to speak to someone in an angry way because you think that they have done something wrong.

scone (*skon*)
a small cake that you can break open and eat with butter or cream and jam.

scooter (*skoot*-er)
a toy that you stand on to ride. It has two wheels with an oblong board in between.

scorch (*skorch*)
to make something so hot that it goes brown: *You might scorch your shirt if you leave the iron on it like that.*

score (*skore*)
the number of points a team or a person makes in a game or contest.

Word building: A person who records the score is called a **scorer**.

scout (*skout*)
1. someone sent to find out things, especially about an enemy.
2. a member of a worldwide club for children that organises fun and interesting activities, especially outdoor activities.

scowl (*skowl*)
to have an angry look on your face.

scramble (*skram*-bel)
1. to climb quickly using your hands to help you: *The children began to scramble down the steep hill to the beach.*
2. to cook eggs by mixing the yolks and whites with milk, and heating the mix.
3. to mix up in a jumbled way.
Word building: I **scrambled**, I am **scrambling**

scrap (*skrap*)
a small piece of something.

scrape (*skrape*)
to rub with something hard or sharp to get off dirt or paint: *We had to scrape our boots on the step to get the mud off them.*
Word building: I **scraped**, I am **scraping**

scratch (*skrach*)
1. to make a mark or cut on something with anything sharp: *Did the kitten scratch your arm with its claws?*
2. to rub your skin with your nails to stop it feeling itchy.

scream (*skreem*)
the loud cry you make when you are frightened or in pain.

screech (*skreech*)
a loud shrill noise: *The car stopped with a screech of brakes.*
Word building: For more than one we use **screeches**.

screen (*skreen*)
1. a smooth surface where moving pictures appear, such as the front of a television set.
2. a thin wall that you use to hide something.
3. a net of thin wire that you put over a window to keep out insects.

screw (*skroo*)
1. a kind of nail that goes into a hole when you twist it around.
2. to turn or twist something: *Screw the lid back on the jar when you've finished.*

scribble (*skribb-l*)
to write or draw something quickly, without trying to be neat.
Word building: I **scribbled**, I am **scribbling**

scrub[1] (*skrub*)
to rub something very hard with a brush to clean it.
Word building: I **scrubbed**, I am **scrubbing**

scrub[2] (*skrub*)
a lot of low trees and shrubs growing together.

scurry (*skurr-ee*)
to move with quick small steps: *At night many little animals scurry about looking for food.*
Word building: I **scurried**, I am **scurrying**

sea (*see*)
a very large area of salt water.

seafood (*see-food*)
food which comes from the sea such as fish, prawns and oysters.

seal[1] (*seel*)
to close something up in such a way that you can't open it again without breaking a part of it: *You press down the flap of the envelope to seal it.*

seal[2] (*seel*)
a sea animal with a long, smooth body covered with short fur.

search (*serch*)
to look carefully for something or someone.

season (*see*-zen)
1. one of the four parts of the year. The seasons are spring, summer, autumn and winter.
2. to make food taste better by adding salt, herbs or spices to it.

seat (*seet*)
something, such as a chair, that is made for people to sit on.

seatbelt
a belt attached to a seat in a car or other vehicle that you wear to keep you safe and secure.

seaweed (*see*-weed)
a plant that grows in the sea.

second[1] (*sek*-ond)
the next one after the first: *I came* *second* *in the race, just behind the winner.*

second[2] (*sek*-ond)
a very small amount of time. There are 60 seconds in one minute.

secondary (*sek*-on-dree)
Something is **secondary** if it comes second. A secondary school is the second school you go to; the school after primary school.

secret (*see*-cret)
Something is **secret** if you don't want other people to know about it: *I kept my diary hidden in a* **secret** *place.*

secretary (*sek*-re-tree)
someone whose job is to write and send letters, answer the phone and look after things in an office.
Word building: For more than one we use **secretaries**.

section (*sek*-shon)
a part of something: *The explosion blew off the roof and top* **section** *of the building.*

secure (*se*-kyoo-a)
safe: *The baby felt* **secure** *in the arms of her mother.*

see
to use your eyes to take information to your mind: *Did you* **see** *Megan's new haircut?*
Word building: I **saw**, I have **seen**, I am **seeing**

seed
a very small part of a plant that you put in the ground so that it can grow into a new plant.

seek
to try to find something.
Word building: I **sought**, I am **seeking**

seem
to appear: *He* **seems** *friendly.* | *I* **seem** *to have left my wallet at home.*

seesaw (*see*-saw)
a plank of wood balanced in the middle, so that it goes up and down when someone sits on each end.

seize (*seez*)
to take hold of someone suddenly.
Word building: I **seized**, I am **seizing**

seldom (*sel*-dom)
hardly ever: *It* **seldom** *rains in the centre of Australia.*

select (*se*-lect)
to decide which one you want: **Select** *a file to open.*
Word building: When you select something, you make a **selection**.

self
a word you use when you are talking about you and your own feelings and thoughts. It is sometimes combined with other words: *After a good long sleep, I felt just like my old* **self** *again.* | *I have good* **self**-control *and good* **self**-esteem.

a
b
c
d
e
f
g
h
i
j
k
l
m
n
o
p
q
r
s
t
u
v
w
x
y
z

selfish *(sel-fish)*
You are **selfish** if you only think about yourself: *It was **selfish** of you to grab the best lollies before we came.*

sell
to give something to someone when they pay you for it: *I'll **sell** my old skateboard to you for $10.*
Word building: I **sold**, I am **selling**

semitrailer *(sem-ee-tray-ler)*
a very large truck with many wheels, for carrying heavy loads. The part where the driver sits joins onto the long trailer at the back.

send
to make someone or something go somewhere: *I'll **send** you to your room if you don't stop shouting. | **Send** me a text message when you get there.*
Word building: I **sent**, I am **sending**

senior *(seen-yor)*
older or more important than the others.

sense
1. the special powers your body has to taste, touch, hear, see and smell: *My **sense** of smell isn't good when my nose is blocked from a cold.*
2. the ability to work out the best thing to say or do: *Have some **sense** and go to bed when you are ill.*

sensible *(sen-si-bl)*
You are **sensible** if you know the best thing to say or do.

sentence *(sen-tence)*
a group of words which belong together and form a whole idea. A sentence starts with a capital letter and usually ends with a full stop.

separate *(sep-a-rate)*
1. to put or keep things or people apart: *I can't **separate** these stamps that are stuck together.*
2. *(sep-ret)* away from something else and not part of it.
Word building: I **separated**, I am **separating**

sergeant *(sar-jent)*
a soldier or a police officer with a high enough rank to be in charge of others.

serial *(seer-ree-al)*
a story in a magazine or on radio or television that you read, hear or see one part at a time.
Word use: Don't confuse this with **cereal**.

series *(seer-reez)*
a number of things that are similar or are joined in some way and that happen in order: *The first cricket match in the **series** will be held in Perth.*
Word building: For more than one we use **series**.

serious *(seer-ree-us)*
1. thoughtful and interested in important things: *The twins are very **serious** and don't laugh much.*
2. You are **serious** about something if you are telling the truth and you're not joking.
3. Something is **serious** if it makes you worried.

servant *(ser-vant)*
someone whose job is to work for someone else, often in their house.

serve
1. to work for someone: *These knights **serve** the king.*
2. to put food on a table: *Can you help me **serve** the dinner to our guests?*
3. to help or assist people in a shop.
Word building: I **served**, I am **serving**

service

1. a helpful act: *You've done me a very kind service.*
2. the supplying of something useful to a large group of people: *The bus service in this town is very reliable.*
3. a religious ceremony: *That was a lovely marriage service.*
4. to fix something or provide it with a service: *The mechanic will service my car.*

serviette *(ser-vee-ett)*

a piece of cloth or paper you use at a meal to wipe your lips and hands and to keep your clothes clean.

session *(sesh-n)*

the length of time you spend doing one thing: *My ice-skating session lasts for one hour.*

set

1. a group of numbers or things that are alike in some way or that you use together: *What is the set of even numbers below 20?*
2. to put someone or something somewhere: *He set the baby down gently on the bed.*
3. to put knives and forks on a table ready for a meal: *I'll set the table for lunch.*
4. to become firm or hard: *Has the jelly set yet?*
5. to sink below the horizon: *The sun will set at 7 o'clock tonight.*
Word building: I **set**, I am **setting**

setting

1. where something is: *This is a lovely setting for your new home.*
2. the time and place in which a play or film takes place.
3. the things such as a knife, fork, and plate used to set someone's place at the table.
4. something on a computer, television or another machine that you can change, like the volume or the speed.

settle *(sett-l)*

1. to decide something: *Let's settle on a good time to meet.*
2. to put something in proper order: *I need to settle all my business before I go away.*
Word building: I **settled**, I am **settling**

settler *(sett-ler)*

someone who goes to live in a new country: *British settlers came to Australia over two hundred years ago.*

several *(sev-ral)*

more than two, but not very many: *Several people came — about four I think.*

severe *(se-veer)*

Something is **severe** if it is so bad that it makes you feel worried: *My friend suffered severe injuries in the crash.*

sew *(rhymes with go)*

to join things together using a needle and thread: *I can sew this button onto my shirt all by myself.*
Word use: Don't confuse this with **so** or **sow**[1].

sex

one of the two groups, male and female, that all humans and animals are divided into: *What's the sex of your new baby — a boy or a girl?*

shabby *(shabb-ee)*

dirty, torn or faded because it's been worn a lot: *What a shabby shirt you're wearing.*
Word building: more shabby = **shabbier**, most shabby = **shabbiest**

shack

a hut made of old pieces of tin or wood.

shade

a place that is darker than the area around it because the light can't reach it: *Come and sit in the shade under these trees.*

Word building: If you're in the shade, then you're in a **shady** place.

shadow *(shad-oe)*

the dark shape of something made when it blocks out the light.

shaggy *(shagg-ee)*

Something or someone is **shaggy** if they are covered with long, rough hair.

Word building: more shaggy = **shaggier**, most shaggy = **shaggiest**

shake

to move quickly backwards and forwards or from side to side: *The leaves began to shake in the wind.*

Word building: I **shook**, I have **shaken**, I am **shaking**

shall *(shal)*

to be going to: *I shall go to the beach this afternoon.*

Word use: This word is a helping word. It is always used with another one in the form **I shall** or **I should** do something.

shallow *(shal-oe)*

Something is **shallow** if it doesn't go a long way down: *This shallow water only reaches my knees.*

shame

the unhappy feeling you have when you know you've said or done a silly or a wrong thing.

shampoo *(sham-poo)*

soap that comes in a bottle, for washing your hair.

shape

the line around the outside edge of something: *This five cent coin has a round shape.*

share *(shair)*

1. the part of something that you get or own: *You have had your share of the cake already.*

2. to use or enjoy something together: *My younger brothers share a bedroom.*

Word building: I **shared**, I am **sharing**

shark

a large fish which is very fierce and sometimes eats people.

sharp

with a thin edge that cuts like a sharp knife or a point that pricks like a sharp needle.

Word building: Something that makes another thing sharp, especially a pencil, is called a **sharpener**.

shave

to cut hair off part of your body leaving your skin very smooth.

Word building: I **shaved**, I am **shaving**

she *(shee)*

a word you use when you are talking about a woman or girl: *She is my best friend.*

shear *(sheer)*

to cut the hair or wool off an animal.

Word building: I **sheared**, I have **sheared** or I have **shorn**, I am **shearing** | Someone whose job is to shear sheep is a **shearer**.

Word use: Don't confuse **shear** with **sheer**.

shed[1]

a simple building used for storing things or sheltering animals.

shed[2]

1. to pour or release: *Bonnie shed some tears during the sad film.*

2. to grow out of and lose a layer of skin or a coat of fur: *Horses will shed their thick winter coats in spring.*

Word building: I **shed**, I am **shedding**

sheep
an animal that farmers keep for its meat and for its thick wool.
Word building: For more than one we use **sheep**.
Word use: A female sheep is a **ewe**. A male sheep is a **ram**.

sheer *(rhymes with **ear**)*
very steep, almost going straight up and down: *I looked over the **sheer** cliff to the rocks far below.*
Word use: Don't confuse this with **shear**.

sheet
1. one of the two large pieces of cloth you sleep between in bed.
2. a large, thin piece of paper, glass or metal.

shelf
a thin flat piece of wood or something like this, joined to a wall or held in a frame. You use it for holding things like books.
Word building: For more than one we use **shelves**.

shell
1. a hard part covering the outside: *The baby bird broke through the **shell** with its beak. | That snail went back into its **shell**.*
2. a large bullet that explodes when it's fired from a big gun.

shelter *(shel-ter)*
a place that protects you from bad weather or that keeps you safe from danger.

she's *(sheeze)*
a short way of saying **she is** or **she has**.

shield *(sheeld)*
anything you use to protect yourself, such as the flat piece of metal, leather or wood that soldiers once carried in battles.

shift
to move something from one place to another.

shine
1. to give out light: *Don't **shine** the torch straight into my eyes.*
2. to rub something until it looks bright.
Word building: I **shone**, I have **shone**, I am **shining** | Something that shines is **shiny**.

ship
a large boat for carrying people or things over the sea.

shirt *(shert)*
something you wear on the top part of your body. It has buttons down the front, sleeves and a collar.

shiver *(shiv-er)*
to shake because you're cold, frightened or very excited.

shock
a sudden bad fright or anything like this that upsets you.

shoe *(shoo)*
a strong covering for your foot. The top part is often made of leather with a rubber part underneath.

shoot
1. to hit or kill something or someone with the bullets from a gun: *Don't **shoot** those rabbits.*
2. to fire a bullet or an arrow from a gun or a bow: *I'll try to **shoot** the arrow at the middle of the target.*
3. a new part growing on a plant.
Word building: I **shot**, I am **shooting**

shop
a place where you can buy the things you need.
Word building: A person who is in charge of a shop is a **shopkeeper**.

a b c d e f g h i j k l m n o p q r **s** t u v w x y z

shopping
1. When you buy things from a shop, you are **shopping**.
2. the things you buy from a shop.

shopping centre *(shopp-ing sent-er)*
a very big building that has many different shops inside it.

Word use: Another word for this is **shopping mall**.

shore *(shor)*
the land along the edge of the sea or a lake.

Word use: Don't confuse this with **sure**.

short
1. not long: *I like to write **short** stories.*
2. not tall: *I know I'm **short** but Mum says I'll grow when I'm older.*

Word building: If you make something short, you **shorten** it.

shorts
short trousers that end above your knees.

shot
1. the shooting of a gun, bow or other weapon.
2. an injection.

Word use: You can also find this word at **shoot**.

should *(rhymes with wood)*
to have a duty to: *You **should** say sorry for hitting your brother.*

shoulder *(shole-der)*
the part of your body that joins your neck to your arm.

shout *(rhymes with out)*
to call or cry out in a loud voice.

shove *(shuv)*
to push something or someone in a rough way.

Word building: I **shoved**, I am **shoving**

shovel *(shuv-l)*
a tool for lifting up and moving heavy things like soil or rubbish.

show *(rhymes with go)*
1. to let someone see something: *Show me your painting.*
2. something you watch, like a play or a program on television: *My favourite **show** is 'The Simpsons'.*

Word building: I **showed**, I have **shown** or I have **showed**, I am **showing**

shower *(rhymes with flower)*
1. a short fall of rain.
2. a wash you have standing under a spray of water that falls down on you.

shriek *(shreek)*
a short, loud cry or noise like the sound of a whistle blowing.

shrill
loud, and like the sound of a whistle.

shrink
to get smaller and smaller.

Word building: I **shrank**, I have **shrunk**, I am **shrinking**

shrub
a small, low tree.

shrug
to make your shoulders go up and then down, to show that you don't know or don't care.

Word building: I **shrugged**, I am **shrugging**

shudder *(shudd-er)*
to shake suddenly because you feel frightened, disgusted or cold.

shut
to bring two parts of something together, or to put something across an opening: *Shut your books now. | Can you please shut the door to keep out the cold air?*

Word building: I **shut**, I am **shutting**

shuttlecock (**shutt**-l-cock)
a piece of rubber or plastic with feathers stuck in it that is used instead of a ball in games like badminton.

shy (rhymes with **my**)
You are **shy** if you are a bit frightened of other people: *Riley was too **shy** to come and meet my new friends.*

sick
You are **sick** if there is something wrong with your body and if your health isn't good.
Word building: When you are sick, you may have a bad **sickness**.

sick bay (**sick** bay)
the place that you go to if you are feeling ill while you are at school.

side
1. one of the edges or lines on the outside of something, but not those on the top, bottom, front or back: *Go in the door on the left **side** of the house.*
2. one of the two outer parts of something flat: *Which **side** of the paper should I draw on?*
3. one of a number of groups or teams that are against each other: *Which **side** do you support in this game?*

sigh (rhymes with **eye**)
to let air out slowly through your mouth with a soft sound, to show that you're tired, sad or no longer worried about something.

sight (site)
your ability to see things.
Word use: Don't confuse this with **site**.

sightseeing (**site**-see-ing)
travelling around looking at objects and places of interest.

sign (sine)
1. anything like a special mark, a movement you make or a notice you read that tells you something important: *There's a 'For Sale' **sign** in front of their house.*
2. to write your name on something in your own writing.

signal (**sig**-nal)
a sound, a light or a movement that tells you something you need to know: *I'll fire this pistol as the **signal** that you should start the race.*

signature (**sig**-na-cher)
the way you write your own name.

silent (**sy**-lent)
1. You are **silent** if you don't talk or make any sound at all.
2. with no sound: *I sat very still in the **silent** room.*
Word building: When everything is silent, then there is **silence**.

silk
a soft, shiny cloth made from the threads a silkworm spins.
Word building: Anything made of or like silk is soft and **silky**.

silkworm (**silk**-werm)
one of the caterpillars that spin soft threads to make their cocoons.

silly (**sill**-ee)
without any good sense: *That **silly** child never listens to the advice people give.*
Word building: more silly = **sillier**, most silly = **silliest** | When people or things are silly, you talk about their **silliness**.

silo (**sy**-lo)
a tower-like building which is used for keeping wheat and other kinds of grain.
Word building: For more than one we use **silos**.

silver (sil-ver)

1. a white, shiny metal that's used for making things like jewellery, coins, knives and forks.

2. shiny grey in colour.

similar (sim-i-lar)

People or things are **similar** if they are alike in some way.

Word building: Things that are similar have great **similarity**.

simple (sim-pl)

easy to understand, do or use.

Word building: more simple = **simpler**, most simple = **simplest**

simply

1. in a plain and simple way: *I like to dress simply because it saves a lot of time.*

2. only: *I am simply watching a bit of television.*

3. absolutely: *This dessert is simply delicious.*

since

from then till now: *It has been years since I saw you.* | *We've been playing since this morning.*

sincere (sin-seer)

full of truth or showing your true feelings: *She is sincere when she says she likes you.*

sing

to use your voice to make music, sometimes with words: *My sister likes to sing in the shower.*

Word building: I **sang**, I have **sung**, I am **singing**

single (sing-gl)

1. one and only: *My single reason for coming is to see you.*

2. not married.

singlet (sing-let or sing-glet)

something you wear on the top part of your body, usually under your other clothes. It has no sleeves, and often has thin straps that go over your shoulders.

sink

1. to go down slowly, the way things go down in water: *I hope my toy boat doesn't sink.* | *Soon the sun will begin to sink below the horizon.*

2. to make a boat go down under the water.

3. a place in a kitchen, a bathroom or a laundry that you can fill with water from the taps above it. You let the water out by taking out the plug from the hole in the bottom.

Word building: I **sank**, I have **sunk**, I am **sinking**

sir (ser)

a polite word you use when you're speaking to a man: *May I take your hat, sir?*

siren (sy-ren)

one of the loud horns used on ambulances, fire-engines and police cars to warn people that they are coming.

sister (sis-ter)

a woman or girl who is part of your family and has the same parents as you.

sit

to rest with the bottom part of your body on something like a chair.

Word building: I **sat**, I am **sitting**

site

1. the land where something is built or will soon be built: *This is a good site for our new house — it's near a big park.*

2. a place on the internet with an address that can be looked up for information and facts.

Word building: Definition 2 is a short way of saying **website**.

Word use: Don't confuse **site** with **sight**.

situation

1. a position: *Her new house has a good* **situation***.*

2. the state of things: *When the car broke down, we were in a difficult* **situation***.*

size

the amount of space that something takes up: *What* **size** *is your room — big or small?*

sizzle *(sizz-l)*

to make a hissing or spitting sound while cooking in oil or fat.

Word building: it **sizzled**, it is **sizzling**

skate

1. a special boot with either a blade on the sole to glide over ice or wheels on the sole to move on the ground.

2. to move swiftly wearing skates.

Word building: I **skated**, I am **skating** | This word is a short way of saying **ice-skate** or **rollerskate**.

skateboard *(skate-bord)*

1. a narrow, wooden or plastic board, with wheels attached to the bottom, which you usually ride while standing up.

2. to move swiftly on the ground, riding a skateboard.

skeleton *(skel-e-ton)*

all the bones inside the body of a person or an animal.

ski *(skee)*

1. a long, thin piece of wood or other material that you join onto your shoe, that lets you move easily over the snow.

2. to move swiftly over the snow, wearing skis.

Word building: For more than one we use **skis**. | I **ski'd** or I **skied**, I am **skiing**

skid

to slide forward on something slippery or smooth.

Word building: I **skidded**, I am **skidding**

skill

You have **skill** if you are able to do something well.

Word building: If you have skill, you are **skilful** or **skilled** at something.

skim

1. to take off something floating on the top of a liquid: *I'll* **skim** *the fat from this gravy with a spoon.*

2. to move in a light way over the top of something: *Look how the birds* **skim** *across the lake.*

Word building: I **skimmed**, I am **skimming**

skin

the layer that covers the outside of people, animals and some fruit and vegetables: *Let me peel the* **skin** *off this banana for you.*

skinny *(skinn-ee)*

You are **skinny** if you're thin and there's not much fat on your body.

Word building: more skinny = **skinnier**, most skinny = **skinniest**

skip

1. to jump lightly, often from one foot to the other.

2. to leave something out: *I'll* **skip** *the next bit because it's too hard to read.*

Word building: I **skipped**, I am **skipping**

skirt *(skert)*

a piece of clothing that women and girls wear. It hangs down from their waist to their knees.

skull

the bony part of your head, covering your brain.

sky *(rhymes with my)*

the part of the air above the earth where the clouds are.

Word building: For more than one we use **skies**.

skydiving *(sky-dive-ing)*

the sport of jumping from a plane and falling through the air before opening your parachute.

slack

1. loose or not tight, like a rope can be.
2. lazy or careless.

slam

to shut something so hard that it makes a loud noise.

Word building: I **slammed**, I am **slamming**

slap

to hit something or someone quickly, usually with your hand spread open.

Word building: I **slapped**, I am **slapping**

slash

to cut something in a violent way with a very sharp blade.

slate

a dark grey rock which is easy to split into thin pieces. It is used to cover roofs and floors.

slave

someone who is the prisoner of another person and who has to work without being paid.

sleep

to rest with your eyes closed and your mind not knowing what is happening around you.

Word building: I **slept**, I am **sleeping** | When you sleep you are **asleep**. If you're tired and you want to sleep, then you're **sleepy**.

sleeve

the part of a shirt, coat or dress that covers your arm.

sleigh *(slay)*

a kind of cart people use for travelling over the snow. It has strips of metal underneath to help it slide and it is usually pulled along by animals.

slender *(slen-der)*

Someone is **slender** if they are slim.

slice

to cut something into thin pieces.

Word building: I **sliced**, I am **slicing**

slide

to move along smoothly: *The drawer should **slide** in and out without getting jammed.*

Word building: I **slid**, I am **sliding**

slight

small: *There's a **slight** chance that it will rain tonight.*

Word building: If there is a slight difference between two things, they are **slightly** different.

slim

thin or not fat: *The ballet dancer had long, **slim** legs.*

Word building: more slim = **slimmer**, most slim = **slimmest**

sling

1. a piece of cloth tied around your neck to hold your arm if it's hurt.
2. to throw something with all your strength: *Watch me **sling** this pebble across the creek.*

Word building: I **slung**, I am **slinging**

slip

1. to slide easily: *Water can **slip** off a duck's smooth feathers.*
2. to fall over: *Be careful not to **slip** on the wet floor.*

Word building: I **slipped**, I am **slipping**

slippery *(slip-ree)*
so smooth or wet that it's hard to hold or to walk on.

slit
a long, straight cut or opening in something.

slope
to be higher at one end than at the other: *The hills **slope** steeply on all sides of the valley.*
Word building: it **sloped**, it is **sloping**

slot
a small slit or opening: *You put the coin in the **slot** and the bubblegum comes out.*

slow *(slo)*
1. Something or someone is **slow** if they take a long time to do something: *The **slow** train stops at every station on the way.*
2. behind the right time: *My watch is always five minutes **slow**.*
Word building: When something or someone is slow, then they go or do things **slowly**.

slug
a small animal that is always slippery and wet, like a snail without its shell.

slum
a dirty place where many poor people live crowded together.

sly *(rhymes with **my**)*
good at tricking people or at making people believe things that aren't true.

smack
to hit someone with your hand spread open.

small *(rhymes with **all**)*
not big or large.

smart
1. clever or quick to understand things: *That **smart** child has learned the whole poem already.*
2. neat and in the latest fashion or style: *What a **smart** new shirt you're wearing.*

smash
to break into pieces with a loud noise.

smell
1. to become aware of something with your nose: *Come and **smell** my new perfume.*
2. to give off something that people can smell: *Fish and chips **smell** delicious.*
3. anything you smell: *These roses have a sweet **smell**.*
Word building: I **smelt** or I **smelled**, I am **smelling** | Anything with a nasty smell is **smelly**.

smile
to show you are happy or friendly, or you find something funny, by making your mouth wide and turning it up at both ends.
Word building: I **smiled**, I am **smiling**

smirk *(smerk)*
to smile in a way that shows you feel pleased with yourself but which annoys other people.

smoke
1. the cloud of gas and ash that floats up into the air when something is burning.
2. to breathe in the smoke from burning tobacco in a cigarette and blow it out again: *It is bad for your health if you **smoke**.*
Word building: he **smoked**, he is **smoking**

smooth *(smoodh)*
with no bumps or lumps: *Stir the cake mixture until it is **smooth**.*

a b c d e f g h i j k l m n o p q r **s** t u v w x y z

smoulder (*smold-er*)
to burn slowly with smoke, but without flame.

SMS message
a text message.

smudge (*smuj*)
a dirty mark or a stain.

smuggle (*smugg-l*)
to take something you shouldn't have into or out of a country without anyone finding out: *People can go to jail if they smuggle parrots out of Australia.*

Word building: I **smuggled**, I am **smuggling** | A person who smuggles is a **smuggler**.

snack
a small meal you eat quickly: *I always have a snack when I come home from school.*

snail
a small animal with a soft body and a shell. You might find one moving slowly along if you look in your garden.

snake
a long creature with a scaly skin. It has no legs and wriggles along the ground.

snap
to break with a sudden cracking sound: *Snap the biscuit in two. | The rubber band will snap if you stretch it too far.*

Word building: it **snapped**, it is **snapping**

snarl
to make a low, angry or fierce sound: *The dog began to snarl as I walked towards it.*

snatch (*snach*)
to take hold of something suddenly: *Hold your purse tightly or a thief might snatch it.*

sneak (*sneek*)
to move or to take something in a quiet or a secret way: *Try to sneak into the room without them hearing you. | I saw you try to sneak a chocolate.*

Word building: I **sneaked**, I am **sneaking** | If you like to sneak about or sneak things, then you're **sneaky**.

sneer
to speak to or to smile at someone in a nasty way that shows you think they are stupid: *Don't sneer at me — you don't know the answer either.*

sneeze
to make a sudden noise, mostly through your mouth, because something is tickling your nose: *The pollen from flowers always makes me sneeze.*

Word building: I **sneezed**, I am **sneezing**

sniff
to breathe in quickly through your nose: *Just sniff that fresh mountain air. | Don't sniff when you have a cold — blow your nose instead.*

snob
someone who thinks that only rich, famous or clever people are important and who won't talk to anyone else.

snore
to breathe in a noisy way while you're asleep: *You wake me up when you snore.*

Word building: I **snored**, I am **snoring**

snorkel (*snor-kl*)
a tube that lets you breathe fresh air as you swim with your face just under the water.

snort
to breathe out hard through your nose with the loud, blowing sound a horse makes: *You always snort when you're angry.*

snow *(rhymes with go)*
raindrops which freeze and fall to the ground as tiny, white flakes.

Word building: There is a lot of snow on a **snowy** day.

snowboard
1. a board for gliding over the snow, which you stand on and strap your feet onto.
2. to glide over the snow on a snowboard.

Word building: I **snowboarded**, I am **snowboarding** | Someone who rides a snowboard is a **snowboarder**.

snuggle
to lie closely together for warmth or comfort: *The puppies **snuggled** together in front of the fire.*

so
1. a word you use to show the reason for something or the cause of something: *I went home straight after school **so** I could get started on my homework.* | *I studied really hard, **so** I got a good mark.*
2. true: *Is that **so**?*
3. very: *That joke is **so** funny!*

Word use: Don't confuse this with **sew** or **sow**[1].

soak *(soke)*
to make something very wet, often by leaving it in water for a long time.

soap *(sope)*
something you use for washing yourself or for cleaning things.

Word building: If you use a lot of soap, then you might get **soapy** hands.

soar *(sor)*
to fly up into the sky the way a bird does: *We watched the kite **soar** higher and higher.*

Word use: Don't confuse this with **saw** or **sore**.

soccer *(sock-er)*
a type of football that two teams play with a round ball they're not allowed to touch with their hands.

society *(so-sy-e-tee)*
a group of people who have something in common or who are interested in the same thing.

Word building: For more than one we use **societies**.

sock
something you wear that covers your foot and ankle and sometimes reaches up to your knee. You wear your shoe over it.

sofa
a long couch with a back and two sides.

soft
1. easy to cut or to press out of shape: *The butter is **soft** and easy to spread.*
2. smooth and nice to touch: *I like to stroke my kitten's **soft** fur.*
3. low in sound: *I can't hear the radio — it's too **soft**.*

softball *(soft-ball)*
a ball game played by two teams in which a long, thin bat is used to hit a ball. This ball is similar to the ball used in baseball, but it's a bit softer. The batter must run around the three bases on the field and return home to score a point.

software *(soft-wair)*
programs that are put into a computer to make it do certain things.

soil
the soft, brown part of the land that plants can grow in.

solar *(sole-ar)*
Something is **solar** if it has to do with the sun: *In our **solar** system all the planets move around the sun.* | *Solar energy is power that is made by the heat of the sun.*

soldier (*sole*-jer)
someone who belongs to an army.

sole
the underneath or bottom part of your foot or of a shoe.

solemn (*sol*-em)
serious or sincere: *I made a **solemn** promise never to tell anybody the secret.*

solid (*sol*-id)
1. anything firm or hard that you can hold in or touch with your hands, like a book or a door.
2. with the inside full of something: *This is a **solid** chocolate egg.*
Word use: Think about how definition 1 is different from **gas** and **liquid**.

solo (*sole*-o)
music you play or a song you sing all by yourself.
Word building: For more than one we use **solos**. | Someone who performs a solo is a **soloist**.

solve (*solv*)
to find the answer to something: *The police are trying to **solve** the mystery of the missing jewels.*
Word building: I **solved**, I am **solving**

some (*sum*)
1. more than one, but not all: ***Some** people like dogs better than cats.* | ***Some** of these apples are rotten.*
2. not particular: *I read about that in **some** book or other.*
Word building: Some kind of thing is **something**. Some person is **someone**.
Word use: Don't confuse this with **sum**.

somersault (*sum*-er-solt)
a way of rolling forward with your heels going over your head.

sometimes (*sum*-times)
some of the time, not always: *We **sometimes** ride our bikes to school.*

somewhere (*sum*-wair)
in a place not known, or not particular: *She lives **somewhere** on the other side of town.*

son (*sun*)
someone's male child.

song
a short piece of music with words that you sing.

soon
in a short time from now: *I'm sure Laxmi will be here **soon**.*

soothe (*soodh*)
to make someone who is sad or hurt feel calm and happy again: *I'll **soothe** the crying boy by rocking him in my arms.*
Word building: I **soothed**, I am **soothing**

sore (*sor*)
1. full of pain or hurting when it's touched: *I bumped my head and it's very **sore** now.*
2. a spot on your skin where the skin is broken and which is sometimes red from infection or swollen from bruising.
Word use: Don't confuse this with **saw** or **soar**.

sorry (*so*-ree)
1. sad because you know you've done something wrong and you wish you hadn't: *I'm **sorry** I was rude.*
2. sad because something bad has happened to someone: *I'm very **sorry** that you have been so sick.*
Word building: more sorry = **sorrier**, most sorry = **sorriest** | When you are sorry, then you feel **sorrow**.

sort
1. one of a group of things: *What **sort** of ice-cream do you like?*
2. to put something with others that are like it: *I have to **sort** my photos before I put them in my album.*

soul *(sole)*
something that is part of you that no-one can see. Some people believe that this part goes on living after you die.
Word use: Another word that means nearly the same is **spirit**. | Don't confuse **soul** with **sole**.

sound
1. anything you can hear with your ears.
2. to seem or appear: *Those voices **sound** angry.*

sound system *(**sound** sis-tem)*
a machine that consists of a CD player and radio.

soup *(soop)*
a food you drink or eat with a spoon, made with meat, fish or vegetables.

sour *(rhymes with **flower**)*
Something is **sour** if it tastes a bit like a lemon.
Word use: The opposite of this is **sweet**.

source *(rhymes with **horse**)*
the place or thing that something comes from: *This river has its **source** high up in the mountains.*
Word use: Don't confuse this with **sauce**.

south *(sowth)*
the direction you will face if you are facing east and you turn to your right.
Word use: The opposite of this is **north**. The other directions are **east** and **west**.

souvenir *(soo-ve-**neer**)*
something you keep to remind you of a place.

sow[1] *(so)*
to spread seeds in the earth so that they'll grow: *The farmer will **sow** this field with wheat.*
Word building: I **sowed**, I have **sown** or I have **sowed**, I am **sowing**
Word use: Don't confuse this with **so** or **sew**.

sow[2] *(rhymes with **cow**)*
a female pig.

soy sauce *(**soy** sorce)*
a dark brown sauce that tastes very salty, used in Chinese cooking.
Word use: This is often called **soya sauce**.

space
1. the place outside the earth's atmosphere, where the moon and the stars are: *They're going to send another rocket into **space**.*
2. the part of a place, or the amount of room a thing takes up: *This table fills a lot of **space**.*
3. an empty place or a part with nothing in it: *Leave a **space** on the page between each word that you write.*

spaceship
a vehicle that can travel to outer space.

spade
1. a tool with a long handle and a wide metal blade, for digging the ground in your garden.
2. a black shape like an upside-down heart with a stem, used on playing cards.

spaghetti *(spa-**get**-ee)*
a food made from flour, water and salt, cut into long, thin strips and cooked in very hot water.

spank
to hit someone with your hand, usually to punish them for something.
Word building: If you spank someone, you give them a **spanking**.

spanner (spann-er)
a tool for holding something tight and turning it around. It's often used for screwing the part that fits onto the end of a bolt.

spare (spair)
extra and not used unless it is needed: *We have a **spare** room in case visitors come to stay.*

spark
1. a tiny piece of burning wood or coal that shoots up from a fire.
2. a sudden flash of light, made by electricity.

sparkle (spark-l)
to shine with little flashes of light: *The sunlight made her diamond ring **sparkle**.*
Word building: it **sparkled**, it is **sparkling**

sparrow (spa-roe)
a small brown bird, common in many parts of the world.

spawn (rhymes with horn)
a mass of eggs given out by fish and other water creatures.

speak (speek)
1. to say words in your ordinary voice: *The baby is learning to **speak**.*
2. to tell someone something or to have a talk with them: *I'll have to **speak** to my mother about that.*
Word building: I **spoke**, I have **spoken**, I am **speaking**

spear (speer)
a long pole with a sharp point at the end used to hunt animals, or to fight with.

special (spesh-l)
1. for one person or group of people or for one kind of thing: *We catch a **special** bus that's only for children going to school. | This is a **special** machine for cutting grass at the edge of a path.*
2. more important than usual: *This is a **special** day — it's my birthday.*
Word building: If you catch a special bus, then it comes **specially** for you.

specialist (spesh-a-list)
a person who is an expert in an area of study or work, such as a doctor who is an expert in one kind of medicine.

species (spee-seez or spee-sheez)
one of the groups into which animals and plants are divided.
Word building: For more than one we use **species**.

speck
a very small spot or bit of something.
Word building: Something with specks on it is **speckled**.

spectacles (speck-ta-kels)
another name for **glasses**.

speech
1. the power that someone has to speak: *Humans have **speech**, but animals don't.*
2. a special talk that someone gives in front of a group of people.

speed
the power to move, go or do something very quickly: *I swim every morning to improve my **speed** for the big race.*
Word building: When someone or something has great speed, they are **speedy** and can move **speedily**.

spell¹
to say or write the letters of a word in the correct order.
Word building: I **spelt** or I **spelled**, I am **spelling** | If you can spell well, then you're good at **spelling**.

spell²

a group of words you say that's supposed to make magic happen: *The witch chanted the **spell** and the prince turned into a frog.*

spend

1. to pay out money buying things: *I'll **spend** this dollar on a comic.*
2. to pass your time in a certain way: *We always **spend** our summer holidays camping.*

Word building: I **spent**, I am **spending**

spice

something you use to make food taste better or to keep it from going bad. Spices come from plants: *Pepper is a **spice** and so is ginger.*

Word building: Food cooked with lots of spices is **spicy**.

spider *(spy-der)*

an animal with eight legs, which usually spins a web and sometimes has a poisonous bite. It is like an insect but it doesn't have wings.

spike

a sharp, pointed bit that sticks out from something.

Word building: Something with spikes is **spiky**.

spill

to let something run or fall from the container that's holding it: *If you trip me I'll **spill** the milk I'm carrying.*

Word building: I **spilt** or I **spilled**, I am **spilling**

spin

1. to turn around and around very fast: *A top can **spin** across the floor.*
2. to make something turn very fast: ***Spin** the coin.*
3. to make thread by twisting and winding long pieces of cotton or wool.
4. Spiders **spin** silk for webs by letting out a long, sticky thread from their bodies.

Word building: I **spun**, I am **spinning**

spinach *(spin-ich)*

a plant with large, green leaves which you can eat as a vegetable.

spine

1. the long row of bones in your back.
2. a sharp thorn on a plant.
3. a stiff spike on an animal such as an echidna.

Word building: Anything with spines or with leaves shaped like spines is **spiny**.

spirit *(spirr-it)*

1. the part of someone that you can't see but that is important in the way they live their life.
2. the soul of a dead person, which some people think comes back to visit people who are alive.
3. courage and energy.

Word building: Someone with a lot of spirit (definition 3) is **spirited**.

spit

to send out liquid or anything else from your mouth: *Don't **spit** at people! | **Spit** your chewing gum into the bin.*

Word building: I **spat**, I am **spitting**

spite

1. a strong wish to hurt someone or to make them cross: *Nadia hit David out of **spite**.*
2. in spite of, You use **in spite of** when you are saying that something is happening even if something else has happened which might have stopped it: *They finished the game **in spite of** the sudden storm.*

Word building: If you are full of spite, then you are **spiteful**.

splash

1. to wet someone or something by scattering drops of liquid on them.
2. a sound like the one the water makes when you jump in.

splendid

extremely good or grand: *There was a **splendid** view of the valley.* | *That was a **splendid** performance!*

Word building: If something is done in a splendid way, it is done **splendidly** and you talk about its **splendour**.

splint

a thin piece of something hard and straight, such as wood, fastened on both sides of a broken bone to hold it in place.

splinter *(splint-er)*

a thin, sharp piece of wood, metal or glass.

split

to break into parts, usually from one end to the other.

Word building: it **split**, it is **splitting**

spoil

1. to hurt or damage something so much that you can't use it.
2. to make someone selfish or rude by always letting them do or say what they like.

Word building: I **spoiled** or I **spoilt**, I am **spoiling**

spoken

Something that is **spoken** is expressed by speaking: *I was given a **spoken** warning about my lateness.*

sponge *(spunj)*

1. a material with lots of holes for taking in water and other liquids. You use it for wiping and cleaning things.
2. a light cake that is easy to chew.

spoon

a tool for eating, stirring and lifting up food and other things. It has a round end joined onto a handle.

sport

something you do to exercise your body. Playing tennis or hockey, riding horses or skating on ice are different kinds of sport.

Word building: A shop where you can buy the clothing and equipment needed for sports is call a **sports store**.

spot

1. a small, round mark: *There's a **spot** of gravy on your shirt.*
2. a place: *What a sunny **spot** for a picnic!*
3. to see or find someone or something: *I can't **spot** her among all those people.*

Word building: I **spotted**, I am **spotting** | Something or someone with spots is **spotted** or **spotty**.

spout *(rhymes with out)*

the part of a jug, kettle, or anything like that, which makes it easy to pour the liquid out.

sprain

to twist and bruise without actually breaking: *I **sprained** my ankle at soccer.*

spray

to scatter tiny drops of water or other liquid on someone or something: *Take the hose and **spray** the roses.*

spread *(spred)*

1. to stretch something out as much as you can: ***Spread** the cloth and see if it will cover the table.*
2. to put something on in a thin layer: *I'll **spread** some jam on my bread.*

Word building: I **spread**, I am **spreading**

spring
1. a piece of wire that's wound around and around. It bounces back when you stretch it or squeeze it.
2. to leap up suddenly.
3. the season of the year, after winter, when it starts to warm up and new leaves start to grow on trees and flowers bloom.
Word building: I **sprang**, I have **sprung**, I am **springing**

sprinkle *(spring-kl)*
to scatter little bits or drops of something: *I'll **sprinkle** some pepper on the chicken.*
Word building: I **sprinkled**, I am **sprinkling**

sprint
to run a short way as fast as you can.

sprout *(rhymes with out)*
to send up new shoots: *The bulb will **sprout** in the spring.*

spurt *(spert)*
to flow or run out suddenly: *Water began to **spurt** from the broken pipe.*

spy *(rhymes with my)*
1. someone who watches people without them knowing and who finds out everything about them.
2. to watch someone in secret and to report everything you find out about them: *Our government sent us to **spy** on you and to find out what secret weapons you are making.*
Word building: I **spy**, he **spies**, I **spied**, I am **spying** | For more than one we use **spies**.

squabble *(skwobb-l)*
to fight or quarrel about little things that aren't important: *They always **squabble** about whose turn it is to use the computer.*
Word building: they **squabbled**, they are **squabbling**

squad *(skwod)*
a small group of people who work or play together.

square *(skwair)*
1. a shape with four straight sides that are all the same length. See the picture at the end of this book.
2. an open place in a town or city where people can meet.

squash *(skwosh)*
1. to make something flat: *Be careful! You'll **squash** the bananas.*
2. a game that two people play in a small court with walls. You use a racquet and a small rubber ball.
3. a fizzy drink made with fruit juice.
4. a small green or yellow vegetable.

squeak *(skweek)*
to make a small, shrill cry or any shrill noise like this: *I heard a mouse **squeak**.* | *Those gates will **squeak** until you oil them.*
Word building: If a gate squeaks, then it is **squeaky**.

squeal *(skweel)*
to make the sudden shrill cry of a person or animal in pain: *I'll **squeal** if you pinch me.*

squeeze *(skweez)*
to press something or someone hard: *Don't **squeeze** me so tightly — you're hurting my arms.*
Word building: I **squeezed**, I am **squeezing**

squid *(skwid)*
a sea animal with a soft body. It has long parts like arms joined to its head.

squirrel *(skwi-rel)*
an animal with a bushy tail, which lives in trees in North America and Europe. It hides nuts and acorns to eat in the winter.

squirt *(skwert)*
to wet someone or something with a jet of water or other liquid.

stable *(**stay**-bl)*
a place for keeping and feeding horses.

stadium *(**stay**-dee-um)*
a large (often indoor) place where sports are played, with seats for people to watch.

staff *(starf)*
all the people who work at a place such as a shop, a school or a hospital.

stag
a male deer.

Word use: The female is a **doe**.

stage
1. the platform in a theatre where the actors or performers stand.
2. one of the important points you must reach if you're going to finish something you've started to do: *I've finished the first **stage** of my art project.*

stagger *(**stagg**-er)*
to walk in a wobbly way as if you are about to fall.

stain *(stane)*
a mark that spoils something: *There is a **stain** on my uniform that I can't get off.*

stairs
a number of steps one after another leading from one level of a house to another.

stake
a stick with a point at one end so that you can push it easily into the ground: *This **stake** will hold up the vine.*

Word use: Don't confuse this with **steak**.

stale
not fresh, or made a long time ago: *This bun is so **stale** that it's too hard to chew.*

Word building: more stale = **staler**, most stale = **stalest**

stalk[1] *(stork)*
the stem of a plant.

stalk[2] *(stork)*
to follow an animal quietly and with so much care that it doesn't hear a sound: *My cat will **stalk** any bird it sees.*

stall *(storl)*
1. a stand or a table for selling things outside: *I bought these roses at a flower **stall** in the city.*
2. a part of a stable or a shed where you keep a horse or a cow.

stallion *(**stal**-yon)*
a male horse that has grown up.

Word use: The female is a **mare**.

stammer *(**stamm**-er)*
to not be able to stop yourself repeating the first letter of some words.

Word use: Another word that means the same is **stutter**.

stamp
1. to push your foot down hard or on top of something on the ground: *Did she **stamp** her foot because she was cross?*
2. a small piece of paper that you buy to stick on the outside of a letter or a parcel.

stand
1. to be on your feet: *I have to **stand** for ages to wait for my bus.*
2. to put up with or bear someone or something: *I can't **stand** that bully.*
3. to be a sign of something: *The pictures of these doves **stand** for peace.*

Word building: I **stood**, I am **standing**

standard *(**stan**-dard)*
how good something usually is: *Your work isn't up to its usual high **standard**.*

star

1. one of the twinkling dots of light that we see shining in the sky at night. Our sun is also one of the many stars in space.
2. someone who is very good at what they do or who is a very famous actor or singer.

starch

a white powder or liquid that people use to make clothes stiff.

stare *(stair)*

to look straight at someone or something for a long time, with your eyes wide open: *I saw them **stare** at my pink hair.*
Word building: I **stared**, I am **staring**

start

1. to begin: *Let's **start** the show now.*
2. to make something begin to move: *The mechanic is trying to **start** the car.*

startle *(star-tl)*

to give a person or an animal a sudden fright: *If you shout like that, you'll **startle** the baby.*
Word building: I **startled**, I am **startling**

starve

to die or to be sick and weak because you don't have enough food to eat: *We need to help the children in some poor countries or they might **starve**.*
Word building: they **starved**, they are **starving** | People who starve die of **starvation**.

state

1. the way someone or something is: *He is in an unhappy **state** because he left his mobile on the bus.*
2. one of the main parts of a country, with its own government: *Tasmania is the **State** of Australia closest to the South Pole.*

statement *(**state**-ment)*

something you say or write down that tells what you think or know about an important thing: *In a **statement** on TV the Prime Minister promised more jobs.*

station *(**stay**-shon)*

1. a place where a train stops to let people get on or off.
2. a farm for keeping sheep or cattle.
3. a place with the special things or machines you need for a certain kind of job: *Go to the police **station** and say that you've been robbed.* | *The power **station** has closed down and no electricity is being made.*
4. a place where radio and television programs are made and sent out.

statue *(**stach**-oo)*

something in the shape of a person or an animal, made out of stone, wood or metal.

stay

1. to keep on being in a place: *You **stay** here while I go and get help.*
2. to live somewhere for a while: *I'd like to **stay** at a hotel by the sea.*

steady *(**sted**-ee)*

1. firm and not likely to move: *I feel safe climbing such a **steady** ladder.*
2. Something is **steady** if it goes on in the same way, without changing: ***Steady** rain has been falling for three days now.*
Word building: more steady = **steadier**, most steady = **steadiest**

steak *(stake)*

a thick slice of meat or fish that you can grill or fry.
Word use: Don't confuse this with **stake**.

steal *(steel)*

to take something that isn't yours.
Word building: I **stole**, I have **stolen**, I am **stealing**
Word use: Don't confuse this with **steel**.

steam *(steem)*

the cloud of gas that is made when water boils. We use it for making machines work and for heating buildings.

Word building: A place with a lot of steam is **steamy**.

steel

iron mixed with other kinds of metal to make it very hard and strong.

Word use: Don't confuse this with **steal**.

steep

Something is **steep** if it rises upwards suddenly and if it's hard to climb.

steer

to make something go the right way by using something like the wheel of a car or the rudder of a boat.

stem

1. the main part of a plant that grows up from the root.
2. the part which joins a flower, a leaf or fruit to a plant.

step

1. the movement you make when you lift your foot and then put it down in a different place.
2. a flat place where you put your foot when you are going up or coming down stairs or a ladder.

step-

a word part that tells you that you are related because a parent has married again, rather than by birth.

Word building: You can have a **step-parent**, **stepmother**, **stepfather**, **stepsister**, **stepbrother**, **stepchild**, **stepdaughter** or **stepson**.

stepfather

A person's **stepfather** is the man who is married to that person's mother, but isn't their father.

stepmother

A person's **stepmother** is the woman who is married to that person's father, but isn't their mother.

stern[1]

strict or firm: *The principal gave the naughty children a **stern** talk about why they should obey the school rules.*

stern[2]

the back of a boat.

stew *(rhymes with **new**)*

food, such as meat and vegetables, that has been cooked slowly in liquid.

stick[1]

a long, thin piece of wood.

stick[2]

1. to press something sharp into or through something: *Your finger will bleed if you **stick** a pin into it.*
2. to attach something with glue or something like glue: ***Stick** a stamp on this envelope.*

Word building: I **stuck**, I am **sticking**

sticker *(stick-er)*

a small piece of paper or plastic that has a printed picture or message on the front and glue on the back.

sticky *(stick-ee)*

Something is **sticky** if it has glue on it or if it feels as if it has glue on it: *Lick the **sticky** side of the stamp. | The floor is **sticky** where I spilt the lemonade.*

Word building: more sticky = **stickier**, most sticky = **stickiest**

sticky tape

tape that is sticky on one side and can be used to stick things together.

stiff

hard or not easy to bend: *This box is made of **stiff** cardboard.*

still

not moving: *The **still** water reflected our faces like a mirror.*

sting

to hurt, with a short, sharp pain: *Your eyes **sting** if you get soap in them.*

Word building: it **stung**, it is **stinging**

stingy *(stin-jee)*

mean about spending money.

Word building: more stingy = **stingier**, most stingy = **stingiest**

stink

to have a very bad smell: *When meat goes bad it begins to **stink**.*

Word building: it **stank**, it has **stunk**, it is **stinking**

stir *(ster)*

to mix something by moving a spoon or stick around in it.

Word building: I **stirred**, I am **stirring**

stockman *(stock-man)*

someone on a farm in the bush, whose job is to look after the cattle.

Word building: For more than one we use **stockmen**.

stomach *(stum-ik)*

the part in the middle of your body where food goes after you have swallowed it.

stone

1. the very hard stuff that rocks are made of: *The wall is made of **stone**.*
2. a piece of this very hard stuff: *Don't throw that **stone**.*
3. the hard, round seed inside fruit such as a cherry, a peach or a plum.

stool *(rhymes with **pool**)*

a seat with no sides or back.

stop

1. to not keep on doing something: *You have to **stop** your game when the bell goes.*
2. to come to rest after moving: *Wait for the bus to **stop** before you get off.*
3. to keep something from happening: *Someone has put a lock on the gate to **stop** us from playing on the court.*

Word building: I **stopped**, I am **stopping**

store

1. to put something away so that you can use it later.
2. a shop.

Word building: I **stored**, I am **storing** | A place where things are stored is called a **storeroom**.

storey *(stor-ree)*

one level of a building and all the rooms that are on it.

Word building: For more than one we use **storeys**.

Word use: Another word that means nearly the same is **floor**. | Don't confuse **storey** with **story**.

storm

a very strong wind, with rain, and sometimes thunder and lightning.

story *(stor-ree)*

something that you write or tell about things that have happened, either made up or in real life.

Word use: Don't confuse this with **storey**.

stove

something that uses gas, electricity or burning wood to give out heat. You cook food on a stove.

straight *(strate)*

1. not bent or curved: *I used my ruler to draw a **straight** line.*
2. without stopping or right now: *Come **straight** home after school.*

strain

1. to separate a liquid from the solid things that are in it: *We cook peas in boiling water and then **strain** them.*
2. to hurt a part of your body by pushing, pulling or stretching it too hard: *You must be careful when you pick up heavy things because you could **strain** your back.*

strange *(straynj)*

1. extraordinary or not usual: *No-one knows what caused the **strange** green light in the sky.*
2. not known or seen before: *When I saw the **strange** car outside our house, I knew that we had a visitor.*

Word building: more strange = **stranger**, most strange = **strangest**

stranger *(strayn-jer)*

1. someone that you haven't met before.
2. someone who has not been in a place before: *You must be a **stranger** to our town.*

strangle *(strang-gl)*

to kill someone by squeezing their throat so that they can't breathe.

Word building: he **strangled**, he is **strangling**

strap

a long, thin piece of leather or some other material that you use to tie or hold things in place: *My watch has a blue **strap**.*

straw

1. a thin, hollow tube, used for sucking drinks.
2. dry stalks of wheat, oats or corn.

strawberry *(straw-be-ree or straw-bree)*

a small, juicy, red fruit that has many tiny seeds on its skin.

Word building: For more than one we use **strawberries**.

stray

an animal, such as a dog or a cat, that is lost and has no home.

streak *(streek)*

a long, thin mark: *You have a **streak** of mud on your cheek.*

stream *(streem)*

a small amount of water that is flowing down to the sea. It is smaller than a river.

street

a road with buildings along one or both sides.

strength

how strong something or someone is: *Jemma has the **strength** to move this table.*

Word building: When you give something extra strength, you **strengthen** it.

stretch *(strech)*

1. to make something bigger by pulling it: ***Stretch** the collar of the jumper and it should go over your head.*
2. to make any part of your body long and straight: *I **stretch** my arms and yawn when I wake up.*

strict

Someone is **strict** if they want you to behave well and follow the rules all the time: *My teacher is **strict** about talking in class.*

strike

1. to give something or someone a hard tap: *I'll throw the ball and you **strike** it with the bat.*
2. the stopping of work by a group of workers until changes they want are made.

Word building: I **struck**, I am **striking**

string

a strong, thick thread used for tying things.

strip[1]

1. to take something off or away: *Mum told me to **strip** the sheets from the beds.*
2. to take off your clothes: *I am going to **strip** and get under the shower.*

Word building: I **stripped**, I am **stripping**

strip[2]

a long, narrow part of something: *Lieng tore a **strip** of paper from the top of the page.*

stripe

a long, narrow part of something that is a different colour from the rest: *I've painted a red **stripe** across this blue wall.*

stroke[1]

a movement where one thing hits another thing: *I chopped the log in two with a **stroke** of the axe.*

stroke[2]

to move your hand along something in an even and gentle way: *The cat purrs when I **stroke** its back.*

Word building: I **stroked**, I am **stroking**

strong

1. Someone or something is **strong** if they have a lot of power: *The wind was so **strong** that it blew our tent over.*
2. not easily broken: *I used a **strong** fishing line to catch the big fish.*

struggle *(strugg-l)*

to fight and push and move your arms and legs to get away.

Word building: I **struggled**, I am **struggling**

stubborn *(stubb-n)*

You are **stubborn** if you won't change your mind about something, even though you might be wrong.

student *(stew-dent)*

a person who is being taught.

study *(stud-ee)*

1. to spend your time learning about something.
2. to look at something very closely: *When you **study** a bubble you can see many different colours.*

Word building: I **studied**, I am **studying**

stuff

1. an everyday word for anything that you can touch, see or use to make things.
2. to push one thing inside another thing: *Can you help me **stuff** my sleeping bag back into its cover?*

stuffy *(stuff-ee)*

without fresh air: *Open the window — this room is very **stuffy**.*

Word building: more stuffy = **stuffier**, most stuffy = **stuffiest**

stump

the part of something that is left after the rest has been cut or broken off: *I sat on the **stump** of the dead tree.*

stupid *(styoo-pid)*

1. Somebody is **stupid** if they take a long time to understand something or to learn things.
2. not sensible: *I was **stupid** to leave my bag where you might trip over it.*

sturdy *(ster-dee)*

strong or tough.

Word building: more sturdy = **sturdier**, most sturdy = **sturdiest**

stutter *(stutt-er)*

to keep repeating the first parts of words: *Some people **stutter** when they are nervous.*

sty *(rhymes with **my**)*

a place where pigs are kept.

Word building: For more than one we use **sties**.

style *(stile)*

the special way something is made or designed: *Which **style** of furniture do you like most — modern or old?*

subject *(sub-ject)*

1. the thing or person that you are talking or writing about: *I'm sick of talking about that — let's change the subject.*

2. something like maths or spelling that you study at school: *My favourite subject is geography.*

submarine *(sub-ma-rine)*

a type of ship that can travel under water.

substance *(sub-stance)*

anything that you can touch or use to make things.

subtract *(sub-tract)*

to take one number or amount away from a larger number or amount: *If you subtract 2 from 6 you get 4.*

Word building: When you subtract one thing from another thing, you make a **subtraction**.

suburb *(sub-erb)*

any part of a city that has its own name, and its own shops, schools and parks.

succeed *(suk-seed)*

to get or do what you were trying to get or do: *I hope you succeed in finding the book you want.*

Word building: If I succeed, I will be very pleased with my **success**.

such

1. You use **such** when you are talking about how much or how big something is, and what happens because of this: *It was such a strong wind that my umbrella blew away.*

2. You use **such** or **such a** to make the next words stronger: *That bush has such beautiful flowers. | It was such a great movie I'm going to see it again next week!*

3. You use **such as** when you are giving examples of something: *She likes sports such as swimming and football.*

suck

to make air or liquid move into your mouth: *I like to suck lemonade through a straw.*

sudden *(sudd-n)*

Something is **sudden** if it happens quickly and without warning.

Word building: If something is sudden, then it happens **suddenly**.

suffer *(suff-er)*

to feel pain or sadness.

suffocate *(suff-o-cate)*

to die because there is not enough air to breathe.

Word building: he **suffocated**, he is **suffocating**

sugar *(shoog-ar)*

a sweet food that is added to other foods and drinks to give them a sweeter taste.

suggest *(su-jest)*

to tell someone your idea about something: *I suggest that we go to the beach.*

Word building: When you suggest something, you make a **suggestion**.

suicide *(soo-i-side)*

a death that happens because a person who wants to die does something that they know will kill them.

suit *(rhymes with boot)*

1. a set of clothes with trousers or a skirt and a jacket to match them.

2. to fit in with what you want to do: *Would it suit you if we changed the time of the meeting to 4 o'clock?*

Word building: If something suits (definition 2), then it is **suitable**.

suitcase *(soot-case; the first part rhymes with boot)*

a large, oblong bag that you use to carry clothes and other things when you travel.

sulk

to stop speaking to someone because you are cross and unhappy about something they've done.

sullen *(sull-n)*

You are **sullen** if you are cross and rude and if you won't talk to people.

sultana *(sul-tarn-a)*

a grape with all the water taken out: *A **sultana** is a dried fruit.*

sum

1. a total: *The **sum** of 14 and 6 is 20.*
2. an exercise in arithmetic: *Can you please help me work out these **sums**?*
3. an amount: *I have won a large **sum** of money!*

Word use: Don't confuse this with **some**.

summer *(summ-er)*

the season of the year when it is hot.

summit *(summ-it)*

the top of a mountain.

sun

the bright, round star that you see in the sky in the daytime. The sun gives heat and light to the earth.

Word use: Something to do with the sun is **solar**.

sunny

Something is **sunny** if it is full of light from the sun: *We wear our hats outside on **sunny** days. | The lizard stretched out on a rock in a **sunny** corner of the garden.*

sunrise

the beginning of the day, when the sun comes up over the horizon.

sunscreen *(sun-screen)*

a cream put on your skin to protect it from the sun.

Word use: This is sometimes called **sunblock**.

sunset

the end of the day, when the sun sinks down below the horizon.

sunshine

the light of the sun.

superior *(su-peer-ree-ar)*

better than someone or something else: *We were beaten by a **superior** team.*

Word use: The opposite of this is **inferior**.

supermarket *(soo-per-mar-ket)*

a large shop where you help yourself to the food and other things that you want to buy.

supersonic *(soo-per-sonn-ic)*

Something is **supersonic** if it travels faster than sound travels: *A **supersonic** plane called the Concorde flew from London to Sydney.*

supper *(supp-er)*

a small meal that you eat in the evening.

supply *(su-ply)*

1. to give or provide things that are needed: *This battery will **supply** electricity to your laptop.*
2. an amount of something that you keep and use when you need to: *We have a **supply** of firewood in the shed for winter.*

Word building: I **supplied**, I am **supplying**

support *(su-port)*

1. to hold something up: *The walls **support** the roof.*
2. to agree with something: *Do you **support** a ban on the killing of whales?*
3. to want something or someone to do well: *I **support** the local football team.*

Word building: A person who supports is called a **supporter**.

suppose (su-**poze**)
to think something is true although you don't know if it really is or not: *I suppose it's always very cold in Alaska.* | *Do you suppose Dad left this cake here for us to eat?*
Word building: I **supposed**, I am **supposing**

sure (shor)
You are **sure** of something if you have no doubt that it is right or true.
Word use: Don't confuse this with **shore**.

surf (serf)
1. the big waves with white foam, that roll onto the beach.
2. to explore the internet: *Let's surf for some information on spiders for our project.*

surface (ser-fiss)
1. the outside of anything: *The surface of the ball is shiny.*
2. the top of something: *A leaf floated on the surface of the water.*

surfboard (serf-bord)
a long, narrow board that you take into the surf so that you can stand or lie on it and let the waves take you back to the shore.

surgeon (ser-jon)
a doctor who is trained to cut open your body to fix an injury or to try to cure an illness.

surgery (ser-je-ree)
1. the room where you see your doctor or dentist.
2. any operation where a doctor cuts open your body to fix an injury or to try to cure an illness.
Word building: For more than one we use **surgeries**.

surname (ser-name)
your last name or the name that most of the people in your family have: *Her first name is Mana and her surname is Yamamoto.*

surprise (su-**prize**)
something that you didn't expect: *We are having a special party as a surprise for Marietta on her birthday.*

surrender (su-**ren**-der)
to stop fighting and to agree to do what the other side wants: *The soldiers defeated the enemy and told them to surrender.*

surround (su-**round**)
to go all around something or someone.

survive (su-**vive**)
to be alive or not damaged after an accident or a disaster: *Daniel was the only one to survive the bus accident.* | *My coin collection survived the fire.*
Word building: I **survived**, I am **surviving** | If you survive something, then you are a **survivor**. The act of surviving is called **survival**.

suspect (su-**spect**)
to think that someone has done something wrong though you don't know for sure: *The police suspect that one of the students stole it.*
Word building: When you suspect someone, you have a **suspicion** (su-**spish**-on) about them.

sustain (sus-**tane**)
to support something or keep it going: *This snack will sustain me until dinner.*

sustainable (sus-**tane**-able)
If something is **sustainable** it can be sustained, which means it can keep going. Natural resources that are **environmentally sustainable**, like the wind and the sun, can keep being used without running out.

swallow (swoll-oe)
to make something go down your throat: *I had a sip of water to help me swallow the medicine.*

swamp *(swomp)*
an area of wet, soft ground.
Word use: Another word that means nearly the same is **marsh**.

swan *(swon)*
a large bird with a long neck that lives near water. Some are white and some are black.

swap *(swop)*
to give one thing and get something else in return: *Would you like to **swap** one of your ham sandwiches for a cheese one of mine?* | *Let's **swap** email addresses.*
Word building: I **swapped**, I am **swapping**

swarm *(rhymes with **form**)*
a large group of insects, such as bees or ants.

swear *(rhymes with **care**)*
1. to use bad words: *It's not very nice to hear people **swear**.*
2. to make a serious promise: *I **swear** that I will always keep the secret.*
Word building: I **swore**, I have **sworn**, I am **swearing**

sweat *(swet)*
tiny drops of salty water that come through your skin when you are very hot or ill or when you've been moving your body a lot.

sweater *(**swet**-er)*
a knitted jumper.

sweep
to use a broom or a brush to move away small bits of dirt or rubbish: *It's your turn to **sweep** the leaves off the front path.*
Word building: I **swept**, I am **sweeping**

sweet
1. Something is **sweet** if it tastes of sugar.
2. a small piece of sweet food made with sugar, honey or chocolate.
Word use: The opposite of this is **sour**. | Another word for definition 2 is **lolly**.

swell
to get bigger: *Dried beans will **swell** if you leave them in water for a day.*
Word building: it **swelled**, it has **swollen**, it is **swelling** | A part of your body that swells is a **swelling**.

swerve *(swerv)*
to turn suddenly and move in a different direction: *The car had to **swerve** to miss the tree.*
Word building: I **swerved**, I am **swerving**

swift
very fast.

swim
to travel through or across water by moving your arms and legs.
Word building: I **swam**, I have **swum**, I am **swimming** | A person who swims is called a **swimmer**.

swimming costume
the piece of clothing that you wear when you go swimming.

swing
1. to move backwards and forwards, from side to side, or in a big curve.
2. a seat that hangs from two ropes. You sit on it and move backwards and forwards for fun.
Word building: I **swung**, I am **swinging**

switch *(swich)*
1. a knob or button that you press or turn to make something go on or off: *Turn the light off at the **switch**.*
2. to change one thing for another thing: *Could I **switch** my appointment from Monday to Thursday?*

sword *(sord)*
a weapon with a long, sharp, pointed blade.

a
b
c
d
e
f
g
h
i
j
k
l
m
n
o
p
q
r
s
t
u
v
w
x
y
z

sympathy *(sim-pa-thee)*

the feeling you have when you are sorry for someone who is sad, ill or in trouble.

Word building: If you feel sympathy, then you're **sympathetic** *(sim-pa-**thet**-ic)*.

synagogue *(sin-a-gog)*

a special place where Jews worship.

syrup *(sirrup)*

a thick, sweet, sticky liquid.

system

1. the way something is organised: *We need to think of a **system** for arranging all these DVDs.*

2. a set of connected parts: *This city has a good transport **system**.*

Word building: If something is arranged according to a system, it is **systematic**.

Tt

Tigers on trampolines teach turtles on tricycles.

tabby *(tabb-ee)*
a cat that has grey or brown fur with dark stripes.
Word building: For more than one we use **tabbies**.

table *(tay-bl)*
a piece of furniture with a flat top and legs.

table tennis
a game like tennis that you play indoors on a table, using small bats and a very light plastic ball.
Word use: Another name for this is **ping-pong**.

tabouli *(ta-**bool**-lee; the middle part rhymes with **pool**)*
a salad of parsley, cracked wheat and lemon.

tack
1. a small nail.
2. to sew together with big, loose stitches: *We'll **tack** the sleeve first, then sew it properly later.*

tackle *(tack-l)*
1. to try to do something that is difficult.
2. to grab someone around their body or legs to make them stop running.
3. all the things that you need to do something: *I keep my fishing **tackle** in a special basket with a lid.*
Word building: I **tackled**, I am **tackling**

taco *(**tar**-ko or **tak**-o)*
a flat piece of crisp, Mexican corn bread folded around spicy meat, lettuce and tomato.
Word building: For more than one we use **tacos**.

tadpole *(**tad**-pole)*
a baby frog or toad. It has a round body and a tail and it lives in water. As it gets bigger it grows legs and is able to leave the water.

tai chi *(ty **chee**)*
a set of exercises in which it is important to move smoothly from one exercise to the next while keeping your balance. It can help keep your mind alert.
Word use: This word comes from the Chinese language and means 'fist of the Great Absolute'.

tail
the part at the end of the body of an animal like a cat, dog or fish, which they can move: *A dog wags its **tail**.*
Word use: Don't confuse this with **tale**.

tailor *(**tay**-lor)*
someone whose job is to make or mend clothes.

a b c d e f g h i j k l m n o p q r s **t** u v w x y z

taipan *(ty-pan; the first part rhymes with eye)*
a long, brown snake whose bite can kill you.

Word use: This word comes from the Wik-Mungkan language of Queensland. See the map of Australian Aboriginal languages at the end of this book.

take
1. to get in your hands: *Take as much as you like because there's plenty here.* | *I can't find my pillow — did you* ***take*** *it?*
2. to bring: *Take your coat because it might get cold.* | *Are you going to* ***take*** *us to the movies tomorrow?*

Word building: I **took**, I have **taken**, I am **taking**

takeaway *(take-a-way)*
a hot or cold meal that you buy at a shop, but take to a different place to eat.

Word use: This is also called **fast food**.

take-off *(take-off)*
when an aeroplane starts its journey by leaving the land and flying into the air.

tale
a story.

Word use: Don't confuse this with **tail**.

talent *(tal-ent)*
what you have if you can do something very well: *The teacher said I have a* ***talent*** *for painting — maybe I'll be a famous artist one day.*

talk *(tork)*
to speak or discuss: *I was too shy to* ***talk*** *to anyone at the party.* | *Alex did not want to* ***talk*** *about sad things.*

tall *(rhymes with ball)*
1. how high someone or something is: *Laura is one metre* ***tall***.
2. higher than usual: *There are many* ***tall*** *buildings in the city.*

tame
An animal is **tame** if it is used to being touched or fed by humans.

Word building: more tame = **tamer**, most tame = **tamest**

tan
1. to let the sun make your skin turn brown.
2. to change the skin of an animal into leather: *After you* ***tan*** *the skin of a cow you can use it to make shoes or coats.*
3. Something is **tan** if it's the brown colour that white skin goes in the sun.

Word building: I **tanned**, I am **tanning**

tangle *(tang-gl)*
to make or get something into a twisted knot: *If you let the kitten play with the knitting wool, it will* ***tangle*** *it.*

Word building: I **tangled**, I am **tangling**

tank
1. a big container for holding petrol or water.
2. a strong, heavy vehicle with armour on the outside and guns on top.

tanker *(tank-er)*
a ship or a truck for carrying a lot of oil or any other kind of liquid.

tap[1]
to hit lightly: *Let's* ***tap*** *on the window to get her attention.*

Word building: I **tapped**, I am **tapping**

tap[2]
1. something used to control the flow of liquid: *Turn off the* ***tap*** *when you brush your teeth.*
2. to get something from a supply: *I will* ***tap*** *my supply of frozen meals to feed the unexpected visitors.*

Word building: I **tapped**, I am **tapping**

tape
1. a long, narrow strip of paper for sticking or cloth for sewing.
2. a long, narrow strip of special plastic that you can use in a machine to record sounds or pictures.

tar
the thick, black, sticky stuff that comes from coal or wood. It is used for making roads.

target *(tar-get)*
something that you aim at and try to hit or reach.

tart
a fruit or jam pie that doesn't have pastry on the top.

task *(rhymes with ask)*
some work that you have to do: *Your next task is to finish your homework.*

Tasmanian devil *(taz-may-nee-an dev-il)*
an animal that is about the size of a small dog, and lives in Tasmania. It has black fur, eats meat and looks very fierce.

taste *(tayst)*
1. the way a food or drink seems to you when you put it in your mouth: *This juice has a very sweet taste.*
2. to take a small bite or sip of something as a test.
Word building: I **tasted**, I am **tasting**

tax
money that people pay each year to the government for them to spend in running the country.

taxi *(tax-ee)*
a car that you can hire to travel in.
Word building: For more than one we use **taxis**.

T-ball *(tee-ball)*
a type of softball for children in which the ball is not thrown to the batter, but is hit from a pole at waist height.

tea *(tee)*
1. a meal that you have in the afternoon or evening.
2. a drink made by pouring boiling water onto the dry leaves of a plant.

teach *(teech)*
to give someone knowledge, to make someone understand something or to show someone how to do something.
Word building: I **taught**, I am **teaching** | Someone whose job is to teach people is a **teacher**.

team *(teem)*
a group of people who do something together: *The team of doctors took turns to rest during the long operation.* | *The school's netball team has a big match tomorrow.*

tear[1] *(teer)*
a drop of water that falls from your eye when you cry.

tear[2] *(tair)*
to pull something and damage it, or to pull something into pieces with rough edges: *That sharp nail could easily tear someone's clothes.* | *Tear the paper into long strips.*
Word building: I **tore**, I have **torn**, I am **tearing**

tease *(teeze)*
to say or do things to annoy someone and to make them embarrassed.
Word building: I **teased**, I am **teasing**

technical *(tek-nik-l)*

1. Something is **technical** if it is connected with science and machinery: *You will need a technical education to work as an engineer.*
2. using words or covering topics that only an expert would understand.

Word building: If someone works in a technical area, they are a **technician** who does things **technically**, and you talk about their **technicality**.

technique *(tek-neek)*

the way of doing or performing something: *Since I learned this new technique for playing my guitar, I have really improved.*

teddy bear

a toy bear.

teenager *(teen-age-er)*

someone who is older than twelve and younger than twenty: *I'm a teenager now that I'm thirteen.*

Word building: A teenager is interested in **teenage** things.

telephone *(tel-e-fone)*

a machine you use to speak to someone who is far away from you.

Word building: This word is often shortened to **phone**.

telescope *(tel-e-scope)*

something you look through, which makes things that are far away seem closer. It is shaped like a tube and it has curved glass at both ends.

television *(tel-e-vizh-on)*

a machine you use to watch films or other shows.

Word building: This word is often shortened to **TV**.

tell

to speak because you want to give someone a picture of something, give them an order or say something: *I'd like to tell you about my dream. | Tell Ali to meet us at the park.*

Word building: I **told**, I am **telling**

temper *(tem-per)*

the way you are feeling at any one time: *If you're smiling, then you must be in a good temper. | I'm in a bad temper because someone broke my CD player.*

temperature *(temp-ra-cher)*

a measure of how hot or cold something or someone is: *The temperature in Darwin reached 39°C today. | The normal temperature of most people when they are well is 37°C.*

temple *(tem-pl)*

a special place where people worship.

temporary *(temp-ree)*

Something is **temporary** if it lasts for only a short time.

Word use: The opposite of this is **permanent**.

tempt *(tempt)*

to try to make someone do something silly or wrong: *Don't tempt me to talk in class.*

Word building: When someone tempts you, they offer you a **temptation**.

tender *(ten-der)*

1. soft and easy to chew or cut.
2. kind and full of love.
3. sore to press or touch.

Word building: If you have a tender heart, you treat people **tenderly** and with a lot of **tenderness**.

tennis *(tenn-is)*

a game for two or four players who use racquets to hit a ball over a net.

tense[1]
1. rigid or stretched tight.
2. feeling nervous or unable to relax:
I felt so tense while I waited for the judge's decision.
Word building: If you feel tense about something, you are suffering from **tension** and you might behave **tensely**.

tense[2]
the form of a verb which shows the time of an action. There is **past tense**, **present tense** and **future tense**.

tent
a shelter made of cloth held up by poles. You can move it easily from place to place when you're camping.

tentacle *(tent-a-kel)*
one of the long, thin parts which some sea animals use to feel or hold things.

term
one of the parts of the year when schools and colleges are open and teachers and their students aren't on holiday.

termite *(ter-mite)*
a white insect that eats wood and which can destroy houses or things like tables and chairs.

terrible *(te-ri-bl)*
very bad.

terrier *(te-ree-er)*
one of the small dogs that were once used for hunting.

terrific *(te-rif-ic)*
1. very great: *The cracker went off with a terrific bang.*
2. very good: *We had a terrific time riding our boogie boards.*

terrify *(te-ri-fy)*
to frighten someone very much.
Word building: it **terrified**, it is **terrifying** | Things that terrify you fill you with **terror**.

territory *(te-ri-tree)*
land thought of as belonging to someone.
Word building: For more than one we use **territories**. | If someone claims that a territory belongs to them then they are **territorial**.

terror
a very strong fear: *I have a terror of spiders.*

terrorist
someone who fights a government by making people very afraid of something: *The terrorist said that he would explode a bomb if the government didn't do what he demanded.*
Word building: A terrorist does acts of **terrorism**.

test
1. a number of questions you have to answer, to show how much you know about something.
2. to try something so that you can find out about it: *Test this bed and tell me if it's too hard to sleep on.*

text
1. the words in a book or on a page, rather than the pictures.
2. a piece of writing.
3. a text message: *I'll send you a text when I find out the time of the concert.*
4. to send a text message: *Don't forget to text me when you get there!*
Word building: Something in a text or based on a text is **textual**.

texta *(tex-ta)*
a thick, brightly coloured pen that is used to fill in the blank parts of a picture.
Word use: This is sometimes called a **felt pen**.

textbook
a book of information on a subject that you are studying.

text message

a message you send on a mobile phone.

than

a word you use to compare one thing to another: *This cake is nicer **than** that one.* | *I am taller **than** you.*

thank

to tell someone how grateful you are for something they've done for you or given you.

that

a word you use to point something out or to show which thing you are talking about: ***That** is a nice coat.* | ***That** is exactly what I mean!*

thaw *(thor)*

to melt: *If you take the meat out of the freezer now, it should **thaw** by dinner time.*

theatre *(theer-ter)*

a building where you can go to see plays, opera, ballet and films.

their *(dhair)*

belonging to them: *These are **their** books.*

Word use: Don't confuse this with **there** or **they're**.

theirs *(dhairs)*

belonging to them: *Those hats are **theirs**.*

them

a word you use when you are talking about other people or things: *Your friends will bring their parents with **them**.* | *You need to water the plants if you want **them** to grow.*

themselves

a word you use when you are talking about something other people have done to their bodies or something they have done without help: *They rubbed sunscreen on **themselves** before heading for the beach.* | *The children grew these vegetables **themselves**.*

then

1. at that time: *We lived by the sea **then**.*
2. soon afterwards: *He put on his coat, **then** rushed out of the house.*
3. in that case: *You forgot your lunch? **Then** you can have some of mine.*

there *(dhair)*

in or at that place: *Your other shoe is **there**, where you left it.*

Word use: Don't confuse this with **their** or **they're**. | The opposite of this is **here**.

therefore

as a result: *Mum ate all the ice-cream, and **therefore** we'll have to find something else for dessert.*

thermometer *(ther-mom-e-ter)*

something for measuring how hot or cold someone or something is.

thesaurus *(the-saw-rus)*

a book of words arranged in groups which have a similar meaning.

these

a word you use to show which things you are talking about: ***These** are my favourite shoes.*

they *(dhay)*

a word you use when you are talking about other people or things: *The teachers said **they** would help us plan the school dance.* | *We need to paint the walls because **they** have become very dirty.*

they're *(dhair)*

a short way of saying **they are**.

Word use: Don't confuse this with **there** or **their**.

thick

Something is **thick** if it measures a lot from one side to the other: *Can you please cut me a **thick** slice of bread?*

Word building: When you make something thick, you **thicken** it so it has a lot of **thickness**.

Word use: The opposite of this is **thin**.

thief *(theef)*

someone who takes things that belong to someone else.

Word building: For more than one we use **thieves**. | If a thief steals something, then they are guilty of **theft**.

thigh *(rhymes with **my**)*

the top part of your leg, above your knee.

thimble *(**thim**-bl)*

a metal cover you wear on your finger so you don't prick it when you're sewing.

thin

1. Something is **thin** if it doesn't measure very much from one side to the other: *This slice of bread is so **thin** that I made a hole in it when I was spreading the butter.*

2. You are **thin** if there isn't much fat on your body and if you don't weigh very much.

Word building: more thin = **thinner**, most thin = **thinnest** | If something is very thin you talk about its **thinness**.

Word use: The opposite of definition 1 is **thick**.

thing

A **thing** is any object, feeling or idea.

think

1. to use your mind to make pictures of things or to find the answer to problems: *I often **think** about my trip to Uluru.* | *Try to **think** what we should do.*

2. to have an idea about something: *Did you **think** of something fun to do on Saturday?*

Word building: I **thought**, I am **thinking**

thirst *(therst)*

the dry feeling you have in your mouth and throat when you need something to drink.

Word building: When you feel thirst, then you're **thirsty**.

this

a word you use to point something out or to show which thing you are talking about: ***This** is my favourite shirt.*

thorn

a bit that sticks out from the stem of some plants and has a sharp point.

those

a word you use to point things out or to show which things you are talking about: ***Those** are my shoes over there.* | ***Those** sorts of lollies are my favourite.*

though *(dhoh)*

1. in spite of the fact that: ***Though** he had plenty of time to get ready, he was still late.*

2. as though, as if: *It rained **as though** it would never stop.*

thought *(thort)*

an idea you have in your mind: *I had a brilliant **thought** about what you should wear to the party.*

thoughtful
1. deep in thought.
2. showing that something has been given a lot of thought: *This is a very **thoughtful** discussion.*
3. considerate: *My neighbours are very kind and **thoughtful**.*

Word use: The opposite of definition 3 is **thoughtless**.

thoughtless *(thort-less)*
If you are thoughtless, you are not thinking carefully, or you are not considering the needs or feelings of other people: *It was very **thoughtless** of you not to invite Toby to your birthday party.*

Word use: The opposite of this is **thoughtful**.

throughout *(throo-out)*
1. everywhere in: *There is interesting wildlife **throughout** Australia.*
2. from the beginning to the end: *I laughed **throughout** the movie.*

thread *(thred)*
a very long thin piece of cotton or anything like this, used for sewing.

thrill
to make someone feel very excited.

Word building: Anything that thrills you is **thrilling**.

throat *(throte)*
1. the front of your neck, under your chin.
2. the part of your body that food passes through on its way from your mouth to your stomach, and air travels down to get to your lungs.

throne
the special chair that a king or a queen sits on at special times.

through *(throo)*
from one side or end of something to the other: *The camels walked **through** the desert.* | *We crawled **through** the pipe.*

throw *(thro)*
to make something go through the air: ***Throw** the ball to me.*

Word building: I **threw**, I have **thrown**, I am **throwing**

thumb *(thum)*
the finger on the inside of your hand, that is much shorter and thicker than the others.

thump
to hit someone or something hard.

thunder *(thun-der)*
the loud, deep noise that comes after a flash of lightning in a storm.

tick[1]
1. the clicking sound a clock makes.
2. a small mark (✓) that shows something has been done the right way.

tick[2]
a tiny animal like an insect, that sucks blood. It can kill dogs and cats.

ticket *(tick-et)*
the small card or piece of paper you get to show that you've paid for something: *Don't forget to buy a train **ticket**.* | *I'd like a **ticket** for the concert on Wednesday.*

tickle *(tick-l)*
to poke someone with your fingers to make them laugh.

Word building: I **tickled**, I am **tickling**

tide
the movement of the seas and oceans up and down. This happens two times each day.

tidy *(tide-dee)*
with everything in the place where it belongs.

Word building: more tidy = **tidier**, most tidy = **tidiest**

tie
1. to fix something firmly in place with a knot or a bow.
2. to get the same number of points in a contest: *If the two teams **tie** they'll both get a prize.*
3. a long, thin piece of cloth you wear around your neck, with a knot under your collar.

Word building: I **tied**, I am **tying**

tiger *(ty-ger)*
an animal with black stripes and yellow fur. It is a large, fierce cat.

tight *(tite)*
Something is **tight** if it fits very closely, with no room to spare.

Word building: If you make something more tight, then you **tighten** it.

tile
a thin piece of baked clay that is used for covering roofs, floors and walls.

till
up to the time of: *I will practise piano **till** dinner time.*

timber *(tim-ber)*
wood which has been sawn into pieces, ready for building things.

time
1. the hours, days, weeks, months and years that pass by.
2. the particular moment that a clock shows: *The **time** now is 2 o'clock.*

time line
1. a line with the dates of important events in history marked on it.
2. a plan of dates for when important things need to happen.

timid *(tim-id)*
A person or an animal is **timid** if they become frightened easily.

Word building: If you are timid you do things **timidly** and with a lot of **timidity** *(ti-mid-i-tee)*.

tin
1. a light silver-coloured metal that cans and cooking pots are made of.
2. a metal container, such as a can: *Did you hide the biscuit **tin**? | Keep the spare buttons together in a **tin**.*

tiny *(tine-ee)*
very small.

Word building: more tiny = **tinier**, most tiny = **tiniest**

tip¹
the pointed part at the end of something: *I've cut the **tip** of my finger.*

tip²
1. to make something slope or fall over: *Be careful not to **tip** the tin of paint.*
2. a place you can take your rubbish.

tip³
1. money you give to thank someone who has done something for you: *I'll leave a **tip** for that helpful waiter.*
2. a piece of useful information: *Can you give me some **tips** on how to use this computer program?*

tiptoe *(tip-toe)*
to walk softly and carefully on the tips of your toes.

Word building: I **tiptoed**, I am **tiptoeing**

tire *(ty-er)*
to make or get sleepy or weak: *Such a long walk will **tire** the children. | I always **tire** quickly after an illness.*

Word building: I **tired**, I am **tiring** | If something tires you, it makes you feel **tired**.

Word use: Don't confuse **tire** with **tyre**.

tissue *(tish-oo)*
soft, thin paper.

title *(tite-l)*
1. the name of a poem, a book, a film or a piece of music.
2. the special name that shows what job someone does or how important they are. Some of the titles people have are **Doctor**, **Mr**, and **Ms**.

to *(rhymes with **you**)*
in the direction of: *Throw the ball **to** me!*
Word use: Don't confuse this with **too** or **two**.

toad *(tode)*
an animal like a big frog.

toadstool *(**tode**-stool; the last part rhymes with **pool**)*
a plant that looks like a mushroom. Some are poisonous. If you eat one of these you could get very sick or die.

toast *(rhymes with **most**)*
bread cut into slices and cooked until it is brown on both sides.

tobacco *(ta-**bak**-o)*
a plant with leaves that are dried and used for smoking in cigarettes, cigars and pipes.

today *(to-**day**)*
this day: ***Today** is Wednesday.*

toe
one of the five parts at the end of your foot.

toffee *(**toff**-ee)*
a sticky, brown sweet.

together *(to-**gedh**-er)*
1. with another person or thing: *They walked **together** in the park.*
2. at the same time: *You must start to sing **together**.*

toilet
1. a bowl connected to a drain for getting rid of waste from your body.
2. a room where people go to use a toilet.
Word use: Another word for this is **lavatory**.

token *(**toe**-ken)*
a ticket or disc used instead of money to pay for something.

tollway *(**toll**-way)*
a road that you must pay money to travel on.

tomato *(to-**mar**-toe)*
a round, red fruit that you can eat.
Word building: For more than one we use **tomatoes**.

tomorrow *(to-**morr**-oe)*
the day after today.

ton *(tun)*
an old-fashioned measure of how heavy things are. One ton is about 1016 kilograms.
Word use: Don't confuse this with **tonne**.

tongue *(tung)*
the soft, wet thing in your mouth, that you use for eating and talking.

tonight
the night following this day.

tonne *(rhymes with **on**)*
a measure you use when you weigh something very heavy. There are 1000 kilograms in a tonne.
Word use: Don't confuse this with **ton**.

tonsil *(**ton**-sel)*
one of the two soft things at the back of your throat.
Word building: If your tonsils are sore, then you might have **tonsillitis** (ton-si-**ly**-tis).

too

1. also: *I like chocolate **too**!*

2. very, or more than is wanted: *You are speaking **too** loudly.*

Word use: Don't confuse this with **to** or **two**.

tool

something you use for doing some kinds of work. Hammers, saws and knives are all tools.

tooth

one of the hard, white parts that grow inside your mouth.

Word building: For more than one we use **teeth**.

toothpaste

a paste you use to clean your teeth.

top

1. the highest part of something: *I'll race you to the **top** of the hill! | Your hat is on the **top** of the cupboard.*

2. a lid for something: *Put the **top** back on the jam jar.*

3. a piece of clothing for the upper part of your body: *I'm going to wear my new green **top**.*

topic *(top-ic)*

the thing that you're talking or writing about: *We chose the environment as a **topic** for discussion.*

topple *(topp-l)*

to fall over or tumble down.

Word building: I **toppled**, I am **toppling**

torch *(torch)*

a light with a battery which you can carry around in your hand.

torpedo *(taw-pee-doe)*

a bomb that a submarine shoots through the water.

Word building: For more than one we use **torpedoes**.

tortoise *(tor-tiss)*

a reptile with a hard shell covering its body. Most of them live on the land.

Word use: Look and see how this animal is different from a **turtle**.

torture *(tor-cher)*

to give someone very great pain usually to find out something from them.

Word building: he **tortured**, he is **torturing**

toss

to throw something: ***Toss** the paper into the bin.*

total *(tote-l)*

1. the whole amount of something when you add it up: *What is the **total** of these numbers?*

2. in every way: *Your room is a **total** mess.*

Word building: If your room is a total mess, then it's **totally** messy.

touch *(tuch)*

1. to feel something or someone with your hand or finger.

2. to be so close that one thing rests against another: *Push the blocks together until the sides **touch**.*

3. the power to feel things with your body, especially your hands.

tough *(tuff)*

hard to break or cut: *Jeans are made of **tough** material.*

tour *(too-er)*

to travel through a place stopping to look at things that interest you: *When we **tour** Queensland we'd like to visit the Great Barrier Reef.*

tourist

someone who travels or tours for pleasure.

Word building: The business of looking after tourists is **tourism**.

tow *(rhymes with go)*
to pull something behind you using a rope or a chain.

towards
in the direction of: *That road leads towards the beach.*

towel *(rhymes with growl)*
a piece of cloth you use for drying something wet.

tower *(rhymes with flower)*
1. a tall, narrow part of a building such as a church or a castle: *The cathedral's bells are in that tower.*
2. any tall, narrow building: *There is a control tower at the airport.*

town
a large group of houses, shops and offices where many people live and work. It is larger than a village and smaller than a city.
Word building: A small town is a **township**.

toy
a thing you play with.

trace
1. a small amount of something: *There is a trace of chocolate on your top lip.*
2. to copy a drawing, a plan or a map by putting a piece of thin paper over it and following along its lines with a pencil.
Word building: I **traced**, I am **tracing**

track
1. a path through the bush or other rough country.
2. the metal rails that a train runs along.
3. marks that show who or what has passed along that way: *The horse left a track of hoof prints in the sand.*
4. the part of a playing field where running takes place.
5. a section of a CD containing one song or piece of music.

tractor *(trak-tor)*
a machine with large wheels and a strong engine. It pulls heavy things on a farm.

trade
1. the buying and selling of things: *Trade at Christmas time was very busy because people were buying lots of presents.*
2. the kind of job you do with your hands or using special tools: *I'll learn a trade and become a carpenter.*

tradition *(tra-dish-on)*
the handing down of beliefs, customs and stories from old people to younger people.
Word building: If something is a tradition among a group of people, it is **traditional** and it is done **traditionally**.

traffic *(traff-ic)*
everything that travels along a road.

tragedy *(traj-e-dee)*
a very sad or dreadful thing that happens.
Word building: For more than one we use **tragedies**. | Any tragedy is **tragic** for the people it happens to.

trail
1. a path made through the mountains or across any rough country.
2. the signs left behind by an animal or a person being hunted.
Word use: Don't confuse this with **trial**.

trailer *(tray-ler)*
something a car or a truck pulls along for carrying heavy loads.

train *(trane)*
1. an engine and the carriages it pulls along a railway track.
2. to teach an animal or a person how to do something.
Word building: When someone trains you, they are giving you **training**.

traitor *(tray-tor)*
  someone who tells an enemy secrets about their friends or their country.

tram
  a passenger vehicle which moves along rails, often on streets and usually powered by electricity from an overhead wire

tramp
  1. to walk with heavy steps: *We heard the soldiers **tramp** down the road in their big boots.*
  2. someone who wanders around without a home.

trampoline *(tramp-o-leen)*
  a frame with material stretched over it and joined to it by springs. You can bounce up and down on it.

trance *(rhymes with dance)*
  the way someone is when they don't know what is happening around them.

transfer *(trans-fer)*
  to send or move someone or something from one place to another: *My dad's boss is going to **transfer** him to a different office. | Can you please **transfer** the money into my bank account?*
  Word building: I **transferred**, I am **transferring**

translate
  to change from one language into another: *She will **translate** the poem from French into English.*
  Word building: I **translated**, I am **translating** | Someone who translates is a **translator** and they make **translations**.

transparent *(trans-pair-rent)*
  Something is **transparent** if you can see through it as if it wasn't there.

transport *(trans-port)*
  to carry or take people, animals or things from one place to another.

trap
  something made for catching animals so that they can't escape.

trapdoor *(trap-door)*
  a small door in a floor or a ceiling.

trapeze *(tra-peze)*
  a short bar that hangs from ropes. Acrobats swing on one while they do their tricks.

travel *(trav-el)*
  to go from one place to another.
  Word building: I **travelled**, I am **travelling** | Someone who travels is a **traveller**.

tray
  a flat piece of wood, plastic or metal used for carrying things.

tread *(tred)*
  to walk or to step on something: *Watch where you **tread**. | Please don't **tread** on my toys.*
  Word building: I **trod**, I have **trodden**, I am **treading**

treasure *(trezh-er)*
  something that's worth a lot of money, such as gold or jewels.

treat *(treet)*
  1. to behave towards someone in a certain way: *I like you, so I will always **treat** you well.*
  2. something special that someone gives you: *I'll take you out to dinner as a **treat** on your birthday.*

tree
  a plant with leaves, branches, roots and a trunk.

tremble *(trem-bl)*
  to shake because you are frightened, weak or• cold: *When I got out of the swimming pool, my knees began to **tremble**.*
  Word building: I **trembled**, I am **trembling**

a b c d e f g h i j k l m n o p q r s **t** u v w x y z

trespass *(tress-pass)*
to go somewhere that you shouldn't, often onto someone's land without asking them.
Word building: If you trespass, then you are a **trespasser**.

trial *(try-al)*
1. the time when a person is brought into a court of law. A judge and a jury have to decide whether or not they have done something wrong.
2. a test to see if something works.
Word use: Don't confuse this with **trail**.

triangle *(try-ang-gl)*
1. a flat shape with three sides. See the picture at the end of this book.
2. a musical instrument with three sides made of steel.

tribe
a group of families that are related to each other. They do things the same way and they live in the same place.

trick
1. something someone does to fool people: *I want to play a funny **trick** on Maya.*
2. something clever that you need a lot of skill to do: *The juggler showed me a great **trick**.*

trickle *(trick-l)*
to flow in a very small or slow stream: *Tears began to **trickle** down his cheeks.*
Word building: it **trickled**, it is **trickling**

tricky
1. difficult to work out: *This is a **tricky** puzzle.*
2. likely to play tricks in order to deceive someone: *My big sister is a very **tricky** person!*

tricycle *(try-sik-l)*
something you ride, with one wheel at the front and two wheels at the back.

trigger *(trigg-er)*
the part on a gun that you press to fire the bullet.

trim
to make something shorter so that it's neat and tidy, usually by cutting it: *Keep still while I **trim** your hair.*
Word building: I **trimmed**, I am **trimming**

trip
1. You take a **trip** when you travel somewhere.
2. to fall over: *Don't **trip** on these rocks.*
Word building: I **tripped**, I am **tripping**

triumph *(try-umf)*
something important that you have done well, such as winning a race.
Word building: If you have a triumph, then you're **triumphant**.

troop
a group of people who do things together: *The **troop** of soldiers marched down the street.*

tropical *(trop-i-cal)*
Something is **tropical** if it comes from one of the hot parts of the world, near the equator: *Pineapples and bananas are **tropical** fruit.*

trot
to move in a way that is fast and steady.
Word building: I **trotted**, I am **trotting**

trouble *(trub-l)*
Someone or something causes **trouble** when they make things difficult for you.
Word building: When something bad is happening to you, then you are **in trouble**.

trousers *(trow-zez)*
something you wear to cover your body from your waist down to your ankles. There is a part for each of your legs.

truck
a special kind of strong car used for carrying heavy loads.

true *(troo)*
1. Something is **true** if it really happened.
2. able to be depended on when you need them: *You are my only **true** friend.*
Word building: more true = **truer**, most true = **truest**

trumpet *(trum-pet)*
a musical instrument that you blow, made of brass.

trunk
1. the main or middle part of something, such as a tree trunk or the trunk of your body.
2. a strong box or chest for keeping or carrying your things in.
3. an elephant's long nose.

trust
to believe that someone or something will help or support you if you need them: *Of course I **trust** my best friend.*
Word building: Someone or something you can trust is **trustworthy**.

truth *(trooth)*
what has really happened: *You must believe that I'm telling the **truth**.*
Word building: If you tell the truth, then you're **truthful**.

try *(rhymes with **my**)*
1. to see if you can do something: ***Try** to read this book and I'll help you with the hard words.*
2. to test something to see what happens: ***Try** this pair of shoes to see if they fit you.*
Word building: I **tried**, I am **trying**

T-shirt
a short-sleeved shirt without a collar.
Word use: Some people spell this **tee-shirt**.

tsunami *(sooh-**nah**-mee)*
a very large wave caused by an earthquake beneath the sea. It can cause a lot of damage.

tuan *(tyoo-an)*
a small marsupial that looks like a mouse with a hairy-tipped tail. It lives mainly in trees and is endangered.
Word use: Another name for this is **phascogale**. The word **tuan** comes from the Wathawurung language of Victoria. See the map of Australian Aboriginal languages at the end of this book.

tub
a container with a round, flat bottom: *You can wash the dog in this **tub** of water. | Here's the lid for that **tub** of butter.*

tube *(tyoob)*
1. a long, thin, empty container that gas or liquid can move through.
2. a soft, thin container for holding something like toothpaste.

tuck
to fold something and put it inside something else in a neat way: ***Tuck** this handkerchief into your pocket.*

tuckshop *(tuck-shop)*
a shop, usually in a school, which sells lunches and snacks.

tuft
a bunch of things like hair, feathers or bits of grass, sticking up in the air.

tug
1. to pull something hard.
2. a small, powerful boat that is used to pull and push big ships.
Word building: I **tugged**, I am **tugging**

tulip *(tyoo-lip)*
a flower that grows from a bulb. It is shaped like a cup.

a b c d e f g h i j k l m n o p q r s **t** u v w x y z

tumble (tum-bl)
to fall and roll over.

Word building: I **tumbled**, I am **tumbling**

tune (tyoon)
musical sounds that go together to make a pleasant pattern for singing or playing.

Word use: Another word that means nearly the same is **melody**.

tunic (tyoo-nic)
a dress that has straight sides and doesn't have sleeves. Girls often wear them to school.

tunnel (tunn-l)
a long hole that goes through the ground. Some are big enough for trains and cars.

turkey (ter-kee)
a large bird that is kept for eating.

Word building: For more than one we use **turkeys**.

turn (tern)
1. to move around: *Turn the handle to open the door.* | *The wheels are starting to turn.*
2. to become: *Do your cheeks turn pink when you giggle?*
3. to change one thing into another thing: *This magic wand can turn a mouse into a horse.*
4. a chance or time for you to do something or get something: *Who wants a turn on the swing?*

turtle (tert-l)
a reptile with a hard shell covering its body, that lives in the sea.

Word use: Look and see how this animal is different from a **tortoise**.

tusk
one of two long, curved teeth that animals such as the elephant and the walrus have.

TV
a machine you use to watch films or other shows.

Word building: This is a short way of saying **television**.

twice
two times: *Knock once for 'no' and twice for 'yes'.*

twig
a small, thin branch of a tree.

twin
one of two children who have the same mother and who were born at the same time.

twinkle (twink-l)
to shine with many quick flashes of light: *Stars twinkle in the sky at night.*

Word building: I **twinkled**, I am **twinkling**

twirl (twerl)
to turn around and around.

twist (twist)
1. to wind things around each other: *To make a rope you twist many strings together.*
2. to turn or bend something: *The bottle top will come off if you twist it around.*

two (rhymes with **you**)
the second number.

Word use: Don't confuse this with **to** or **too**.

type (tipe)
1. a kind or sort: *Is this the type of paper that you wanted?*
2. to write with a machine which has keys you press down to make letters and numbers: *Type this letter, please.*

Word building: I **typed**, I am **typing**

typewriter

a machine with keys that you press down to type letters and numbers.

tyre *(rhymes with **fire**)*

a ring of rubber that goes around the edge of a wheel.

Word use: Don't confuse this with **tire**.

a
b
c
d
e
f
g
h
i
j
k
l
m
n
o
p
q
r
s
t
u
v
w
x
y
z

Uu

Umpires in uniform upset unicorns in underwear.

ugly (*ug-lee*)
not attractive to look at: *I have an **ugly** scar on my knee from where I fell over.*
Word building: more ugly = **uglier**, most ugly = **ugliest**

Uluru (*ool-u-roo*)
a very big, red rock in the middle of Australia that is a very special place for Aboriginal people.
Word use: This word comes from the Luritja language of the Northern Territory. See the map of Australian Aboriginal languages at the end of this book.

umbrella (*um-brell-a*)
a circle of cloth or plastic stretched over a metal frame that has a short pole in the centre for a handle. You use an umbrella to keep off the rain or to protect you from the sun.

umpire (*um-py-er*)
someone who makes sure that you keep to the rules when you play games like tennis or cricket.
Word use: Another word that means nearly the same is **referee**.

uncle (*ung-kel*)
1. the brother of your father or mother.
2. your aunt's husband.

unconscious (*un-con-shus*)
You are **unconscious** when you look as if you are asleep, but you have fainted or have had a hard knock on the head: *I was **unconscious** for a few minutes after the car crash.*

under (*un-der*)
in a place below: *The cat curled up and went to sleep **under** my chair.*

underground (*un-der-ground*)
under the ground.

undergrowth (*un-der-growth*)
plants and bushes that grow underneath tall trees.

underline (*un-der-line*)
to draw a line under a word.
Word building: I **underlined**, I am **underlining**

underneath (*un-der-neeth*)
below or under: *Write your address **underneath** your name. | The key is **underneath** the yellow pot.*

understand (*un-der-stand*)
1. to know why someone is thinking, feeling or doing something: *I **understand** why you were upset.*
2. to know what something means or how something works: *I can **understand** a bit of French. | I don't **understand** how this new program works.*
Word building: I **understood**, I am **understanding**

upper

underwear *(un-der-wair)*
clothes such as singlets and underpants that you wear under your other clothes.

undo *(un-doo)*
to open or untie: *Undo the buttons and take off your coat.* | *I can't undo this knot in my laces.*
Word building: I **undid**, I have **undone**, I am **undoing**

unemployed *(un-em-ployd)*
Someone is **unemployed** if they do not have a job.

unfair
not fair or just: *I think that decision is very unfair.*

unicorn *(yoo-ni-corn)*
an animal in stories that looks like a horse with a long, straight horn.

uniform *(yoo-ni-form)*
a set of clothes that you wear to show what job you do, which sports team you belong to, or which school you go to.

union *(yoon-yon)*
workers who have joined together to form a group to ask for more pay or other things that are a problem for them all.
Word building: This is short for **trade union**.

unique *(yoo-neek)*
Something is **unique** if there is no other thing like it.

unit *(yoo-nit)*
1. an amount used when you count or measure: *A cent is a unit of money.* | *A metre is a unit of length.*
2. a single part out of a set or a whole thing: *Kim is in the rescue unit of the police force.*
3. one of several homes that are all in one large building.
Word building: Definition 3 is short for **home unit**.

unite *(yoo-nite)*
to join together to make one: *The two clubs will unite to form one big club.*
Word building: they **united**, they are **uniting**

universe *(yoo-ni-vers)*
the whole of space with the stars, planets and everything else that is in it.

university
a place where you can study and do research after you have left school.

unknown *(un-nohn)*
not known.

unleaded petrol *(un-led-ed pet-rol)*
petrol that does not contain tiny bits of lead and is therefore not as harmful to people.
Word use: Compare this with **leaded petrol**.

unless *(un-less)*
except if: *I'm not going unless Ashley comes too.*

until *(un-til)*
up to the time of: *I will read until bedtime.*

unusual *(un-yoo-zhoo-al)*
not usual.

up
1. towards the sky: *The bird flew up.* | *Put your hand up if you know the answer.*
2. from low to high: *Please turn the volume up.*
Word use: The opposite of this is **down**.

upon *(u-pon)*
on or on top of: *The new holiday cabin was built upon a hill.*

upper *(up-er)*
higher than something else: *I sleep on the upper bunk and my brother sleeps on the lower one.*

upright *(up-rite)*
Something is **upright** if it goes straight up: *Two **upright** poles hold up the tent.*

uproar *(up-raw)*
a lot of noise made by a crowd of people.

upset *(up-set)*
1. to knock something over.
2. to make someone feel sad or hurt.
Word building: I **upset**, I am **upsetting**

upstairs
up the stairs: *I'm going **upstairs**.* | *The bathroom is **upstairs**.*

upwards *(up-wards)*
from a low to a high place: *The rocket flew **upwards**.*
Word use: The opposite of this is **downwards**.

urge *(erge)*
1. to try hard to make someone do something: *I **urge** you to read this excellent book.*
2. a strong wish to do something: *Kelly had a sudden **urge** to sneeze.*
Word building: I **urged**, I am **urging**

urgent *(er-jent)*
Something is **urgent** if it has to be done at once.
Word building: Something urgent must be done **urgently**.

us
a word you use when you are talking about yourself and another person or people: *Is there enough cake for all of **us**?* | *Dad asked **us** to tidy our bedrooms.*

USB stick *(yooh es bee stick)*
a memory stick that you connect to a part of a computer called the USB port.

use *(yooz)*
1. to make something work for you: *We are learning to **use** a computer.* | ***Use** a sharp knife to cut the rope.*
2. *(yooz)* the act of using something: *I clean my paintbrushes after each **use**.*
Word building: I **used**, I am **using** | Something you can use is **useful**. Something you can't use may be **useless**.

used *(yoozed)*
not new: *He bought a **used** car because he couldn't afford a new one.*

usual *(yoo-zhoo-al)*
Something is **usual** if it's what people expect because it's what most often happens: *The mail will be here by 10 o'clock if the postman comes at his **usual** time.* | *It's **usual** to bring a gift to a birthday party.*
Word building: If it's usual for you to do something, then it's something that you **usually** do.

Vv

Vultures on vacation visit volcanoes.

vacant *(vay-kent)*
empty, or not being used.

vacation
a holiday.

vacuum *(vak-yoom)*
an empty space with no air or any other gas in it.

vacuum cleaner *(vak-yoom cleen-er)*
a machine that sucks up dirt from floors.

vain *(vane)*
You are **vain** if you are too proud of yourself and of the way you look.
Word use: If you do something **in vain**, you do it without success. | Don't confuse **vain** with **vein**.

valley *(vall-ee)*
the low land between hills or mountains.
Word building: For more than one we use **valleys**.

valuable
1. worth a lot of money: *The king's crown was very **valuable**.*
2. useful or important: *Don't waste **valuable** time.*

value *(val-yoo)*
1. the amount of money that something is worth.
2. to feel that something is important or special: *I **value** the time I spend with my grandmother.*
Word building: I **valued**, I am **valuing**

van
a covered truck that is used for carrying things like furniture.

vanilla *(va-nill-a)*
a liquid that is used to give a special taste to food like ice-cream or milk drinks.

vanish *(van-ish)*
to go out of sight suddenly.

vapour *(vay-por)*
a cloud of steam, mist or fog.

variety *(va-ry-e-tee)*
a number of things of many different kinds: *We looked at a **variety** of watches before we chose this one.*
Word building: For more than one we use **varieties**.

various
more than one and different: *The explorers visited **various** parts of the island.*

vary *(vair-ree)*
to make something different: *I like to **vary** the way I look by changing the style of my hair.*
Word building: I **varied**, I am **varying**

vase *(varz)*
a container for water and flowers.

vast *(varst)*
very great: *It takes days to drive across the* **vast** *desert.* | *The storm caused a* **vast** *amount of damage.*

veal *(veel)*
meat from a calf.

vegetable *(vej-ta-bel)*
part of some plants that is used as food.

vegetarian *(vej-e-**tair**-ree-an)*
someone who does not eat meat.

vehicle *(**vee**-i-kl)*
a machine with wheels that can travel on land from one place to another. Cars, bicycles, buses and trains are vehicles.

veil *(vale)*
a piece of thin material that some women and girls use to cover their faces or heads.

vein *(vane)*
one of the small tubes inside your body that carry blood to your heart.
Word use: The tubes that carry blood from your heart are **arteries**. | Don't confuse **vein** with **vain**.

venom *(**ven**-om)*
the poison that a spider or snake puts into the body of something or something that it bites.
Word building: A creature that can put venom into the body of something that it bites is **venomous** *(**ven**-om-us)*.

verandah *(ve-**ran**-da)*
a part on the outside of a house, that is covered by the roof but doesn't have walls.
Word use: People spell this **verandah** or **veranda**.

verb
a word in a sentence which tells you what someone or something does or feels, such as 'hear' and 'walks'.

verdict *(**ver**-dict)*
what a judge or a jury decides about a prisoner in a court of law: *The* **verdict** *was 'not guilty' and the prisoner went free.*

verse
a part of a song or a poem.

vertical *(**ver**-ti-cal)*
Something is **vertical** if it stands straight up.
Word use: Think about how this is different from **horizontal**.

very
extremely: *I'm* **very** *excited about going on holiday!*

Vesak *(**ve**-sahk)*
a Buddhist festival celebrating the life of the Buddha. It is held in May or June.

vessel *(**vess**-el)*
1. a ship or boat.
2. a container, such as a cup or bottle, that can hold liquid.

vet
someone whose job is to try to make animals that are sick or hurt well again.
Word building: This word is short for **veterinary surgeon** *(vet-e-ren-ree ser-jen)* or **veterinarian** *(vet-e-re-**nair**-ree-an)*.

vibrate *(vy-**brate**)*
to tremble or shake quickly: *The boat began to* **vibrate** *when the captain started the engine.*
Word building: it **vibrated**, it is **vibrating**

victim *(**vic**-tim)*
someone who has something bad happen to them: *The shop assistant was the* **victim** *of a cruel thief.*

victory *(vic-tree)*
a win in a game or a fight.
Word building: For more than one we use **victories**.

video *(vid-ee-o)*
1. a machine that can record pictures and sounds on a special tape and play them back on your television.
2. the special tape with a film on it: *My parents kept a **video** of me as a baby taking my first steps.*
Word building: You play or record a video on a **video recorder**.

view *(vyoo)*
everything you can see from one place: *You get a wonderful **view** of the city from the top of the tower.*

village *(vill-age)*
a small town in the country.

villain *(vill-in)*
a bad person: *Nobody liked the **villain** in the play.*

vine
a kind of plant with thin branches that can twist around sticks and cling to walls.

vinegar *(vin-e-gar)*
a sour liquid that you use to flavour food.

violent *(vy-o-lent)*
strong and dangerous: *A **violent** storm knocked over our trees.*
Word building: Anything that's violent can cause **violence**.

violet *(vy-o-let)*
a small plant with purple flowers.

violin *(vy-o-lin)*
a musical instrument with strings. You hold it between your shoulder and chin and play it with a bow.

virus *(vy-rus; the first part rhymes with **eye**)*
1. a very tiny living thing that causes disease and is easily caught from someone else: *The common cold is a **virus**.*
2. a small program that can get into your computer over the internet or from a disk and cause lots of damage to your files and other programs.
Word building: For more than one we use **viruses**.

visible *(viz-i-bel)*
Something is **visible** if you can see it.

vision *(vizh-en)*
the power you have to see things with your eyes: *Cats have good **vision** in the dark.*

visit *(viz-it)*
to go to see a person or a place.
Word building: Someone who visits is a **visitor**.

voice
the sound you make with your mouth when you speak or sing.

voicemail
a spoken message you receive on your telephone that you can save and listen to later.

volcano *(vol-kay-no)*
a mountain with an opening in the top. Sometimes gases, rocks and very hot liquids burst out of it.
Word building: For more than one we use **volcanoes**.

volleyball *(voll-ee-ball)*
a team game in which a large ball is hit over a high net with the hand or lower arm.

volume *(vol-yoom)*
1. a book or one of a set of books.
2. how loud a sound is: *He turned up the **volume** of the radio to listen to the music.*

a b c d e f g h i j k l m n o p q r s t u **v** w x y z

volunteer *(vol-un-teer)*
someone who offers to do something that they don't have to do.

vote
to say which person or plan you want to choose, by putting up your hand or by marking it on a piece of paper: *I'll **vote** for you as class captain.*
Word building: I **voted**, I am **voting**

vowel *(vow-el)*
one of a special group of five letters of the alphabet. The vowels are **a**, **e**, **i**, **o** and **u**.
Word use: Look at **consonant**.

voyage *(voy-ij)*
a long journey over water.

vulnerable *(vul-ne-ra-bl)*
1. Something is **vulnerable** if it is not strong or protected, and so is likely to be hurt.
2. A type of animal is **vulnerable** if it might soon become endangered unless action is taken.
Word use: Compare this with **endangered**.

vulture *(vul-cher)*
a large bird that eats dead animals.

Ww

Whales with whiskers wink at wizards with wands.

waddle *(wod-l)*
to walk with short steps, swinging from side to side like a duck: *If that goose sees your sandwich, it will **waddle** over to steal it as fast as it can!*
Word building: it **waddled**, it is **waddling**

waddy *(wodd-ee)*
a heavy, wooden stick traditionally used by Aboriginal people in war.
Word use: This word comes from the Dharug language of New South Wales. See the map of Australian Aboriginal languages at the end of this book.

wade
to walk through water: *She took off her shoes so that she could **wade** across the creek.*
Word building: I **waded**, I am **wading**

wage
the money that is paid to someone for the job that they do.

wagon *(wag-on)*
a cart with four wheels, that is pulled by horses.

wail
to make a long sad cry.
Word use: Don't confuse this with **whale**.

waist
the middle part of your body, just above your hips.
Word use: Don't confuse this with **waste**.

wait
to stay somewhere until something happens: ***Wait** here until I come back.*
Word use: Don't confuse this with **weight**.

waiter
a person who serves food and drink to you at your table in a restaurant or hotel.
Word building: Some people call a woman waiter a **waitress**.

wake
to stop someone from being asleep: *That noise will **wake** the baby.*
Word building: I **woke**, I have **woken**, I am **waking**

walk *(rhymes with **fork**)*
to move along by putting one foot in front of the other: *My little brother is learning to **walk**.*

wall
1. one of the sides of a room or a building.
2. a fence made of brick or stone.

wallaby *(wol-a-bee)*
an Australian animal that is like a kangaroo. The female carries her babies in a pouch.
Word building: For more than one we use **wallabies**.
Word use: This word comes from the Dharug language of New South Wales. See the map of Australian Aboriginal languages at the end of this book.

wallaroo *(woll-a-roo)*
a large kangaroo with shaggy, dark fur that lives in rocky or hilly land.
Word use: This word comes from the Dharug language of New South Wales. See the map of Australian Aboriginal languages at the end of this book.

wallet *(wol-et)*
a small, flat bag for paper money. You can fold it and put it in your pocket.

wand *(wond)*
a thin stick that fairies, witches or magicians use to make spells and magic.

wander *(won-der)*
to move about without wanting to go anywhere in a hurry: *I like to wander along the beach looking for shells.*
Word use: Don't confuse this with **wonder**.

want *(wont)*
to feel that you would like something or to do something: *I want to go swimming.*

war *(rhymes with saw)*
a long fight between the armies of different countries.

waratah *(wo-ra-tar)*
an Australian shrub that has big, red flowers.

wardrobe *(wor-drobe)*
a large cupboard where you hang your clothes.

warm *(rhymes with form)*
You are **warm** if you can feel some heat: *Come and get warm by the fire.*
Word building: Something that makes you warm gives you **warmth**.

warn *(worn)*
to tell someone to be careful because they might be in danger.
Word building: If you warn someone, you give them a **warning**.

warrior *(wo-ree-or)*
a soldier or fighter.

wash *(wosh)*
to make something clean using water and sometimes soap: *Wash your hands before you eat your sandwich.*

washing machine *(wosh-ing ma-sheen)*
a machine that washes clothes automatically.

wasp *(wosp)*
an insect with wings, that can sting you.

waste *(wayst)*
to use up something in a foolish way: *Dad told us not to waste electricity by leaving the lights on.*
Word building: I **wasted**, I am **wasting**
Word use: Don't confuse this with **waist**.

watch *(woch)*
1. to look at something: *Watch the soup and tell me when it starts to boil.* | *Let's watch a DVD tonight.*
2. a small clock that you wear on your wrist.

water *(wor-ter)*
the clear liquid that falls from the sky when it rains. It makes the seas, rivers and lakes.

watermelon
a large melon with green skin and a dark pink juicy part inside.

waterproof *(wor-ter-proof)*
Something is **waterproof** if water can't go through it.

wattle *(wott-l)*
a shrub with fluffy, round, yellow flowers, that grows in Australia.

wave
1. to move your hand up and down or from side to side: *Wave goodbye to your friends.*
2. a ridge of water that moves across the top of the sea: *A wave splashed against the side of the boat.*
Word building: I **waved**, I am **waving**

wax
thick, greasy stuff that is easy to melt. Candles are made of wax.

way
1. the path you take to get somewhere: *Which way is the airport?*
2. how something is done: *The teacher showed him the way to do the sum.*
Word use: Don't confuse this with **weigh**.

we
a word you use when you are talking about yourself and another person or people: *We had a great time at the pool today.*

weak
not strong or powerful: *My legs felt weak after I had been ill in bed. | The light of the candle is too weak to use for reading.*
Word use: Don't confuse this with **week**.

wealth *(welth)*
a lot of money.
Word building: If you have wealth, then you are **wealthy**.

weapon *(wep-on)*
something that is used in a fight to hurt somebody.

wear *(wair)*
to put something on your body: *Did you wear your new suit?*
Word building: I **wore**, I have **worn**, I am **wearing**
Word use: Don't confuse this with **where** or **we're**.

weary *(weer-ree)*
very tired.
Word building: more weary = **wearier**, most weary = **weariest**

weather *(wedh-er)*
how it is outside. Wind, rain, snow, sun, clouds, heat and cold are all part of the weather.
Word use: Don't confuse this with **whether**.

weave
to make things like wool, cotton, or thin cane into material by passing the threads under and over each other: *I can weave straw into a basket.*
Word building: I **wove**, I have **woven**, I am **weaving**

web
1. the sticky net that spiders make to catch insects.
2. the, the system of storing the information on the internet so that people all around the world can find it.
Word building: Definition 2 is a short way of saying **the World Wide Web**.

webbed
Fingers and toes are **webbed** if they are joined together by a flap of skin: *Ducks have webbed feet.*

webcam
a video camera attached to a computer that you can use to send a video picture over the internet.
Word building: This word is a short way of saying **web camera**.

web page

a section of a website that you can access on the internet.

website *(web-site)*

a place on the internet with an address that can be looked up for information and facts.

Word building: This word is often shortened to **site**.

wedding *(wedd-ing)*

the time when a man and a woman get married.

weed

a plant that you can't use and that grows where you don't want it.

week

the seven days from Sunday to the next Saturday. It is a measure of time.

Word building: If something happens once a week, then it happens **weekly**.

Word use: Don't confuse **week** with **weak**.

weekend

the time from Friday evening to Sunday evening, when most people do not have to work or go to school.

weep

to cry, with tears coming out of your eyes.

Word building: I **wept**, I am **weeping**

weigh *(way)*

to find out how heavy something is: *I stood on the scales to weigh myself.*

Word use: Don't confuse this with **way**.

weight *(wate)*

how heavy something is: *The weight of this bag of oranges is five kilograms.*

Word use: Don't confuse this with **wait**.

weird *(weerd)*

very strange: *I had a weird dream about witches and fairies.*

welcome *(wel-cum)*

to greet someone in a friendly way and show that you are pleased to see them: *Stand at the door and welcome the guests.*

Word building: I **welcomed**, I am **welcoming**

well^1

1. healthy: *They looked happy and well after their holiday.*

2. in a way that shows skill: *She swims well.*

well^2

a hole dug into the ground to get water or oil.

well-known

1. clearly or fully known: *That story is well-known to me.*

2. famous or known by many people: *My brother is a well-known artist.*

we're *(wair)*

a short way of saying **we are**.

Word use: Don't confuse this with **wear** or **where**.

west

the direction opposite to east, where you face if you are watching the sun set in the evening.

Word use: The opposite to this is **east**. The other directions are **north** and **south**.

wet

1. covered or soaked with liquid: *I got caught in the rain and my clothes are wet.*

2. not yet dry: *Watch out for the wet paint.*

3. the wet, the rainy season in central and northern Australia, from December to March.

wetland *(wet-land)*

a natural area where the ground is usually wet, such as a swamp.

whale *(wale)*

a very large animal that lives in the sea.

Word use: Don't confuse this with **wail**.

wharf *(worf)*
a place built on the shore of a harbour where ships are loaded and unloaded.
Word building: For more than one we use **wharves**.

what *(wot)*
You use **what** when asking about something: *What time is lunch?*

whatever
1. anything: *Take **whatever** you like from the fridge.*
2. no matter what: ***Whatever** happens, make sure you take care of yourself.*

wheat *(weet)*
a plant that grows hard seeds which people grind into flour.

wheel *(weel)*
1. a circle of wood or metal with a hole in the middle.
2. to push something with wheels, like a cart or a bicycle: ***Wheel** your bicycle up the steep hill.*

wheelchair
a chair on wheels that people who can't walk use to get around.

when *(wen)*
1. at what time: ***When** are we going to the beach?*
2. at the time that: ***When** I grow up I want to be a movie star.*

whenever
at any time: *You can visit **whenever** you like.*

where *(wair)*
at what place: ***Where** is my other shoe?*
Word use: Don't confuse this with **wear** or **we're**.

wherever
any place: *We can have lunch **wherever** you like.*

whether
a word you use when you talk about two things that might happen: *I will find out **whether** we are leaving today or leaving tomorrow.*
Word use: Don't confuse this with **weather**.

which *(wich)*
what one: ***Which** CD do you want to play?*
Word use: Don't confuse this with **witch**.

while *(wile)*
for the length of time that: *Can you dance **while** I sing?*

whimper *(wim-per)*
to cry softly.

whine *(wine)*
to make a long, high sound: *The dog began to **whine** to be let in the house.*
Word building: I **whined**, I am **whining**
Word use: Don't confuse this with **wine**.

whip *(wip)*
1. a long piece of rope or leather joined to a handle. It is used for hitting animals.
2. to stir cream or any food like this with quick, light movements until it is thick.
Word building: I **whipped**, I am **whipping**

whiskers *(wiss-kers)*
the long, thick hairs that grow on the faces of some animals. Cats have whiskers.

whisper *(wiss-per)*
to speak very softly.

whistle *(wiss-l)*
1. to make a sound like a bird's call, by blowing through a round opening you make with your lips and your teeth: *My dog comes running when I **whistle**.*
2. a small pipe which makes high-pitched sounds when you blow through it.
Word building: I **whistled**, I am **whistling**

white *(wite)*
Something is **white** if it's the colour of milk.
Word building: more white = **whiter**, most white = **whitest**

whiteboard *(wite-bord)*
a large, white, plastic board used for writing or drawing on with a special felt pen.

white-out *(wite-out)*
a thin, white paint that is used to cover written mistakes on paper.
Word use: Another word for this is **liquid paper**.

whiz *(wizz)*
to move with a humming or hissing sound: *We heard your train **whiz** past the station.*
Word building: I **whizzed**, I am **whizzing**

who *(hoo)*
which person or people: ***Who** wants some ice-cream?*

whole *(hole)*
1. Something is **whole** if all of it is there: *The **whole** school has come to watch the parade.*
2. in one piece: *My dog swallows his dog biscuits **whole**.*

whose *(hooz)*
You use **whose** to talk about someone owning something: ***Whose** bike is that?*

why *(wy; rhymes with **eye**)*
for what reason: ***Why** do birds fly?*

wicked *(wick-ed)*
evil or bad.

wicket *(wick-et)*
a set of three sticks standing in a row with two small pieces of wood resting on top. In cricket the bowler tries to hit it with the ball.

wide
1. Something is **wide** if it measures a lot from one side to the other: *We have to row across this **wide** river.*
2. as far as or as much as it can be: *The clown's mouth is **wide** open.*
Word building: more wide = **wider**, most wide = **widest** | If you make something wide, you **widen** it and increase its **width**.
Word use: The opposite of definition 1 is **narrow**.

widow *(wid-oe)*
a woman whose husband is dead.

widower *(wid-o-er)*
a man whose wife is dead.

width
how wide something is from one side to the other: *What's the **width** of this room?*
Word use: Another word that means nearly the same is **breadth**.

wife
the woman a man marries.
Word building: For more than one we use **wives**.

wig
a covering of hair that is made to wear on the head.

wild
Something is **wild** if it lives or grows by itself, without people to take care of it: *Lions and tigers are **wild** animals.*

wildlife *(wild-life)*
animals, birds and insects living in their natural habitat.

will[1]
to be going to do something: *I **will** go shopping this afternoon.*
Word use: This is a helping word. It is always used with another one in the form **I will** or **I would**. You can say **won't** and **wouldn't** for 'will not' and 'would not'.

will²

1. the power of choosing your own actions.

2. a written statement of what a person wants done with their possessions after they die.

willing *(will-ing)*

Someone is **willing** if they agree to do something in a happy way: *I am **willing** to help with the washing-up.*

willy-willy *(will-ee-will-ee)*

a strong wind that moves around in circles.

Word use: This word possibly comes from either the Yindjibarndi language of Western Australia, or the Wembawemba language of Victoria. See the map of Australian Aboriginal languages at the end of this book.

win

to do better than anyone else in something.

Word building: I **won**, I am **winning** | If you win something, then you are the **winner**.

wind¹

air that moves along and blows things about.

Word building: When the wind is blowing, then it's **windy**.

wind² *(rhymes with **dined**)*

to turn one way and then another way: *The rivers **wind** down to the sea.*

Word building: I **wound**, I am **winding**

window *(win-doe)*

an opening in a wall for light and air to come in. It is usually covered with glass.

wine

a drink with alcohol in it that some adults drink. It is made from grapes.

Word use: Don't confuse this with **whine**.

wing

1. the part on each side of a bird or an insect that it uses for flying.

2. one of the long, flat parts that stick out on both sides of a plane.

wink

to close and open one eye quickly, often as a signal to a friend.

winter *(win-ter)*

the season of the year when it is cold.

wipe

to rub something gently to get it clean or dry.

Word building: I **wiped**, I am **wiping**

wire *(rhymes with **fire**)*

a long piece of thin metal that you can bend.

wise *(wize)*

able to decide what is true or right: *That judge is a **wise** person.*

Word building: more wise = **wiser**, most wise = **wisest** | If you are wise, you have a lot of **wisdom**.

wish

to want something very much: *I **wish** I could fly!*

wisp

a small piece of something: *A **wisp** of smoke rose from the chimney.*

witch

a woman who does magic.

Word use: Don't confuse this with **which**.

with

as well as, together: *She is going skating **with** her friends. | Can I please have yoghurt **with** my fruit?*

within

inside: *The dog is asleep **within** the kennel.*

without

not with, or not having: *I won't go **without** you. | Have you got any biscuits **without** nuts?*

a
b
c
d
e
f
g
h
i
j
k
l
m
n
o
p
q
r
s
t
u
v
w
x
y
z

witness (wit-ness)

someone who sees or hears something that happens: *I was a **witness** to the robbery.*

wizard (wiz-ard)

someone who does magic: *The **wizard** turned the mouse into a unicorn.*

wobble (wobb-l)

to move from side to side: *The bike began to **wobble** and I fell off.*

Word building: I **wobbled**, I am **wobbling** | If something wobbles, then it's **wobbly**.

wolf (woolf)

a large animal like a big dog, that eats meat and that howls.

Word building: For more than one we use **wolves**.

woman (woom-an)

a female grown-up person.

Word building: For more than one we use **women** (wim-en).

wombat (wom-bat)

a short, heavy, Australian animal that digs its burrow under the ground. The female carries her babies in a pouch.

Word use: This word comes from the Dharug language of New South Wales. See the map of Australian Aboriginal languages at the end of this book.

wonder (wun-der)

to think about something with interest or surprise: *I **wonder** what will happen next.*

Word use: Don't confuse this with **wander**.

wonderful (wun-der-ful)

very good: *I enjoyed that meal — you're a **wonderful** cook.*

wood (rhymes with good)

the hard stuff that the trunk and branches of trees are made of.

Word building: If something is made of wood, then it's **wooden**.

wool (rhymes with full)

the soft, curly hair that grows on sheep and some other animals.

Word building: If something is made from sheep's wool, then it's **woollen**.

woomera (woom-e-ra)

a strong piece of wood with a notch at the end, traditionally used by Aboriginal people to help throw a spear.

Word use: This word comes from the Dharug language of New South Wales. See the map of Australian Aboriginal languages at the end of this book.

word (werd)

1. a sound or a group of sounds that means something.

2. the group of letters you use to write down these sounds.

work (werk)

1. something that takes a lot of effort: *Digging up these weeds is hard **work**.*

2. a job you do to earn money: *I'm a teacher so I have to be at **work** by 9 o'clock.*

3. to go the way it should: *This torch doesn't **work**.*

worker

1. someone or something that works.

2. someone who has a particular job: *The trains were full of office **workers** on their way to the city.*

3. someone who is employed in a factory or does work with their hands: *The **workers** gathered to listen to what the bosses had to say.*

world (werld)

the earth and everything on it.

World Wide Web (werld wide web)

the, a system of storing the information on the internet so that people all around the world can find it.

Word building: This is often shortened to **the web** or **WWW**.

worm *(werm)*
a long, thin animal with a soft body and no legs. It slides along like a snake does.

worry *(wu-ree)*
to feel afraid that something bad might happen: *My parents **worry** when I don't come straight home from school.*
Word building: I **worried**, I am **worrying**

worse *(werse)*
more bad: *Is your cold **worse** today or do you feel better?*
Word use: You can find this word at **bad** as well.

worship *(wer-ship)*
to feel or show great love for God or for anyone you love as if they were God.
Word building: I **worshipped**, I am **worshipping**

worst *(werst)*
most bad: *This is the **worst** pie I've ever tasted!*
Word use: You can find this word at **bad** as well.

worth *(werth)*
1. equal to the amount of money you've paid for something: *These lollies aren't **worth** $1.*
2. good enough for something: *This bike isn't **worth** fixing.*
Word building: If something isn't worth anything, then it's **worthless**.

would *(wood)*
See **will**¹.

wound *(woond)*
a place on your body where you have a deep cut or severe damage to skin and flesh.

wrap *(rap)*
to fold paper or material around something or someone to cover them.
Word building: I **wrapped**, I am **wrapping**

wreath *(reeth)*
flowers and leaves tied together to make a ring: *They put the **wreath** on the soldier's grave.*

wreck *(rek)*
to spoil or break something so that it can't be used.

wren *(ren)*
a very small bird with a long tail sticking up in the air.

wrestle *(ress-l)*
to fight with someone and try to throw them to the ground.
Word building: I **wrestled**, I am **wrestling** | People who wrestle in a ring are **wrestlers** and they take part in a game of **wrestling**.

wriggle *(rigg-l)*
to twist and turn like a snake.
Word building: I **wriggled**, I am **wriggling**

wrinkle *(rink-l)*
a line or a fold on something that is usually smooth.

wrist *(rist)*
the part of your body where your hand joins onto your arm.

write *(rite)*
1. to make letters or words with a pen, a pencil or anything like this: ***Write** your name at the top of the page.*
2. to make something using words: *I'll **write** a poem about my friend.*
Word building: I **wrote**, I have **written**, I am **writing** | When you write, you do some **writing**. Someone who writes stories and poems is a **writer**.

wrong *(rong)*
1. very bad: *It is **wrong** to copy other people's work and say it is yours.*
2. not correct: *You have given the **wrong** answer.*
Word use: The opposite of definition 2 is **right**.

a
b
c
d
e
f
g
h
i
j
k
l
m
n
o
p
q
r
s
t
u
v
w
x
y
z

a
b
c
d
e
f
g
h
i
j
k
l
m
n
o
p
q
r
s
t
u
v
w
x
y
z

X-ray *(ex-ray)*
a photograph of the inside of someone's body, taken with a special machine. Doctors look at them to see if anything is wrong and needs fixing.

xylophone *(zy-lo-fone)*
a musical instrument with a row of wooden bars that get longer to make deeper sounds. You hit these with small wooden hammers.

yabby *(yabb-ee)*
a crayfish.
Word use: This word comes from the Wembawemba language of Victoria. See the map of Australian Aboriginal languages at the end of this book.

yacht *(yot)*
a boat with a sail.

yard[1]
the ground around your house. It often has a fence around it.

yard[2]
an old-fashioned measure of how long things are. One yard is about 91 centimetres.

yawn *(yorn)*
to take a long deep breath through your mouth when you are bored or tired.

year
the twelve whole months from the first day of January to the last day of December. It is a large measure of time.

yeast *(yeest)*
the stuff that you add to dough so that it swells up when you make bread.

yell
to call out loudly.

yellow *(yell-oe)*
Something is **yellow** if it has the bright colour that butter and lemons have.

yes
a word you use when you agree with something or agree to do something, or if you allow someone to do something: *Yes, that is correct.* | *Yes, I will feed your goldfish while you are away.* | *Yes, you can borrow my bike.*
Word use: The opposite of this is **no**.

yesterday
the day before today: *Jonah came to see us yesterday.*

yet
1. at this time: *Don't go yet.*
2. at a particular time in the past: *He hadn't arrived yet.*
3. but: *Your school work is good, yet it could be even better.*

Zz

Xylophones are played while yabbies visit the zoo.

yoghurt *(yoe-get)*
a creamy food that is made from milk.

yolk *(yoke)*
the yellow part of an egg.

Yom Kippur *(yom **kip**-a)*
a very important day of fasting and prayer for Jewish people, in September or October of each year.

you *(yoo)*
a word you use when you are talking to someone, or to a group of people: *You play the piano well.* | *I'll lend **you** my pencil.* | *When I blow the whistle, **you** should all start running.*

young *(yung)*
A person or an animal is **young** if they are not very old.
Word building: When you are young, then you're in your **youth**.

your *(rhymes with **saw**)*
a word you use when you are talking about something that belongs to the person you are talking to: *That is **your** jacket.*
Word use: Don't confuse this with **you're**.

you're *(rhymes with **saw**)*
a short way of saying **you are**.
Word use: Don't confuse this with **your**.

yours *(rhymes with **saws**)*
a word you use when you are talking about something that belongs to the person you are talking to: *That jacket is **yours**.*

yourself *(your-**self**)*
a word you use when you are talking to somebody about something they have done to their body or something they have done without help: *Have you hurt **yourself**?* | *Did you make that bookmark **yourself**?*

yourselves *(your-**selves**)*
a word you use when you are talking to some people about something they do to themselves or something they do by themselves without help: *Have you hurt **yourselves**?* | *Do the dishes **yourselves**.*

youth
1. a young person or young people.
2. the time when you are young: *I spent my **youth** living with my grandfather.*
Word building: If you are in your youth, or act or look like you are in your youth, you are **youthful**.

zebra *(**zeb**-ra)*
a kind of horse that comes from Africa and has black and white stripes on its body.

a
b
c
d
e
f
g
h
i
j
k
l
m
n
o
p
q
r
s
t
u
v
w
x
y
z

zero *(zeer-roe)*
'0' or the number you use when there is nothing to count.

Word building: For more than one we use **zeros** or **zeroes**.

zigzag
a line that goes up and down into sharp points.

zinc *(zink)*
a bluish-white metal that is mixed with copper to make brass.

zone
an area: *You must drive more slowly in the school **zone**.*

zoo
a place where you can go and see many different animals, especially wild ones.

zucchini *(zu-kee-nee)*
a long, thin vegetable with a green skin.

Appendix

Theme word lists

Australiana

Anzac	didjeridu	kangaroo	parrot
bandicoot	digger	koala	platypus
banksia	dillybag	kookaburra	possum
barramundi	dingo	kowari	quokka
bilby	dot painting	kurrajong	quoll
bindi-eye	echidna	lorikeet	rock art
blue-tongue	emu	magpie	rosella
boomerang	eucalypt	mammal	settler
bottlebrush	galah	marsupial	stockman
brolga	goanna	monotreme	Tasmanian devil
budgerigar	grazier	mulga	
bunyip	gum tree	national park	wallaby
bushranger	humpy	nulla-nulla	wombat
churinga	jabiru	numbat	woomera
cockatiel	jackaroo		
cockatoo	jarrah		
colony	jillaroo		
convict	joey		
cooee			
coolibah			
corroboree			

Celebrations

anniversary
balloon
birthday
cake
camera
candle
card
confetti
congratulations
decorations
festival
fireworks
gift
Halloween
holiday
invitation
New Year
party
photograph
present
wedding

Environment

adaptation	evolution	rain
air pollution	extinction	recycling
atmosphere	fire	resource
autumn	flame	season
avalanche	flood	shade
burn	food chain	snow
bushcare	fossil fuel	solar
bushfire	freeze	spring
carbon footprint	global warming	steam
cloud	grassland	storm
compost	greenhouse effect	summer
conservation		survival
cyclone	habitat	temperature
desert	hail	thunder
drought	icicle	time
earthquake	inferno	tsunami
eco-friendly	light	vapour
ecology	lightning	volcano
ecosystem	litter	vulnerable
endangered	lunar	waste
erosion	national park	water
	natural	weather
	nature	wetland
	pollution	winter
	protection	

Theme word lists

Food

appetite	fish	nachos	salad
banquet	flavour	noodles	sandwich
barbecue	fork	nuts	saucer
bistro	fried rice	pasta	sausage roll
bowl	fruit	pavlova	seafood
bread	gelato	picnic	spoon
butter	glass	pizza	straw
cafe	hamburger	plate	supermarket
cake	herb	poultry	tabouli
canteen	hot dog	recipe	tacos
cereal	hummus	restaurant	takeaway
cheese	ice-cream		tuckshop
chocolate	ingredient		vegetables
chopsticks	kebab		yoghurt
cook	knife		
cup	lamington		
delicatessen	lasagne		
dessert	licorice		
diet	meat		
dish	menu		
drink	mug		
egg			

Health and safety

abdomen	collapse	head lice	patient
abrasion	collision	heart	scab
accident	conscious	height	scar
ache	deaf	hospital	skeleton
AIDS	diarrhoea	human	specialist
allergy	diet	illness	splint
ambulance	disease	infection	splinter
antibiotic	doctor	invalid	sprain
appendix	Down	itch	sting
asthma	syndrome	measles	stomach
bacteria	drown	medicine	thermometer
bandage	emergency	mumps	tonsillitis
bandaid	exercise	nurse	tonsils
bleed	fever	ointment	virus
blind	grommet	operation	weight
blister			
body			
bone			
brain			
broken			
bruise			
cancer			
casualty			
cerebral palsy			
chickenpox			
clinic			

Theme word lists

Jobs

actor	farmer
architect	grocer
astronomer	hairdresser
baker	jeweller
barber	judge
builder	lawyer
butcher	mechanic
carpenter	model
chemist	musician
cleaner	nurse
dentist	police
detective	reporter
doctor	secretary
drycleaner	tailor
electrician	teacher
engineer	vet

Money

account	euro
ATM	fare
bank	fine
bill	income
cash	job
cash register	PIN
cent	pocket money
change	pound
charge	price
cheque	profit
coin	purse
credit card	receipt
customer	refund
deposit	salary
docket	shops
dollar	tax
economy	tip
EFTPOS	wage
	wallet

Ice-cream
Single . . . $3.00
Double . . . $4.00

Religion

altar	Christian	hymn	priest
baptism	Christianity	imam	rabbi
bar mitzvah	Christmas	Islam	Ramadan
bat mitzvah	church	Jew	synagogue
Buddhism	Deepavali	Judaism	temple
Buddhist	Easter	minister	veil
cathedral	Hanukkah	mosque	Vesak
celebrant	Hindu	Muslim	worship
ceremony	Hinduism	Pesach	Yom Kippur
christening	holy	prayer	

Theme word lists

School

activity	highlighter	pencil	scissors
addition	homework	playground	secondary
after-school care	information	poetry	sharpener
assembly	kindergarten	preschool	sick bay
atlas	library	primary	sport
author	liquid paper	principal	stadium
before-school care	maths	projector	student
blackboard	measure	publish	subtraction
classroom	multiplication	punctuation	teacher
cleaner	music	reference	texta
craft	nonfiction	research	thesaurus
day care	office	ruler	uniform
deputy	PE	science	whiteboard
dictionary			
division			
education			
encyclopedia			
equipment			
eraser			
excursion			
fact			
fiction			
game			
graph			

Sport and leisure

aerobics

athlete

audience

Australian
  Rules

badminton

baseball

basketball

bike rack

blog

boogie board

bronze

champion

cheer squad

cinema

coach

competitor

computer
  game

cricket

crowd

dance

disco

drawing

field

finalist

football

goal

gold

guide

hockey

ice skates

kanga cricket

karate

match

medallion

music

netball

Olympic
  Games

opponent

painting

personal best

rap

reading

record

referee

rock

rollerblades

Rugby
  League

Rugby Union

scorer

scout

sightseeing

silver

skateboard

skiing

snowboard

soccer

supporter

surfing

swimmer

swimming

table tennis

T-ball

team

tennis

track

umpire

uniform

video

volleyball

waves

wharf

world

writing

Theme word lists

Technology and machines

access

air conditioner

automatic

broadcast

byte

cable

calculator

camera

cassette
 recorder

CD

CD-ROM

click

communication

computer

computer game

computer
 program

design

dishwasher

disk

DVD

electricity

electronic
 whiteboard

email

experiment

fax

font

format

hard disk

hard drive

home page

icon

industry

internet

laptop

log in

log off

machine

manual

manufacture

mechanical

metal

microphone

microwave

mobile phone

modem

monitor

mouse

online

printer

prototype

radiator

refrigerator

remote control

satellite

scanner

screen

SMS message

software

sound system

surf

telephone

telescope

television

USB stick

vacuum cleaner

vibrate

video

voicemail

washing
 machine

web

webcam

web page

BUZZ...
CLICK...

Transport

aeroplane	flight attendant	ocean liner	station
aircraft		parachute	submarine
airport	float	passenger	take-off
automatic	freeway	petrol station	taxi
battery	garage	pilot	ticket
bicycle	gas	propeller	token
boat	glider	railway	tollway
buoy	handlebars	road	traffic
captain	helicopter	rocket	trailer
car	hovercraft	route	train
carriage	hydrofoil	runway	tram
car wash	jetty	scooter	unleaded petrol
coach	landing	seatbelt	
container ship	leaded petrol	signal	yacht
cruise ship	licence		
detour	manual		
diesel oil	mechanic		
dinghy	monorail		
emergency exit	motorbike		
engine			
ferry			

Types of writing and speaking

Discussion

Writing or speaking which gives more than one opinion on something

Example: debate, conversation about the causes of climate change

Explanation

Writing or speaking which tells how or why something happens

Example: explaining why ice melts, explaining how a computer works

Exposition

Writing or speaking which gives only one opinion on something

Example: advertisement, election speech

Information report

Writing or speaking which gives facts on something

Example: project on endangered animals, information sheet on sport

Procedure

Writing or speaking which tells how to do or make something

Example: recipe, instructions for making a kite, rules for playing a game

Recount

Writing or speaking which explains exactly how things happened

Example: news item, diary entry, excursion report

Drama

Writing or speaking which is meant to be acted out

Example: play, mime

Narrative

Writing or speaking which tells a story

Example: Fairytale, Dreaming story, novel

Poetry

Writing or speaking which expresses feelings and thoughts, especially your own feelings and thoughts

Example: ballad, limerick, rhyme

Prepositions

A preposition is a word placed before a noun to show its relation to other words in the sentence. Here are some common prepositions with illustrations to show their meaning.

above my head

beneath the trees

inside the box

across the river

beside the chair

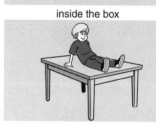
on the table

along the path

between the posts

off the ladder

at the corner

by the window

over the wall

behind the door

down the hole

through the window

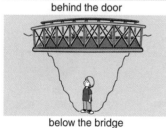
below the bridge

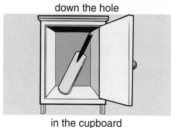
in the cupboard

up the hill

Some of our endangered and vulnerable mammals

Australian sea lion

black-flanked rock wallaby

blue whale

Boullanger Island dunnart

brush-tailed rabbit-rat

burrowing bettong

Carpentarian antechinus

Christmas Island shrew

dibbler

dusky hopping mouse

eastern barred bandicoot

fin whale

fluffy glider

greater bilby

greater stick-nest rat

Hastings River mouse

humpback whale

Julia Creek dunnart

Kangaroo Island dunnart

kowari

large-eared pied bat

Leadbeater's possum

long-footed potoroo

mahogany glider

mountain pygmy possum

mulgara

northern bettong

northern hairy-nosed wombat

northern hopping mouse

northern quoll

numbat

Pilbara leaf-nosed bat

plains rat

quokka

red-tailed phascogale

rufous hare-wallaby

sei whale

Semon's leaf-nosed bat

southern elephant seal

southern marsupial mole

southern right whale

spectacled flying fox

spot-tailed quoll

subantarctic fur seal

Tasmanian devil

tiger quoll

western quoll

western ringtail possum

woylie

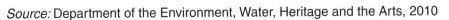

Source: Department of the Environment, Water, Heritage and the Arts, 2010

Map showing the Aboriginal languages referred to in this dictionary

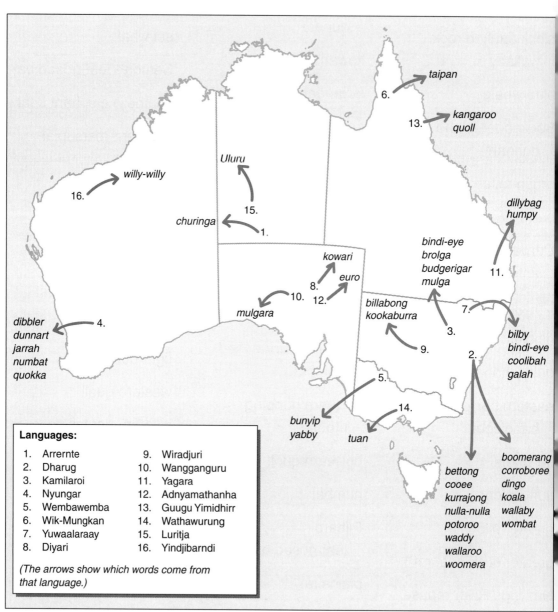

taipan
6.

kangaroo
quoll
13.

Uluru

willy-willy
16.

15.

churinga
1.

dillybag
humpy

kowari

bindi-eye
brolga
budgerigar
mulga
11.

euro
8.
10. 12.

billabong
kookaburra

mulgara

7.

dibbler
dunnart
jarrah
numbat
quokka
4.

3.

bilby
bindi-eye
coolibah
galah

9.
2.

5.

14.

bunyip
yabby

tuan

boomerang
corroboree
dingo
koala
wallaby
wombat

bettong
cooee
kurrajong
nulla-nulla
potoroo
waddy
wallaroo
woomera

Languages:

1.	Arrernte	9.	Wiradjuri
2.	Dharug	10.	Wangganguru
3.	Kamilaroi	11.	Yagara
4.	Nyungar	12.	Adnyamathanha
5.	Wembawemba	13.	Guugu Yimidhirr
6.	Wik-Mungkan	14.	Wathawurung
7.	Yuwaalaraay	15.	Luritja
8.	Diyari	16.	Yindjibarndi

(The arrows show which words come from that language.)

Facts

Continents

Africa

Antarctica

Asia

Australia

Europe

North America

South America

Days of the week

Sunday

Monday

Tuesday

Wednesday

Thursday

Friday

Saturday

Months of the year

January

February

March

April

May

June

July

August

September

October

November

December

Oceans

Arctic

Atlantic

Indian

Pacific

Southern

Planets

Mercury

Venus

Earth

Mars

Jupiter

Saturn

Uranus

Neptune

Shapes

Flat shapes

square	
rectangle	
triangle	
pentagon	
hexagon	
heptagon	
octagon	
circle	
semicircle	
oval	

Solid shapes

cube	
pyramid	
cone	
prism	
cylinder	
sphere	
hemisphere	

Maths facts

Mathematical signs

+	plus	=	equals
−	minus	≠	not equal to
÷	divide	<	less than
×	multipy	>	greater than

Measurements

Length
1 millimetre (mm)
1 centimetre (cm) = 10 mm
1 decimetre (dm) = 10 cm
1 metre (m) = 10 dm
1 decametre (dam) = 10 m
1 hectometre (hm) = 100 m
1 kilometre (km) = 1000 m

Area
1 are = 100 square metres
1 hectare = 100 ares
1 square kilometre = 100 hectares

Time
60 seconds = 1 minute
60 minutes = 1 hour
24 hours = 1 day
365 days = 1 year
366 days = 1 leap year
10 years = 1 decade
10 decades = 1 century

Numbers

1	one	1st	first
2	two	2nd	second
3	three	3rd	third
4	four	4th	fourth
5	five	5th	fifth
6	six	6th	sixth
7	seven	7th	seventh
8	eight	8th	eighth
9	nine	9th	ninth
10	ten	10th	tenth
20	twenty	20th	twentieth
40	forty	40th	fortieth
50	fifty	50th	fiftieth
100	hundred	100th	hundredth
1000	thousand	1000th	thousandth

Mass
1 milligram (mg)
1 centigram = 10 mg
1 decigram = 10 cg
1 gram = 10 dg
1 decagram = 10 g
1 hectogram = 100 g
1 kilogram = 1000 g
1 tonne (metric ton) = 1000 kg

Capacity
1 millilitre (mL)
1 centilitre = 10 mL
1 decilitre = 10 cL
1 litre = 10 dL
1 decalitre = 10 L
1 hectolitre = 100 L
1 kilolitre = 1000 L

Helpful hints to the spelling of tricky words

If you can't easily find the word you're looking up, it might be that the word begins with a letter or letters that you say in a different way to normal or which may be completely silent. Here is a table to help you track down those tricky words.

The sound the word begins with	The possible first letters of the word	Example
f	ph	**ph**otograph
g	gh	**gh**ost
g	gu	**gu**ide
h	wh	**wh**ole
j	g	**g**em
k	ch	**ch**aracter
k	qu	**qu**ay
kw	qu	**qu**ite
n	gn	**gn**ome
n	kn	**kn**ee
r	rh	**rh**yme
r	wr	**wr**ite
s	c	**c**ereal
s	sc	**sc**ience
sh	s	**s**ugar
sk	sch	**sch**ool
w	wh	**wh**ite
z	x	**x**ylophone